JANE AUSTE

SELECTED LETTERS
1796–1817

MARILYN BUTLER is the author of *Maria Edgeworth: a Literary Biography* (1972), *Jane Austen and the War of Ideas* (1975), and *Romantics, Rebels and Reactionaries* (1981), among other books and articles on the novel or on Romanticism. She is Professor of English Literature at Cambridge and a Fellow of King's College.

JANE AUSTEN

Born, Steventon, Hants, 16 December 1775
Died, Winchester, 18 July 1817

JANE AUSTEN

Selected Letters 1796–1817

Edited by
R. W. CHAPMAN

With an Introduction by
MARILYN BUTLER

Oxford   New York
OXFORD UNIVERSITY PRESS

Oxford University Press, Walton Street, Oxford OX2 6DP

Oxford New York
Athens Auckland Bangkok Bombay
Calcutta Cape Town Dar es Salaam Delhi
Florence Hong Kong Istanbul Karachi
Kuala Lumpur Madras Madrid Melbourne
Mexico City Nairobi Paris Singapore
Taipei Tokyo Toronto

and associated companies in
Berlin Ibadan

Oxford is a trade mark of Oxford University Press

First published 1955
First issued as an Oxford University Press paperback
with a new Introduction by Marilyn Butler 1985

British Library Cataloguing in Publication Data

Data available

Library of Congress Cataloging in Publication Data
Austen, Jane, 1775-1817,
Selected letters, 1796-1817.
Bibliography: p.
Includes index.
1. Austen, Jane, 1775-1817—Correspondence.
2. Novelists, English—19th century—Correspondence.
I. Chapman, R. W. (Robert William), 1881-1960.
II. Title.
PR4036.A4 1985 823'.7 84-1184
ISBN 0-19-281485-0 (pbk.)

9 10

Printed in Great Britain by
Biddles Ltd
Guildford and King's Lynn

PREFACE

THIS selection of about one-third of Jane Austen's letters known to be extant is designed as an introduction to her life and letters. For further information I may refer to my own editions of the novels, minor writings, and letters; to the *Memoir* (1870, 1871, and Oxford 1926) by her nephew J. E. Austen-Leigh; to the *Life and Letters* (1913) by two members of the Austen-Leigh family; to Miss C. L. Thompson's *Survey* (1929); to Miss Elizabeth Jenkins's *Life* (1938, 1948); to *My Aunt Jane Austen* by her niece Caroline (published 1952 by the Jane Austen Society of Chawton); and to my own *Facts and Problems* (1948) and *Critical Bibliography* (1953).

Annotation has been reduced to a minimum, and is mainly limited to the identification of persons obscurely or ambiguously named. The reader should remember that 'my Uncle', 'my Aunt' almost always means Mr. and Mrs. Leigh-Perrot; that Mary is likely to be either James Austen's wife or Frank Austen's (but they are often distinguished as Mrs. J. A., Mrs. F. A.); that Elizabeth is either Edward Austen's wife (his daughter is always Lizzie) or Elizabeth Bigg, Mrs. Heathcote; that Eliza is either Mrs. Henry Austen or Mrs. Fowle, and that Edward is either JA's brother, or his son, or James's son James Edward.

Fuller information will be found in the selective indexes.

Jane Austen did not break her letters into paragraphs; she wrote to get as much as she could into a single sheet, since a second sheet would cost her corre-

spondent double postage. In the letters which depend
on Lord Brabourne's edition of 1884 I have retained
his paragraphing.

The numbers of the letters are those of my complete
edition.

R. W. C.

1954

CONTENTS

INTRODUCTION

JANE AUSTEN's letters have been highly controversial. Even before they became available in Chapman's larger collected edition of 1932, their imminence started a literary fracas, in the course of which insults were flung that put many readers off Austen in the 1930s, and perhaps put some off still. The letters trangressed against the received notions of what a great writer's letters were like; more particularly, they were not what 'gentle Jane's' letters should have been like. 'A desert of trivialities', H. W. Garrod called them in 1928, 'punctuated by occasional oases of clever malice'. In a review of Chapman's edition, E. M. Forster thought he also detected 'ill breeding', and gave a lofty explanation of Jane Austen's 'fundamental weakness as a letter writer'—'She has not enough subject-matter on which to exercise her powers'. It was in the light of the impression left by the letters that D. W. Harding read the novels in 1939 as studies in 'regulated hatred'. When critics gradually returned to the theme of Jane Austen the peerless artist (perhaps *the* artist among our novelists, the English Flaubert), they rarely mentioned the letters at all. Even if an unfavourable impression of the woman lingered, it was tacitly agreed to be irrelevant. In that case, why bother to read the letters? No one seemed to argue that they rated attention on their own account as literature.

Anyone coming fresh to the letters now, complete or, as here, in Chapman's own careful selection, is surely in for a pleasant surprise. They may not match

ix

the idealized received view of Jane Austen; that does not make them untruthful, and it is anything but uninteresting. In any case, much of their charm lies in their content, and it has been obscured by so much discussion of the character of the writer. Chapman in first introducing the *Letters* declared that his years of work on them had been delightful, for it had admitted him into a world as 'real' and as pleasing as Trollope's Barsetshire. His selection, of about one-third of the surviving letters, preserves the diurnal detail and omits some of the waspish touches which literary critics made so much of. We do not find here, for example, Jane Austen's notorious quip to her sister Cassandra, on 27 October 1798: 'Mrs. Hall, of Sherborne, was brought to bed yesterday of a dead child, some weeks before she expected, owing to a fright. I supposed she happened unawares to look at her husband' (*Collected Letters*, p. 24). Nor do we have her reaction to newspaper reports of the Battle of Albuera, in the Peninsular War, on 31 May 1811, strangely sandwiched between a message from Mrs Cooke of Bookham, and a description of Miss Harriot Webb, 'who is short & not quite straight': 'How horrible it is to have so many people killed!—And what a blessing that one cares for none of them!' (*Collected Letters*, p. 286). It might have been better to include both of these: Jane Austen on childbirth and on war must be interesting. But Chapman has not been false to the overall impression left by the *Collected Letters*, and he has seized upon their intrinsic popular appeal. You do not have to be a professional, whether a literary critic or a social historian, to read them with pleasure, for they satisfy a basic human curiosity about other people's lives. Here, anticipating the twentieth-century soap opera, is a family saga which introduces a range of characters in different generations; births, marriages, and deaths; family tensions and the occasional whiff of scandal. Like all the best soap operas, this one is located in a world different from our own but easily imaginable and distinctly enviable— the great houses, rectories, and small houses of rural southern England. And when the saga occurs in real life, its details become the stuff of social history. Who visits whom? What conventions govern visits? What did a family eat, at what time, and how much did it cost? How did a portionless and discriminating woman set about acquiring a husband?

The chief protagonists described in the letters are the members of Jane Austen's immediate family. Her surviving correspondence begins in 1796, when she was already twenty-one, and her brothers and sister also grown up. They were the children of the Revd George Austen (1731–1805), who came of a Kentish family with wealthy connections. George Austen inherited no money, and owed a great deal to the patronage of two Kentish relatives. His uncle Francis Austen, a wealthy Sevenoaks solicitor, paid for him to attend Tonbridge School, and later, in 1773, presented him with the living of the Hampshire parish of Deane. Well before that, in 1761, while he was a Fellow of St John's College, Oxford, he was made rector of the adjoining parish of Steventon, the gift of a second cousin, Thomas Knight I. George Austen's solid prospects and good connections were enough to win him a similarly well-bred and well-connected (though also portionless) wife, Cassandra Leigh (1739–1827), the niece of Dr Theophilus Leigh, Master of Balliol, and sister of James Leigh, later Leigh-Perrot, who owned two substantial houses, Paragon, Bath, and Scarlets, in Berkshire.

To the small adjoining parishes, Steventon and Deane, which are on the edge of the chalk uplands seven miles from Basingstoke, the newly married Austens came in 1764, and there eight children were born: James, born 1765, who became a clergyman and succeeded his father as rector of Steventon; George, born 1766, who was mentally retarded and never lived with the family; Edward, born 1767, afterwards adopted by the childless Thomas Knight II, and eventually the owner of Godmersham Park, Kent, and Hampshire estates at Steventon and Chawton; Henry, born 1771, who became successively a soldier, banker, bankrupt, and clergyman; the sailors Frank, born 1774, and Charles, born 1779, both of whom eventually rose to be admirals; and the two sisters, neither of whom married, Cassandra, born 1773, and Jane, born 1775. Four of the brothers married and had children, and of these James's daughter Anna (later Lefroy) and (James) Edward (later Austen-Leigh), and Edward's eldest child Fanny Knight (later Knatchbull) figure most prominently in the letters. Another name of note is that of the Lloyd sisters, especially Mary, who married James in 1797, and is often referred to as Mrs J. A., and the unmarried Martha, who lived with Mrs Austen and her daughters during Jane's last years.

Jane Austen's life began and ended in the Hampshire countryside, with an eight-year interlude from her late twenties in Bath and Southampton. Until early 1801 she lived with her parents and her sister Cassandra at Steventon rectory, the house where she was born. Then George Austen decided to retire with his wife and daughters to a succession of lodgings at Bath, where, after four years, he died. Mrs Austen, Cassandra, and Jane would have been left with a mere £210 a year, had it not been more than doubled by contributions from Edward, James, Henry, and Frank. Between 1807 and 1809 they shared lodgings at Southampton with the newly-married Frank. From 1809 until Jane's death in 1817 from Addison's disease, a kidney complaint, they lived in a six-bedroomed house belonging to Edward in the Hampshire village of Chawton.

Almost all the surviving letters pass between these households and those of George Austen's other children. It was a very important part of the family ethos to keep together. This indeed is the rationale behind the letters, the reason they needed to be written and sent: they are reports to one branch of a scattered family on the doings and concerns of another. The unmarried, unoccupied sisters Cassandra and Jane played a key role as travellers between the households and assiduous correspondents, Cassandra specializing a little more in visiting Edward's household and connections in Kent, Jane somewhat closer to and more preoccupied with two of the younger brothers—Henry, said to have been her favourite, who lived in London, and the sailor Frank, who reported to her from various war fronts, the Kentish coastal defences, the Trafalgar campaign, the West Indies, the Peninsular War and the Baltic. The sisters made good aunts and friends to the next generation, especially to the children of James and Edward, the only ones Jane lived to see grow up: the socialite Fanny Knight made her a confidante in romantic matters (pp. 172–80, 190–7), while James's more literary children Anna and Edward consulted her about their novels (pp. 162ff., 169ff., 187ff.). The letters, which characteristically pass between two Austen households—Steventon, Godmersham, Southampton, Chawton—and between Jane in one and Cassandra in another, bond the family closer together by acting as news-sheets, very consciously for family news only. Jane sends details about Frank's promotion (pp. 18–24), not opinions about the war. Personalities and events outside the family ambit, local or national, have little significance, and the affairs of mere acquaintances often fail to come into focus—'we met . . . Dr. Hall in such very deep mourning that either his mother, his wife, or himself must be dead' (p. 25).

The reader of the saga made by the letters soon learns to locate the various branches of Austens and to characterize the different households, with their neighbourhood worlds. At Steventon rectory Jane Austen had enjoyed a happy, gregarious childhood rather like that attributed to Catherine Morland in *Northanger Abbey*: she learnt boys' games, rolled down the slope behind the house, and watched the older children acting comedies in her father's barn. But by the 1790s, with the boys gone, the girls and their parents lived more sedately in the roomy house, where Mrs Austen, having lost her occupation as a cheerful and competent mother, became hypochondriac and depressed. The family circle became less agreeable with the second marriage of James in 1797 to the former Mary Lloyd, a woman whom Jane Austen characterizes as domineering (p. 81), uncultivated (p. 72), and obsessed with money (p. 73). Their 'neighbourhood', the families they visited, consisted of the scattered landed gentry, the well-off tenants and the clergy of adjoining parishes: the Lefroys, more Kentish protégés of Frank Austen, from the adjoining parish of Ashe; the Digweeds, tenants of Steventon Manor, and Mr Holder, tenant of Ashe Park; the Lloyds at Ibthorp, the Fowles at Kintbury, and the Biggs at Manydown. Since the main landowner at Steventon was the absentee Edward Knight, and after 1797 his heir, Jane Austen's brother Edward, the rector's family had the enhanced prestige of being effectively the representatives of the local magnate. This put them on visiting terms with grander families, such as the Lady Dortchester who invites Jane to a ball on 8 January 1799 (p. 24). The sisters also attend regular assemblies in the nearest town, Basingstoke, in the hope, candidly revealed by the letters, of finding husbands. Jane Austen conducts a cheerful flirtation with Tom Lefroy, nephew of the rector of Ashe—'Imagine to yourself everything most profligate and shocking in the way of dancing and sitting down together' (p. 3). Cassandra became engaged to the Revd Thomas Fowle, but he died in the West Indies in 1797. A niece was told by Cassandra how Jane received a proposal from another neighbour, Harris Bigg-Wither of Manydown, in 1802, when he was twenty-one and she was twenty-seven; she accepted him, thought it over, and refused him the following morning.

The Austens may have moved to Bath to give their daughters a wider circle in which to look, but no offer was forthcoming there; it was at the seaside that Jane Austen met the young man whom the family believed she might have married (for Chapman's account, see p. 47). Bath society comes across in the letters as tedious, formal, and elderly: 'Another stupid party last night . . . I cannot anyhow continue to find people agreable' (p. 54). As contacts, the wealthy maternal uncle and aunt, the Leigh-Perrots, must have left something to be desired; the few surviving references to them are unenthusiastic, as though Jane Austen regarded them much as Anne Elliot in *Persuasion* regards Viscountess Dalrymple and the Hon. Miss Carteret, grand relations it is not quite worth keeping up with.

For the rest of her life Jane Austen had repeatedly to face the fact, somewhat masked in her youth at Steventon, that she was what a hierarchical society termed a poor relation. Edward's loyal invitations to his sisters to visit Godmersham enlarged their social horizons, but involved them in subtle humiliations. The coach fare to Kent was expensive, and they were given it by kind old Mrs Knight; dressing up to the standard of the great East Kent houses was evidently a perennial problem, on a personal allowance of £20 a year apiece. Their eldest Knight niece, Fanny, confided to a sister long afterwards that in good society they were 'below par': 'They were not rich & the people around with whom they chiefly mixed, were not at all high bred, or in short anything more than *mediocre* & they of course tho' superior in *Mental powers* & *cultivation* were on the same level as far as *refinement* goes—but . . . Aunt Jane was too clever not to put aside all possible signs of "common-ness" (if such an expression is allowable) & teach herself to be more refined, at least in intercourse with people in general' (*Cornhill*, 973 (1947–8), 72–3). One of Jane Austen's letters from Southampton betrays her dislike of being patronized on account of her poverty: 'They live in a handsome style and are rich, and she seemed to like to be rich, and we gave her to understand that we were far from being so; she will soon feel therefore that we are not worth her acquaintance' (pp. 74–5). It is an encounter that conveys the same sense of shame and resentment as *The Watsons*, the unfinished novel about a family of impecunious spinsters that she wrote some time after 1803.

Jane Austen's life is often described as even and her world as unchanging, but reading through the letters suggests otherwise; both her mood and her world change considerably. While she may have had personal reasons to feel sad as she grew older, she also caught a seriousness of tone which became common in polite society during her lifetime. Prosperity had enlarged the leisured class, promoting into it commercial and professional families whose background and experience made them critical of an older aristocracy they perceived as extravagant, frivolous, and often morally or religiously corrupt. Between 1793 and 1815, war with France, an atheistic and democratic enemy, gave a strong fillip to those moral crusaders who hoped to preserve the conservative status quo in Britain by ensuring that the propertied classes were fit to lead. It was precisely a family like the Austens, both gentry and professional, surviving on a combination of patronage and personal talent, which was likely to feel the call of Evangelicalism; and so the Austens did, or at least the poorer ones did.

When Jane Austen was growing up, her father and her clerical brothers James were both strictly speaking pluralists: they each had more than one church living, and so did not reside in one parish for which they were responsible. Criticism of pluralism and non-residence grew both inside and outside the Church during these years. George Austen, though a conscientious and pious clergyman, encouraged secular pursuits in his family, such as the reading of sensational Gothic novels and the acting of plays which were almost invariably light comedies. The newer, stricter attitude to clerical duties and to private theatricals manifests itself in *Mansfield Park* (1814). Frank and Cassandra Austen both seem to have been touched by evangelicalism before Jane was, and to have influenced her to follow their lead. The Admiral Gambier who appears in the letters as Frank's patron was a notable evangelical; Frank seems sometimes to have written home in an evangelical tone, as he did for example when he condemned slavery after a visit to Antigua in 1806; and Jane goes out of her way in writing to him to sympathize with the pleasure he must feel at visiting Sweden, 'so zealous as it was for Protestantism!' (p. 143). Jane read the evangelical Hannah More and Thomas Gisborne at Cassandra's suggestion, in 1805 and 1809. But the most direct evidence of Jane Austen's adoption of the evangelical goals and values, if not of the style, occurs when her Godmersham niece Fanny Knight asks her advice over a young man who is courting her, John Pemberton Plumtre. The fashionable Fanny must have represented John Plumtre's tendency to evangelicalism as ridiculous. Jane Austen in reply civilly but firmly disagrees: 'I am by no means convinced that we ought not all to be Evangelicals' (p. 174).

It is hard to tell whether Jane Austen underwent anything so dramatic as a 'conversion' in her middle years. In her youth she was, surely, already pious, but in the reticent eighteenth-century style; the letters show her engaged all her life in the visits and charitable giving expected of gentlewomen, especially of clergy families. But her tone as a correspondent certainly becomes more serious. In the 1790s and as late as 1801 she allows herself some saucy jokes in the Mary Crawford vein: 'I am proud to say that I have a very good eye at an Adultress, for tho' repeatedly assured that another in the same party was the *She*, I fixed upon the right one from the first . . . She . . . looked rather quietly & contentedly silly than anything else. Mrs. Badcock & two young women were of the same party, except when Mrs. Badcock thought herself obliged to leave them to run round the room after her drunken Husband. His avoidance, & her pursuit, with the probable intoxication of both, was an amusing scene' (p. 53). In 1807 she still finds neat ways of introducing scandal: ' . . . I see nothing to he glad of, unless I make it a matter of Joy that Mrs. Wylmot has another son, & that Ld Lucan has taken a Mistress, both of which Events are of course joyful to the Actors' (p. 75). Perhaps she later came to feel remorse for these flashes of malice; so, at least, the prayers she composed for her own use suggest—'Incline us oh God! to think humbly of ourselves, to be severe only in the examination of our own conduct, to consider our fellow-creatures with kindness.'

The deepening seriousness of tone accompanied a widening in social experience. After her first visit to Godmersham in 1798 Jane Austen cannot be described as a woman who had lived a retired life. She moved in East Kent great houses, Bath assembly rooms, occasionally London drawing-rooms; she could compare south-coast resorts like Lyme and Dawlish with a dockyard town like Southampton. Jane Austen wrote her first two books—*Sense and Sensibility* (1811) and *Pride and Prejudice* (1813)—soon after settling at Chawton, and these two, like the later *Northanger Abbey* (1818), are revamped versions of novels already substantially written in the 1790s; they have many sharply observed scenes, but they do not read like representative impressions of gentry life, as do the novels written entirely at Chawton—*Mansfield Park* (1814), *Emma* (1816), *Persuasion* (1818), and the fragment of 1817, *Sanditon*. Of these, *Mansfield Park* appears to deal with a restricted setting, a series of houses and their grounds, yet it confidently pronounces on the internal weaknesses of the gentry, even as victory over France was leaving them safe from outside enemies. *Emma*, *Persuasion*, and *Sanditon* are more open and documentary studies of contemporary life in three counties which border Hampshire and resemble it, Surrey, Dorset, and Sussex.

Chawton was a bigger village than Steventon, more prosperous and also far busier, for it was on the main road from London to Winchester. It was to just such villages, resembling Highbury in *Emma*, that London professional people, or half-pay officers, or clergy and clergy widows, might think of retiring. The Austens had no carriage now; instead of going far afield to do rather select visiting, as they had done from Steventon, they walked about the village or the two miles into the bustling small town of Alton, shopping, exchanging library books, and calling on Miss Benn, Chawton's real-life Miss Bates, whom everyone in the village seems to have felt responsible for. Jane Austen evidently had an acute eye for the social nuances of the heterogeneous, socially mobile community she encountered at Chawton, a countryside turning sub-

urban, its cottages and farmhouses converting to
villas. She captures the social unease in *Emma*, the
architectural disarray in the houses at Uppercross
in *Persuasion*, the fads, entrepreneurship and con-
sumerism in her portrayal of the ex-fishing village,
Sanditon, where progress becomes visible when the
shoemaker's window sports an expensive pair of
nankin boots.

Admittedly, these powers of observation, description,
and comment are displayed in the novels, not the
letters. We have to deduce from reading of her
activities and contacts what Chawton was like; she
was not one of those informed observers who noted
significant details like wages, rents, prices, and the
state of the harvest. Comparing two such onlookers,
Arthur Young in 1767 and William Cobbett in 1821,
we get an impression of economic decline in much of
rural Hampshire during her lifetime. Reports to the
Board of Agriculture in 1816, the year of *Emma*,
describe Hampshire businesses failing, farms aban-
doned, and labourers-turned-vagrants roaming the
lanes looking for work. It is not Jane Austen but her
nephew Edward Austen-Leigh who informs us that
weaving in the cottages, the means whereby labourers'
families supplemented their incomes in winter, ceased
at Steventon early in the 1800s, when it was rendered
unprofitable by the new mechanized industry further
north. Jane Austen may have avoided sociological
comment as she avoided political comment, because it
was ladylike to do so. But she is also silent on the
landscape, which in a time of enclosure must have
changed considerably, a fact which distressed John
Clare in Northamptonshire. The letters are considerably more reticent than the novels when it comes to

making general pronouncements, including visual ones, about her world.

They are reticent about emotions too. Cassandra thought otherwise, and burnt 'the greater part' of the letters addressed to her because they revealed too much. Yet the tone everywhere is so non-committal and the matter so prosaic that it is reasonable to doubt that Jane Austen ever wrote letters in the expressive autobiographical vein of her contemporaries Cowper, Lamb, and Keats, or that she offered opinions on general issues, like her fellow-novelist Maria Edgeworth. The style has evolved to transmit discrete items of news, not comment; it leaves scant room for the subjective. Chapman defends this feature of the letters by saying that, when postage costs were high, the recipient could not be expected to pay for mere opinions. This is an argument which applies equally to other letter-writers of the period, and it does not explain why some of them do write about themselves, while Jane Austen does not. More relevant is the fact that all those contemporaries with whom she is usually compared unfavourably were published writers. In that age of intense biographical curiosity, a celebrity's letters would be circulated, and sooner or later (if the writer was successful) would appear in print. The writer knew his correspondence to be, from the outset, part of his *œuvre*, and a uniquely influential means of commanding admiration: no one who has read the letters of Lamb, Byron, Keats, even Edgeworth, can doubt that each of these is aware of the public over the shoulder of the addressee. But Jane Austen wrote to her older sister and to other siblings, to whom she was not a professional writer, but a domestic figure, and a junior one; no one, in or out of the family, could have viewed her as an author until the last six years of her life. The Austen letters are unusual precisely because they do communicate with the private addressee, above all with Cassandra.

The critics of the 1930s who disliked the letters were comparing them, either explicitly or implicitly, with letters of the same period by writers; they sought, and failed to find, 'literariness', self-analysis, self-characterization, stylistic self-consciousness—those traits which reveal that a letter-writer is not addressing the addressee but the public. As an influential addressee, Cassandra came in for criticism: Jane's teasing 'I know your starched notions' (p. 134) was taken literally rather than ironically, and Cassandra subtly became her sister's censor even in the act of writing. Chapman himself joined the lobby against Cassandra—'I must add, though with reluctance, my impression that Cassandra Austen was not the correspondent who best evoked her sister's powers' (*Collected Letters*, p. xl). Instead he singles out the letters to her nieces, Fanny Knight and Anna Lefroy, for their 'flow of fancy', and also, presumably, for their treasured asides about novel-writing, like the fact that '3 or 4 families in a Country Village is the very thing to work on' (p. 170). Writing to young people, especially to novelists, Jane Austen was for once authoritative, in the role of a published professional writer. But to describe these as her best letters, attractive though they are, is to belittle the rest.

The charge that she lacks 'niceness' loses most of its point when we consider how much motive comparable letter-writers had to manufacture their images for the public and for posterity. She had her motives too—overtly, to keep up family connections; privately, to order her world in terms that made sense of it for herself and Cassandra. Far from reproducing the social scene photographically, Jane Austen shows it perspectively, with the nearest objects only in focus. Outsiders, whether peers or peasants, are named and given perhaps a single attribute. But she notices childbirth, a woman's experience, especially death in childbirth, just as she notices eligibility in young men. She does not look for new friends—'Miss Blachford is agreeable enough. I do not want people to be very agreeable, as it saves me the trouble of liking them a great deal' (p. 19). But she shows charity to the ageing women, Miss Benn and Mrs Stent, because there is a resemblance between their situation and the Austen sisters': 'Poor Mrs Stent! it has been her lot to be always in the way; but we must be merciful, for perhaps in time we may come to be Mrs Stents ourselves, unequal to anything & unwelcome to everybody' (p. 63).

She even makes distinctions within the family. The letters to Cassandra are surely written in a style to facilitate quotation but to deter reading aloud; they are too note-like and discontinuous to be followed except with the eye. If this convention had not been understood, she would have been less able to convey reservations about one sibling to another. Henry, she tells Frank, is getting over his grief for his wife Eliza rather quickly (pp. 144–5); having James to stay gives no pleasure, she observes to Cassandra, because he fidgets and bangs doors and remains under the influence of his disagreeable wife Mary (p. 81). On the Godmersham family the letters as we now have them are unfailingly polite, but somewhat distant. It was these two older branches who afterwards presented the 'family' Jane Austen to posterity. James's children Edward (Austen-Leigh) and Caroline wrote down the two most valuable firsthand accounts of her, Fanny Knight's son Lord Brabourne edited (1884) the first selection of letters. Naturally these relatives made no fine distinctions between their own senior branches, which inherited landed wealth, and the less secure junior ones. They presented Jane Austen as an acknowledged country gentlewoman, Fanny Knight's social equal, not the uneasy and marginal figure Fanny Knight actually remembered. But the letters tell another story.

As time goes on, Jane Austen writes most warmly to and about the brothers and sisters closest to her in age: a little quizzically, about Henry; more admiringly, about the sailors Frank and Charles, whose style as letter-writers she praises—'They are such thinking, clear, considerate Letters as Frank might have written' (p. 159), and of Charles, 'How pleasantly & how naturally he writes! and how perfect a picture of his Disposition & feelings, his style conveys!' (p. 184). She does not write of her *alter ego* Cassandra but only to her, in dense, allusive, non-descriptive language appropriate for a sister who grew up sharing a room and all confidences. In structure and content the later letters to the adoptive sister Martha Lloyd take on some similar characteristics: that of 29 November 1812 (pp. 123 ff.) is typical, and contains brisk business about village charity; an equally brisk and businesslike account of the new novel—'P. & P. is sold' (p. 125); and some tart village news—'Happy Woman! to stand the gaze of a neighbourhood as the Bride of such a pink-faced, simple young Man!' (p. 126). By now Jane Austen's writing for publication makes the most significant topic in the letters, the one that distinguishes the innermost from the second ring of intimacy. Only to Cassandra does she fully reveal her emotions about the novels—'I can no more forget it [S. & S.] than a mother can forget her sucking child' (p. 114); 'I have got my own darling child [P. & P.] from London' (p. 131). But she confides to both Cassandra and Martha that making money from the novels is essential to her pleasure in them; they understand her poverty, and Fanny Knight does not—'as you are much above caring about money, I shall not plague you with any particulars' (pp. 175–6). The sum Jane Austen left in her will, about £400, is approximately the sum she made from writing. Without it, she was economically dependent. With it, she was beginning to be, although a woman, the kind of effective professional her brothers in the Navy were. It would not have been easy to convey her understanding and delight in this transformation to anyone except Cassandra.

If these least manufactured of family and personal letters failed to meet some expectations of them, it was surely because the expectations were wrong. The bulk of the letters are bulletins upon the social world, not in a form intended for that world, as the novels are, but interestingly shaped as a dialogue with a sister whose worldly situation duplicated Austen's own. The 'gentle Jane' the world expected to meet in the letters was not an entire fabrication, but the civilized, pleasant, and charitable woman her neighbours, friends, and wider family saw, and some admirers, nostalgic for Regency elegance, still see. Those qualities are felt in the novels, for when Jane Austen wrote for publication she was on her guard. When she

wrote to Cassandra, it was not to please other people
but to resist, to challenge, and, in her private mental
universe, to master them. The family's Jane Austen
would have been the easier woman to meet, but
Cassandra's Jane Austen wrote *Mansfield Park* and
Emma.

MARILYN BUTLER

FURTHER READING

The following suggestions supplement books recommended by R. W. Chapman on p. v. On Jane Austen and her family: Jane Aiken Hodge, *The Double Life of Jane Austen* (1952); Lord David Cecil, *A Portrait of Jane Austen* (1978); George Holbert Tucker, *A Goodly Heritage: A History of Jane Austen's Family* (Manchester, 1983); Park Honan, *Jane Austen: Her Life* (1987).

For the historical context, see J. David Grey, A. Walton Litz and B. Southam (eds.), *The Jane Austen Companion* (NY, 1986; in UK, *The Jane Austen Handbook*, London, 1986); Oliver MacDonagh, *Jane Austen: Real and Imagined Worlds* (New Haven and London, 1991); Ellen Moers, *Literary Women* (1976); Jane Rendall, *The Origins of Modern Feminism: Women in Britain, France and the United States, 1780–1860* (1985); Warren Roberts, *Jane Austen and the French Revolution* (1979); Jane Spencer, *The Rise of the Woman Novelist* (1986); *Victoria County History: Hampshire and the Isle of Wight*, 6 vols., (1900–12), especially vol. 5.

I. STEVENTON

1796–1801: *Twenty to Twenty-five*

THE Steventon letters are full of the family and of the names of friends and neighbours, most of whom may be allowed to remain mere names. But we shall hear more of such intimates as the Lloyds at Ibthorp (which JA writes phonetically Ibthrop), the Fowles at Kintbury, the Lefroys at Ashe hard by, and the Biggs of Manydown (whose father and brother are, disconcertingly, Bigg-Wither). See the Introduction and Index.

Letters 1 and 2 tell of dancing and (probably very mild) flirting. The quality of Jane's affair with Tom Lefroy (of the Irish branch) was much debated in the family later; it was probably not serious. Mrs. Lefroy's 'friend' of 11, Samuel Blackall, reappears in 81; *he* seems to have had serious intentions, not reciprocated; but later and confused recollections connected him, wrongly, with what was almost certainly Jane's only real love-affair; see any Life, or the 'Romance' chapter in my *Facts and Problems*.

7 gives us our first glimpse of Kent, where Edward and his bride (daughter of one of several Kentish baronets who appear in the letters) had set up house.

Philadelphia Walter (8) was the daughter of George Austen's half-brother.

11, 12, 15, 16 are to Cassandra at Godmersham near Canterbury, where Edward had entered on his inheritance and was to bring up a large family. In 12

1

we hear of books: Egerton Brydges (brother of Jane's dear Mrs. Lefroy), Boswell, Cowper.

15 and 16 are full of the two sailors' affairs. 19 introduces Bath, where Jane was the guest of Edward, in search of health from the Pump. 24, 25, 27, 29 are from Steventon to Godmersham. They show George Austen's decision to retire to Bath; and though Jane shared Anne Elliot's dislike of Bath, she makes the best of it, and looks forward to seaside holidays.

26 is the first of the few surviving letters to Martha Lloyd, sister of James Austen's second wife and of Mrs. Eliza Fowle; she joined forces with Mrs. Austen, then widowed, and her daughters at Southampton and Chawton, later becoming Frank's second wife and so ultimately Lady Austen.

The only references, in these early letters, to Jane's novels are in letters (17, 21, not in this selection) of 1799, where *First Impressions* (the early name of *Pride and Prejudice*) is mentioned as having been read by Cassandra and Martha.

It is significant, both for Jane's love-affair and for her assumed abstinence from literary work in the long interval between Steventon and Chawton, that between May 1801 and January 1805 we have only one letter, from Lyme in 1804.

1. *To Cassandra Austen.*[1] *Saturday* 9 *Jan.* ⟨1796⟩

Steventon: Saturday January 9

In the first place I hope you will live twenty-three years longer. Mr. Tom Lefroy's birthday was yesterday, so that you are very near of an age.

[1] Staying with the Fowles at Kintbury.

After this necessary preamble I shall proceed to inform you that we had an exceeding good ball last night, and that I was very much disappointed at not seeing Charles Fowle of the party, as I had previously heard of his being invited. In addition to our set at the Harwood's ball, we had the Grants, St. Johns, Lady Rivers, her three daughters and a son, Mr. and Miss Heathcote, Mrs. Lefevre, two Mr. Watkins, Mr. J. Portal, Miss Deanes, two Miss Ledgers, and a tall clergyman who came with them, whose name Mary[1] would never have guessed.

We were so terrible good as to take James in our carriage, though there were three of us before; but indeed he deserves encouragement for the very great improvement which has lately taken place in his dancing. Miss Heathcote is pretty, but not near so handsome as I expected. Mr. H. began with Elizabeth,[2] and afterwards danced with her again; but *they* do not know how *to be particular*. I flatter myself, however, that they will profit by the three successive lessons which I have given them.

You scold me so much in the nice long letter which I have this moment received from you, that I am almost afraid to tell you how my Irish friend[3] and I behaved. Imagine to yourself everything most profligate and shocking in the way of dancing and sitting down together. I *can* expose myself, however, only *once more*, because he leaves the country soon after next Friday, on which day we *are* to have a dance at Ashe after all. He is a very gentlemanlike, good-looking, pleasant young man, I assure you. But as to our having ever met, except at the three last balls, I

---

[1] Lloyd, soon to be the second Mrs. James Austen.
[2] Bigg.   [3] Tom Lefroy.

cannot say much; for he is so excessively laughed at about me at Ashe, that he is ashamed of coming to Steventon, and ran away when we called on Mrs. Lefroy a few days ago.

We left Warren at Dean Gate, in our way home last night, and he is now on his road to town. He left his love, &c., to you, and I will deliver it when we meet. Henry goes to Harden[1] to-day in his way to his Master's degree. We shall feel the loss of these two most agreeable young men exceedingly, and shall have nothing to console us till the arrival of the Coopers on Tuesday. As they will stay here till the Monday following, perhaps Caroline will go to the Ashe ball with me, though I dare say she will not.

I danced twice with Warren last night, and once with Mr. Charles Watkins, and, to my inexpressible astonishment, I entirely escaped John Lyford. I was forced to fight hard for it, however. We had a very good supper, and the greenhouse was illuminated in a very elegant manner.

We had a visit yesterday morning from Mr. Benjamin Portal, whose eyes are as handsome as ever. Everybody is extremely anxious for your return, but as you cannot come home by the Ashe ball, I am glad that I have not fed them with false hopes. James danced with Alithea,[2] and cut up the turkey last night with great perseverance. You say nothing of the silk stockings; I flatter myself, therefore, that Charles[3] has not purchased any, as I cannot very well afford to pay for them; all my money is spent in buying white gloves and pink persian. I wish Charles had been at Manydown, because he would have given you some description of

[1] To the Coopers.   [2] Bigg.
[3] Fowle.

4

my friend, and I think you must be impatient to hear
something about him.

Henry is still hankering after the Regulars, and as
his project of purchasing the adjutancy of the Oxfordshire is now over, he has got a scheme in his head about
getting a lieutenancy and adjutancy in the 86th, a
new-raised regiment, which he fancies will be ordered
to the Cape of Good Hope. I heartily hope that he will,
as usual, be disappointed in this scheme. We have
trimmed up and given away all the old paper hats of
Mamma's manufacture; I hope you will not regret the
loss of yours.

After I had written the above, we received a visit
from Mr. Tom Lefroy and his cousin George. The
latter is really very well-behaved now; and as for the
other, he has but *one* fault, which time will, I trust,
entirely remove—it is that his morning coat is a great
deal too light. He is a very great admirer of Tom
Jones, and therefore wears the same coloured clothes,
I imagine, which *he* did when he was wounded.

Sunday. By not returning till the 19th, you will
exactly contrive to miss seeing the Coopers, which I
suppose it is your wish to do. We have heard nothing
from Charles[1] for some time. One would suppose they
must have sailed by this time, as the wind is so favourable. What a funny name Tom[2] has got for his vessel!
But he has no taste in names, as we well know, and
I dare say he christened it himself. I am sorry for the

---

[1] Austen.

[2] *Tom* is either Thomas Williams, R.N., who married JA's first
cousin Jane Cooper, or Thomas Fowle, Cassandra's fiancé, who at about
this time sailed, as chaplain, to the West Indies, where he died in 1797.
When Cassandra believed herself to have destroyed all very intimate
letters from her sister, she might overlook this reference; she certainly
overlooked that to her 'wedding-clothes' in the letter of 1 Sept. 1796.

Beaches' loss of their little girl, especially as it is the one so much like me.

I condole with Miss M. on her losses and with Eliza[1] on her gains, and am ever yours,

J. A.

2. *To Cassandra Austen. Thursday ⟨14⟩ Jan. ⟨1796⟩*

Steventon: Thursday January 16

I have just received yours and Mary's letter, and I thank you both, though their contents might have been more agreeable. I do not at all expect to see you on Tuesday, since matters have fallen out so unpleasantly; and if you are not able to return till after that day, it will hardly be possible for us to send for you before Saturday, though for my own part I care so little about the ball that it would be no sacrifice to me to give it up for the sake of seeing you two days earlier. We are extremely sorry for poor Eliza's illness. I trust, however, that she has continued to recover since you wrote, and that you will none of you be the worse for your attendance on her. What a good-for-nothing fellow Charles[1] is to bespeak the stockings! I hope he will be too hot all the rest of his life for it!

I sent you a letter yesterday to Ibthorp, which I suppose you will not receive at Kintbury. It was not very long or very witty, and therefore if you never receive it, it does not much signify. I wrote principally to tell you that the Coopers were arrived and in good health. The little boy is very like Dr. Cooper, and the little girl is to resemble Jane, they say.

Our party to Ashe to-morrow night will consist of

---

[1] Fowle.

Edward Cooper, James (for a ball is nothing without *him*), Buller, who is now staying with us, and I. I look forward with great impatience to it, as I rather expect to receive an offer from my friend in the course of the evening. I shall refuse him, however, unless he promises to give away his white coat.

I am very much flattered by your commendation of my last letter, for I write only for fame, and without any view to pecuniary emolument.

Edward is gone to spend the day with his friend, John Lyford, and does not return till to-morrow. Anna[1] is now here; she came up in her chaise to spend the day with her young cousins, but she does not much take to them or to anything about them, except Caroline's[2] spinning-wheel. I am very glad to find from Mary that Mr. and Mrs. Fowle are pleased with you. I hope you will continue to give satisfaction.

How impertinent you are to write to me about Tom,[3] as if I had not opportunities of hearing from him myself! The *last* letter that I received from him was dated on Friday the 8th, and he told me that if the wind should be favourable on Sunday, which it proved to be, they were to sail from Falmouth on that day. By this time, therefore, they are at Barbadoes, I suppose. The Rivers are still at Manydown, and are to be at Ashe to-morrow. I intended to call on the Miss Biggs yesterday had the weather been tolerable. Caroline, Anna, and I have just been devouring some cold souse, and it would be difficult to say which enjoyed it most.

Tell Mary that I make over Mr. Heartley and all his estate to her for her sole use and benefit in future, and not only him, but all my other admirers into the

---

[1] James's daughter.   [3] Cooper.
[2] See note on p. 5.

bargain wherever she can find them, even the kiss which C. Powlett wanted to give me, as I mean to confine myself in future to Mr. Tom Lefroy, for whom I do not care sixpence. Assure her also, as a last and indubitable proof of Warren's indifference to me, that he actually drew that gentleman's picture for me, and delivered it to me without a sigh.

Friday. At length the day is come on which I am to flirt my last with Tom Lefroy, and when you receive this it will be over. My tears flow as I write at the melancholy idea. Wm. Chute called here yesterday. I wonder what he means by being so civil. There is a report that Tom[1] is going to be married to a Lichfield lass. John Lyford and his sister bring Edward[2] home to-day, dine with us, and we shall all go together to Ashe. I understand that we are to draw for partners. I shall be extremely impatient to hear from you again, that I may know how Eliza is, and when you are to return.

With best love, &c., I am affectionately yours,

J. Austen

7. *To Cassandra Austen. Sunday* 18 *Sept.* 1796

Rowling: Sunday 18th Septr

My dear Cassandra

This morning has been spent in Doubt & Deliberation; in forming plans, and removing Difficulties, for it ushered in the Day with an Event which I had not intended should take place so soon by a week. Frank has recd his appointment on Board the Captain John Gore, commanded by the Triton, and will therefore

---

[1] Chute. [2] Cooper.

be obliged to be in Town on wednesday—and tho' I have every Disposition in the world to accompany him on that day, I cannot go on the Uncertainty of the Pearsons being at Home; as I should not have a place to go to, in case they were from Home. I wrote to Miss P. on friday, and hoped to receive an answer from her this morning, which would have rendered everything smooth and Easy, and would have enabled us to leave this place to-morrow, as Frank on first receiving his Appointment, intended to do. He remains till Wednesday merely to accomodate me. I have written to her again to-day and desired her to answer it by return of post—On Tuesday therefore I shall positively know whether they can receive me on Wednesday—If they cannot, Edward has been so good as to promise to take me to Greenwich on the Monday following which was the day before fixed on, if that suits them better. If I have no answer at all on Tuesday, I must suppose Mary[1] is not at Home, and must wait till I do hear; as after having invited her to go to Steventon with me, it will not quite do, to go home and say no more about it.

My Father will be so good as to fetch home his prodigal Daughter from Town, I hope, unless he wishes me to walk the Hospitals, Enter at the Temple, or mount Guard at St. James. It will hardly be in Frank's power to take me home; nay, it certainly will not. I shall write again as soon as I get to Greenwich.

What dreadful Hot weather we have!—It keeps one in a continual state of Inelegance. If Miss Pearson should return with me, pray be careful not to expect too much Beauty. I will not pretend to say that on a *first veiw*, she quite answered the opinion I had formed of her. My Mother I am sure will be disappointed, if

[1] Pearson.

she does not take great care. From what I remember
of her picture, it is no great resemblance. I am very
glad that the idea of returning with Frank occurred
to me, for as to Henry's coming into Kent again, the
time of its taking place is so very uncertain, that I
should be waiting for *Dead-men's Shoes.*

I had once determined to go with Frank to-morrow
and take my chance &c.; but they dissuaded me from
so rash a step—as I really think on consideration it
would have been; for if the Pearsons were not at home,
I should inevitably fall a Sacrifice to the arts of some
fat Woman who would make me drunk with Small
Beer.

Mary is brought to bed of a Boy; both doing very
well. I shall leave you to guess what Mary, I mean.—
Adieu, with best Love to all your agreable Inmates.
Do not let the Lloyds go on any account before I
return, unless Miss P. is of the party.

How ill I have written. I begin to hate myself.

Yrs ever,

J: Austen

The Triton is a new 32 Frigate, just launched at
Deptford.—Frank is much pleased with the prospect
of having Capt: Gore under his command.

8. ⟨*To Philadelphia Walter*⟩. *Sunday 8 April* ⟨1798⟩

Steventon Sunday April 8th

⟨1798 in another hand⟩

My dear Cousin

As Cassandra is at present from home, you must
accept from my pen, our sincere Condolance on the

10

melancholy Event which Mrs Humphries Letter announced to my Father this morning. The loss of so kind & affectionate a Parent, must be a very severe affliction to all his Children, to yourself more especially, as your constant residence with him has given you so much the more constant & intimate Knowledge of his Virtues. But the very circumstance which at present enhances your loss, must gradually reconcile you to it the better; the Goodness which made him valuable on Earth, will make him Blessed in Heaven. This consideration must bring comfort to yourself, to my Aunt, & to all his family & friends; & this comfort must be heightened by the consideration of the little Enjoyment he was able to receive from this World for some time past, & of the small degree of pain attending his last hours. I will not press you to write before you would otherwise feel equal to it, but when you can do it without pain, I hope we shall receive from you as good an account of my Aunt & yourself, as can be expected in these early days of Sorrow. My Father & Mother join me in every kind wish, & I am my dear Cousin,

Yours affec:^{tely}

Jane Austen

11. *To Cassandra Austen. Saturday* 17 *Nov.* 1798

Saturday, November 17, 1798.

My dear Cassandra

If you paid any attention to the conclusion of my last letter, you will be satisfied, before you receive this, that my mother has had no relapse, and that Miss Debary comes. The former continues to recover, and though she does not gain strength very rapidly, my expectations are humble enough not to outstride her improvements. She was able to sit up nearly eight hours yesterday, and to-day I hope we shall do as much. . . . So much for my patient—now for myself.

Mrs. Lefroy did come last Wednesday, and the Harwoods came likewise, but very considerately paid their visit before Mrs. Lefroy's arrival, with whom, in spite of interruptions both from my father and James, I was enough alone to hear all that was interesting, which you will easily credit when I tell you that of her nephew[1] she said nothing at all, and of her friend[2] very little. She did not once mention the name of the former to *me*, and I was too proud to make any enquiries; but on my father's afterwards asking where he was, I learnt that he was gone back to London in his way to Ireland, where he is called to the Bar and means to practise.

She showed me a letter which she had received from her friend a few weeks ago (in answer to one written by her to recommend a nephew of Mrs. Russell to his notice at Cambridge), towards the end of which was a sentence to this effect: 'I am very sorry to hear of Mrs. Austen's illness. It would give me particular pleasure to have an opportunity of improving my acquaintance with that family—with a hope of creating to myself a nearer interest. But at present I cannot indulge any expectation of it.' This is rational enough; there is less love and more sense in it than sometimes appeared before, and I am very well satisfied. It will all go on exceedingly well, and decline away in a very reasonable manner. There seems no likelihood of his coming into Hampshire this Christmas, and it is therefore most probable that our indifference will soon be mutual,

---

[1] Tom Lefroy.   [2] Blackall, see p. 146.

unless his regard, which appeared to spring from knowing nothing of me at first, is best supported by never seeing me.

Mrs. Lefroy made no remarks on the letter, nor did she indeed say anything about him as relative to me. Perhaps she thinks she has said too much already. She saw a great deal of the Mapletons while she was in Bath. Christian is still in a very bad state of health, consumptive, and not likely to recover.

Mrs. Portman is not much admired in Dorsetshire; the good-natured world, as usual, extolled her beauty so highly, that all the neighbourhood have had the pleasure of being disappointed.

My mother desires me to tell you that I am a very good housekeeper, which I have no reluctance in doing, because I really think it my peculiar excellence, and for this reason—I always take care to provide such things as please my own appetite, which I consider as the chief merit in housekeeping. I have had some ragout veal, and I mean to have some haricot mutton to-morrow. We are to kill a pig soon.

There is to be a ball at Basingstoke next Thursday. Our assemblies have very kindly declined ever since we laid down the carriage, so that dis-convenience and dis-inclination to go have kept pace together.

My father's affection for Miss Cuthbert is as lively as ever, and he begs that you will not neglect to send him intelligence of her or her brother, whenever you have any to send. I am likewise to tell you that one of his Leicestershire sheep, sold to the butcher last week, weighed 27 lb. and ¼ per quarter.

I went to Deane with my father two days ago to see Mary, who is still plagued with the rheumatism, which she would be very glad to get rid of, and still more glad

13

to get rid of her child,[1] of whom she is heartily tired. Her nurse is come, and has no particular charm either of person or manner; but as all the Hurstbourne world pronounce her to be the best nurse that ever was, Mary expects her attachment to increase.

What fine weather this is! Not very becoming perhaps early in the morning, but very pleasant out of doors at noon, and very wholesome—at least everybody fancies so, and imagination is everything. To Edward, however, I really think dry weather of importance. I have not taken to fires yet.

I believe I never told you that Mrs. Coulthard and Anne, late of Manydown, are both dead, and both died in childbed. We have not regaled Mary with this news. Harry St. John is in Orders, has done duty at Ashe, and performs very well.

I am very fond of experimental housekeeping, such as having an ox-cheek now and then; I shall have one next week, and I mean to have some little dumplings put into it, that I may fancy myself at Godmersham.

I hope George[2] was pleased with my designs. Perhaps they would have suited him as well had they been less elaborately finished; but an artist cannot do anything slovenly. I suppose baby[3] grows and improves.

Sunday. I have just received a note from James to say that Mary was brought to bed last night, at eleven o'clock, of a fine little boy, and that everything is going on very well. My mother had desired to know nothing of it before it should be all over, and we were clever enough to prevent her having any suspicion of

[1] James Edward.
[2] Edward's boy.
[3] Edward's infant son William.

14

it, though Jenny, who had been left here by her mistress, was sent for home. . . .

I called yesterday on Betty Londe, who enquired particularly after you, and said she seemed to miss you very much, because you used to call in upon her very often. This was an oblique reproach at me, which I am sorry to have merited, and from which I will profit. I shall send George another picture when I write next, which I suppose will be soon, on Mary's account. My mother continues well.

Yours,
J. A.

12. *To Cassandra Austen. Sunday* 25 *Nov.* ⟨1798⟩

Steventon: Sunday November 25

My dear Sister

I expected to have heard from you this morning, but no letter is come. I shall not take the trouble of announcing to you any more of Mary's children, if, instead of thanking me for the intelligence, you always sit down and write to James. I am sure nobody can desire your letters so much as I do, and I don't think anybody deserves them so well.

Having now relieved my heart of a great deal of malevolence, I will proceed to tell you that Mary continues quite well, and my mother tolerably so. I saw the former on Friday, and though I had seen her comparatively hearty the Tuesday before, I was really amazed at the improvement which three days had made in her. She looked well, her spirits were perfectly good, and she spoke much more vigorously than Elizabeth[1] did when we left Godmersham. I had only a

[1] Edward's wife.

glimpse at the child, who was asleep; but Miss Debary told me that his eyes were large, dark, and handsome. *She* looks much as she used to do, is netting herself a gown in worsteds, and wears what Mrs. Birch would call a *pot hat*. A short and compendious history of Miss Debary!

I suppose you have heard from Henry himself that his affairs are happily settled. We do not know who furnishes the qualification. Mr. Mowell[1] would have readily given it, had not all his Oxfordshire property been engaged for a similar purpose to the Colonel. Amusing enough!

Our family affairs are rather deranged at present, for Nanny has kept her bed these three or four days, with a pain in her side and fever, and we are forced to have two charwomen, which is not very comfortable. She is considerably better now, but it must still be some time, I suppose, before she is able to do anything. You and Edward will be amused, I think, when you know that Nanny Littlewart dresses my hair.

The ball on Thursday was a very small one indeed, hardly so large as an Oxford smack.[2] There were but seven couples, and only twenty-seven people in the room.

The Overton Scotchman has been kind enough to rid me of some of my money, in exchange for six shifts and four pairs of stockings. The Irish is not so fine as I should like it; but as I gave as much money for it as I intended, I have no reason to complain. It cost me 3*s.* 6*d.* per yard. It is rather finer, however, than our last, and not so harsh a cloth.

We have got 'Fitz-Albini;' my father has bought it

---

[1] Probably Morrell; the MS. is untraced.
[2] Not explained.

against my private wishes, for it does not quite satisfy
my feelings that we should purchase the only one of
Egerton's works of which his family are ashamed. That
these scruples, however, do not at all interfere with my
reading it, you will easily believe. We have neither of
us yet finished the first volume. My father is disappointed—*I* am not, for I expected nothing better.
Never did any book carry more internal evidence of
its author. Every sentiment is completely Egerton's.[1]
There is very little story, and what there is told in a
strange, unconnected way. There are many characters
introduced, apparently merely to be delineated. We
have not been able to recognise any of them hitherto,
except Dr. and Mrs. Hey and Mr. Oxenden, who is not
very tenderly treated.

You must tell Edward that my father gives 25*s.*
a piece to Seward for his last lot of sheep, and, in
return for this news, my father wishes to receive some
of Edward's pigs.

We have got Boswell's 'Tour to the Hebrides,' and
are to have his 'Life of Johnson;' and, as some money
will yet remain in Burdon's hands, it is to be laid out
in the purchase of Cowper's works. This would please
Mr. Clarke, could he know it.

By the bye, I have written to Mrs. Birch among my
other writings, and so I hope to have some account of
all the people in that part of the world before long.
I have written to Mrs. E. Leigh[2] too, and Mrs. Heathcote has been ill-natured enough to send me a letter
of enquiry; so that altogether I am tolerably tired of
letter-writing, and, unless I have anything new to tell

[1] Brydges.
[2] Elizabeth L. of Adlestrop, an elderly spinster, Cassandra's godmother.

you of my mother or Mary, I shall not write again for many days; perhaps a little repose may restore my regard for a pen. Ask little Edward whether Bob Brown wears a great coat this cold weather.

15. *To Cassandra Austen. Monday* 24 *Dec.* ⟨1798⟩

Steventon: Monday night December 24.

My dear Cassandra

I have got some pleasant news for you which I am eager to communicate, and therefore begin my letter sooner, though I shall not *send* it sooner than usual.

Admiral Gambier, in reply to my father's application, writes as follows:—'As it is usual to keep young officers in small vessels, it being most proper on account of their inexperience, and it being also a situation where they are more in the way of learning their duty, your son has been continued in the "Scorpion;"[1] but I have mentioned to the Board of Admiralty his wish to be in a frigate, and when a proper opportunity offers and it is judged that he has taken his turn in a small ship, I hope he will be removed. With regard to your son now in the "London"[2] I am glad I can give you the assurance that his promotion is likely to take place very soon, as Lord Spencer has been so good as to say he would include him in an arrangement that he proposes making in a short time relative to some promotions in that quarter.'

There! I may now finish my letter and go and hang myself, for I am sure I can neither write nor do anything which will not appear insipid to you after this. *Now* I really think he will soon be made, and only wish we could communicate our foreknowledge of the event

[1] Charles.   [2] Frank.

to him whom it principally concerns. My father has
written to Daysh to desire that he will inform us, if
he can, when the commission is sent. Your chief wish
is now ready to be accomplished; and could Lord
Spencer give happiness to Martha[1] at the same time,
what a joyful heart he would make of yours!

I have sent the same extract of the sweets of
Gambier to Charles, who, poor fellow, though he sinks
into nothing but an humble attendant on the hero of
the piece, will, I hope, be contented with the prospect
held out to him. By what the Admiral says, it appears
as if he had been designedly kept in the 'Scorpion.'
But I will not torment myself with conjectures and
suppositions; facts shall satisfy me.

Frank had not heard from any of us for ten weeks
when he wrote to me on November 12 in consequence
of Lord St. Vincent being removed to Gibraltar. When
his commission is sent, however, it will not be so long
on its road as our letters, because all the Government
despatches are forwarded by land to his lordship from
Lisbon with great regularity.

I returned from Manydown this morning, and found
my mother certainly in no respect worse than when I
left her. She does not like the cold weather, but that
we cannot help. I spent my time very quietly and very
pleasantly with Catherine. Miss Blachford is agreeable
enough. I do not want people to be very agreeable, as
it saves me the trouble of liking them a great deal. I
found only Catherine and her when I got to Manydown on Thursday. We dined together and went
together to Worting to seek the protection of Mrs.
Clarke, with whom were Lady Mildmay, her eldest
son, and a Mr. and Mrs. Hoare.

[1] See note, p. 213.

Our ball was very thin, but by no means unpleasant. There were thirty-one people, and only eleven ladies out of the number, and but five single women in the room. Of the gentlemen present you may have some idea from the list of my partners—Mr. Wood, G. Lefroy, Rice, a Mr. Butcher (belonging to the Temples, a sailor and not of the 11th Light Dragoons), Mr. Temple (not the horrid one of all), Mr. Wm. Orde (cousin to the Kingsclere man), Mr. John Harwood, and Mr. Calland,[1] who appeared as usual with his hat in his hand, and stood every now and then behind Catherine and me to be talked to and abused for not dancing. We teased him, however, into it at last. I was very glad to see him again after so long a separation, and he was altogether rather the genius and flirt of the evening. He enquired after you.

There were twenty dances, and I danced them all, and without any fatigue. I was glad to find myself capable of dancing so much, and with so much satisfaction as I did; from my slender enjoyment of the Ashford balls (as assemblies for dancing) I had not thought myself equal to it, but in cold weather and with few couples I fancy I could just as well dance for a week together as for half an hour. My black cap was openly admired by Mrs. Lefroy, and secretly I imagine by everybody else in the room.

Tuesday. I thank you for your long letter, which I will endeavour to deserve by writing the rest of this as closely as possible. I am full of joy at much of your information; that you should have been to a ball, and have danced at it, and supped with the Prince,[2] and that you should meditate the purchase of a new muslin gown, are delightful circumstances. *I* am determined

[1] See note, p. 213.   [2] Prince William of Gloucester.

to buy a handsome one whenever I can, and I am so tired and ashamed of half my present stock, that I even blush at the sight of the wardrobe which contains them. But I will not be much longer libelled by the possession of my coarse spot; I shall turn it into a petticoat very soon. I wish you a merry Christmas, but *no* compliments of the season.

Poor Edward! It is very hard that he, who has everything else in the world that he can wish for, should not have good health too. But I hope with the assistance of stomach complaints, faintnesses, and sicknesses, he will soon be restored to that blessing likewise. If his nervous complaint proceeded from a suppression of something that ought to be thrown out, which does not seem unlikely, the first of these disorders may really be a remedy, and I sincerely wish it may, for I know no one more deserving of happiness without alloy than Edward is.

I cannot determine what to do about my new gown; I wish such things were to be bought ready-made. I have some hopes of meeting Martha at the christening at Deane next Tuesday, and shall see what she can do for me. I want to have something suggested which will give me no trouble of thought or direction.

Again I return to my joy that you danced at Ashford, and that you supped with the Prince. I can perfectly comprehend Mrs. Cage's distress and perplexity. She has all those kind of foolish and incomprehensible feelings which would make her fancy herself uncomfortable in such a party. I love her, however, in spite of all her nonsense. Pray give 't'other Miss Austen's' compliments to Edward Bridges when you see him again.

I insist upon your persevering in your intention of

buying a new gown; I am sure you must want one, and as you will have 5*l.* due in a week's time, I am certain you may afford it very well, and if you think you cannot, I will give you the body-lining.

Of my charities to the poor since I came home you shall have a faithful account. I have given a pair of worsted stockings to Mary Hutchins, Dame Kew, Mary Steevens, and Dame Staples; a shift to Hannah Staples, and a shawl to Betty Dawkins; amounting in all to about half a guinea. But I have no reason to suppose that the *Battys* would accept of anything, because I have not made them the offer.

I am glad to hear such a good account of Harriet Bridges; she goes on now as young ladies of seventeen ought to do, admired and admiring, in a much more rational way than her three elder sisters, who had so little of that kind of youth. I dare say she fancies Major Elkington as agreeable as Warren, and if she can think so, it is very well.

I was to have dined at Deane to-day, but the weather is so cold that I am not sorry to be kept at home by the appearance of snow. We are to have company at dinner on Friday: the three Digweeds and James. We shall be a nice silent party, I suppose. Seize upon the scissors as soon as you possibly can on the receipt of this. I only fear your being too late to secure the prize.

The Lords of the Admiralty will have enough of our applications at present, for I hear from Charles that he has written to Lord Spencer himself to be removed. I am afraid his Serene Highness will be in a passion, and order some of our heads to be cut off.

My mother wants to know whether Edward has ever made the hen-house which they planned together.

I am rejoiced to hear from Martha that they certainly continue at Ibthorp, and I have just heard that I am sure of meeting Martha at the christening.

You deserve a longer letter than this; but it is my unhappy fate seldom to treat people so well as they deserve. . . . God bless you!

Yours affectionately,

Jane Austen

Wednesday. The snow came to nothing yesterday, so I *did* go to Deane, and returned home at nine o'clock at night in the little carriage, and without being very cold.

16. *To Cassandra Austen. Friday* 28 *Dec.* 1798

My dear Cassandra

Frank is made. He was yesterday raised to the Rank of Commander & appointed to the Petterel Sloop, now at Gibraltar. A Letter from Daysh has just announced this, & as it is confirmed by a very friendly one from Mr Mathew to the same effect transcribing one from Admiral Gambier to the General, We have no reason to suspect the truth of it. As soon as you have cried a little for Joy, you may go on, & learn farther that the India House have taken *Captn Austen's* Petition into consideration—this comes from Daysh—& likewise that Lieut: Charles John Austen is removed to the *Tamer* Frigate—this comes from the Admiral. We cannot find out where the Tamer is, but I hope we shall now see Charles here at all Events.

This letter is to be dedicated entirely to good News. If you will send my father an account of your Washing & Letter expences &c, he will send you a draft for the

amount of it, as well as for your next quarter, & for
Edward's rent. If you don't buy a muslin Gown now
on the strength of this Money, & Frank's promotion,
I shall never forgive you.

Mrs Lefroy has just sent me word that Lady Dortchester means to invite me to her Ball on the 8th of
January, which tho' an humble Blessing compared
with what the last page records, I do not consider as
any Calamity. I cannot write any more now, but I have
written enough to make you very happy, & therefore
may safely conclude.——

Yours affec^ly

Jane

Steventon Friday Decr 28th

19. *To Cassandra Austen. Friday* 17 *May* ⟨1799⟩

13, Queen's Square, Friday May 17

My dearest Cassandra

Our journey yesterday went off exceedingly well;
nothing occurred to alarm or delay us. We found the
roads in excellent order, had very good horses all the
way, and reached Devizes with ease by four o'clock.
I suppose John has told you in what manner we were
divided when we left Andover, and no alteration was
afterwards made. At Devizes we had comfortable
rooms and a good dinner, to which we sat down about
lobster, which made me wish for you, and some
cheese-cakes, on which the children made so delightful a supper as to endear the town of Devizes to them
for a long time.

Well, here we are at Bath; we got here about one

o'clock, and have been arrived just long enough to go over the house, fix on our rooms, and be very well pleased with the whole of it. Poor Elizabeth has had a dismal ride of it from Devizes, for it has rained almost all the way, and our first view of Bath has been just as gloomy as it was last November twelvemonth.

I have got so many things to say, so many things equally unimportant, that I know not on which to decide at present, and shall therefore go and eat with the children.

We stopped in Paragon[1] as we came along, but as it was too wet and dirty for us to get out, we could only see Frank, who told us that his master was very indifferent, but had had a better night last night than usual. In Paragon we met Mrs. Foley and Mrs. Dowdeswell with her yellow shawl airing out, and at the bottom of Kingsdown Hill we met a gentleman in a buggy, who, on minute examination, turned out to be Dr. Hall—and Dr. Hall in such very deep mourning that either his mother, his wife, or himself must be dead. These are all of our acquaintance who have yet met our eyes.

I have some hopes of being plagued about my trunk; I *had* more a few hours ago, for it was too heavy to go by the coach which brought Thomas and Rebecca from Devizes; there was reason to suppose that it might be too heavy likewise for any other coach, and for a long time we could hear of no waggon to convey it. At last, however, we unluckily discovered that one was just on the point of setting out for this place, but at any rate the trunk cannot be here till to-morrow; so far we are safe, and who knows what may not happen to procure a farther delay?

[1] The Leigh-Perrots.

25

I put Mary's letter into the post-office at Andover with my own hand.

We are exceedingly pleased with the house; the rooms are quite as large as we expected. Mrs. Bromley is a fat woman in mourning, and a little black kitten runs about the staircase. Elizabeth has the apartment within the drawing-room; she wanted my mother to have it, but as there was no bed in the inner one, and the stairs are so much easier of ascent, or my mother so much stronger than in Paragon as not to regard the double flight, it is settled for us to be above, where we have two very nice-sized rooms, with dirty quilts and everything comfortable. I have the outward and larger apartment, as I ought to have; which is quite as large as our bedroom at home, and my mother's is not materially less. The beds are both as large as any at Steventon, and I have a very nice chest of drawers and a closet full of shelves—so full indeed that there is nothing else in it, and it should therefore be called a cupboard rather than a closet, I suppose.

Tell Mary that there were some carpenters at work in the inn at Devizes this morning, but as I could not be sure of their being Mrs. W. Fowle's relations, I did not make myself known to them.

I hope it will be a tolerable afternoon. When first we came, all the umbrellas were up, but now the pavements are getting very white again.

My mother does not seem at all the worse for her journey, nor are any of us, I hope, though Edward seemed rather fagged last night, and not very brisk this morning; but I trust the bustle of sending for tea, coffee, and sugar, &c., and going out to taste a cheese himself, will do him good.

There was a very long list of arrivals here in the

newspaper yesterday, so that we need not immediately dread absolute solitude; and there is a public breakfast in Sydney Gardens every morning, so that we shall not be wholly starved.

Elizabeth has just had a very good account of the three little boys.[1] I hope you are very busy and very comfortable. I find no difficulty in doing my eyes. I like our situation very much; it is far more cheerful than Paragon, and the prospect from the drawing-room window, at which I now write, is rather picturesque, as it commands a perspective view of the left side of Brock Street, broken by three Lombardy poplars in the garden of the last house in Queen's Parade.

I am rather impatient to know the fate of my best gown, but I suppose it will be some days before Frances can get through the trunk. In the meantime I am, with many thanks for your trouble in making it, as well as marking my silk stockings,

Yours very affectionately,

Jane

A great deal of love from everybody.

24. *To Cassandra Austen. Saturday* 1 *Nov.* 1800

Steventon: Saturday Nov. 1st.

My dear Cassandra

You have written I am sure, tho' I have received no letter from you since your leaving London; the Post, & not yourself must have been unpunctual. We have at last heard from Frank; a letter from him to you

---

[1] Fanny and Edward were of the Bath party, leaving George, Henry, and William at home.

came yesterday, & I mean to send it on as soon as I can get a ditto, (*that* means a frank,) which I hope to do in a day or two. En attendant, You must rest satisfied with knowing that on the 8th of July the Petterell with the rest of the Egyptian Squadron was off the Isle of Cyprus, whither they went from Jaffa for Provisions &c., & whence they were to sail in a day or two for Alexandria, there to wait the result of the English proposals for the Evacuation of Egypt. The rest of the letter, according to the present fashionable stile of Composition, is cheifly Descriptive; of his Promotion he knows nothing, & of Prizes he is guiltless. Your letter is come; it came indeed twelve lines ago, but I could not stop to acknowledge it before, & I am glad it did not arrive till I had completed my first sentence, because the sentence had been made ever since yester-day, & I think forms a very good beginning. Your abuse of our Gowns amuses, but does not discourage me; I shall take mine to be made up next week, & the more I look at it, the better it pleases me. My Cloak came on tuesday, & tho' I expected a good deal, the beauty of the lace astonished me. It is too handsome to be worn, almost too handsome to be looked at. The Glass is all safely arrived also, & gives great satis-faction. The wine glasses are much smaller than I expected, but I suppose it is the proper size. *We* find no fault with your manner of performing any of our commissions, but if you like to think yourself remiss in any of them, pray do. My Mother was rather vexed that you could not go to Penlington's, but she has since written to him, which does just as well. Mary is disappointed of course about her Locket, & of course delighted about the Mangle which is safe at Basing-stoke. You will thank Edward for it on their behalf &c.

&c., & as you know how much it was wished for, will
not feel that you are inventing Gratitude. Did you
think of our Ball on thursday evening, & did you suppose me at it? You might very safely, for there I was.
On wednesday morning it was settled that Mrs. Harwood, Mary & I should go together, and shortly afterwards a very civil note of invitation for me came from
Mrs. Bramston, who wrote I beleive as soon as she
knew of the Ball. I might likewise have gone with Mrs.
Lefroy, & therefore with three methods of going, I
must have been more at the Ball than anybody else.
I dined & slept at Deane. Charlotte & I did my hair,
which I fancy looked very indifferent; nobody abused
it however, & I retired delighted with my success. It
was a pleasant Ball, & still more good than pleasant,
for there were nearly 60 people, & sometimes we had
17 couple. The Portsmouths, Dorchesters, Boltons,
Portals & Clerks were there, & all the meaner & more
usual &c. &c.'s. There was a scarcity of Men in
general, & a still greater scarcity of any that were
good for much. I danced nine times out of ten, five
with Stephen Terry, T. Chute & James Digweed &
four with Catherine. There was commonly a couple of
Ladies standing up together, but not often any so
amiable as ourselves. I heard no news, except that Mr.
Peters who was not there, is supposed to be particularly attentive to Miss Lyford. You were enquired after
very prettily, & I hope the whole assembly now understands that you are gone into Kent, which the families
in general seemed to meet in ignorance of. Lord Portsmouth surpassed the rest in his attentive recollection
of you, enquired more into the length of your absence,
& concluded by desiring to be 'remembered to you when
I wrote next.' Lady Portsmouth had got a different

29

dress on, & Lady Bolton is much improved by a wig. The three Miss Terries were there, but no Anne; which was a great disappointment to me; I hope the poor girl had not set her heart on her appearance that Even^g so much as I had. Mr. Terry is ill, in a very low way. I said civil things for Edward to Mr. Chute, who amply returned them by declaring that had he known of my brother's being at Steventon he should have made a point of calling on him to thank him for his civility about the Hunt. I have heard from Charles, & am to send his shirts by half dozens as they are finished; one sett will go next week. The Endymion is now waiting only for orders, but may wait for them perhaps a month. Mr. Coulthard was unlucky in very narrowly missing another unexpected Guest at Chawton, for Charles had actually set out & got half the way thither in order to spend one day with Edward, but turned back on discovering the distance to be considerably more than he had fancied, & finding himself & his horse to be very much tired. I should regret it the more if his friend Shipley had been of the party, for Mr. Coulthard might not have been so well pleased to see only one come at a time.

Miss Harwood is still at Bath, & writes that she never was in better health & never more happy. Jos: Wakeford died last Saturday, & my father buried him on Thursday. A deaf Miss Fonnereau is at Ashe, which has prevented Mrs. Lefroy's going to Worting or Basingstoke, during the absence of Mr. Lefroy. My Mother is very happy in the prospect of dressing a new Doll which Molly has given Anna. My father's feelings are not so enviable, as it appears that the farm cleared 300£ last year. James & Mary went to Ibthrop for one night last monday, & found Mrs. Lloyd not in very good looks. Martha has been lately at Kintbury, but is probably at home by this time. Mary's promised maid has jilted her, & hired herself elsewhere. The Debaries persist in being afflicted at the death of their Uncle, of whom they now say they saw a great deal in London. Love to all. I am glad George remembers me.

Yours very affec:^{tley}

J. A.

I am very unhappy. In re-reading your letter I find I might have spared myself my Intelligence of Charles. To have written only what you knew before! You may guess how much I feel.

I wore at the Ball your favourite gown, a bit of muslin of the same round my head, border'd with Mrs. Cooper's band—& one little Comb.

25. *To Cassandra Austen.* *Saturday* 8 *Nov.* 1800

Steventon Saturday Even^g—Novr 8

My dear Cassandra,

Having just finished the first volume of Les Veillees du Chateau, I think it a good opportunity for beginning a letter to you while my mind is stored with Ideas worth transmitting. I thank you for so speedy a return to my two last, & particularly thank you for your anecdote of Charlotte Graham & her cousin Harriet Bailey, which has very much amused both my Mother & myself. If you can learn anything farther of that interesting affair I hope you will mention it. I have two messages; let me get rid of them, & then my paper will be my own. Mary fully intended writing to you by Mr Chute's frank, & only happened intirely to forget it— but will write soon—& my father wishes Edward to send him a memorandum in your next letter, of the price of the hops. The Tables are come, & give general contentment. I had not expected that they would so perfectly suit the fancy of us all three, or that we should so well agree in the disposition of them; but nothing except their own surface can have been smoother; The two ends put together form our constant Table for everything, & the centre peice stands exceedingly well under the glass; holds a great deal most commodiously, without looking awkwardly. They are both covered with green baize & send their best Love. The Pembroke has got its destination by the sideboard, & my mother has great delight in keeping her money & papers locked up. The little Table which used to stand there, has most conveniently taken itself off into the best bed-room, & we are now in want only of the chiffoniere, which is neither finished nor come. So much for that subject; I now come to another, of a very different nature, as other subjects are very apt to be. Earle Harwood has been again giving uneasiness to his family, & Talk to the Neighbourhood; in the present instance however he is only unfortunate & not in fault. About ten days ago, in cocking a pistol in the guard-room at Marcou, he accidentally shot himself through the Thigh. Two young Scotch Surgeons in the Island were polite enough to propose taking off the Thigh at once, but to that he would not consent; & accordingly in his wounded state was put on board a Cutter & conveyed to Haslar Hospital at Gosport; where the bullet was extracted, & where he now is I hope in a fair way of doing well. The surgeon of the Hospital wrote to the family on the occasion, & John Harwood went down to him immediately, attended by James, whose object in going was to be the means of bringing back the earliest Intelligence to M^r and Mrs Harwood, whose anxious sufferings particularly those of the latter, have of course been dreadful. They went down on tuesday, & James came back the next day, bringing such favourable accounts as greatly to lessen the distress of the family at Deane, tho' it will probably be a long while before Mrs Harwood can be quite at ease. *One* most material comfort however they have; the assurance of it's being really an accidental wound, which is not only positively declared by Earle himself, but is likewise testified by the particular direction of the bullet. Such a wound could not have been received in a duel. At present he is going on very well, but the Surgeon will not declare him to be in no danger. John Harwood came back last night, & will probably go to him again soon. James had not time at Gosport to take any other steps towards seeing Charles, than the very few which conducted him to the door of the assembly room in the Inn, where there happened to be a Ball on the night of their arrival. A likely spot enough for the discovery of a Charles: but I am glad to say that he was not of the party, for it was in general a very ungenteel one, & there was hardly a pretty girl in the room. I cannot possibly oblige you by not wearing my gown, because I have it made up on purpose to wear it a great deal, & as the discredit will be my own, I feel the less regret. You must learn to like it yourself & make it up at Godmersham; it may easily be done; it is only protesting it to be very beautiful, & you will soon think it so. Yesterday was a day of great business with me; Mary drove me all in the rain to Basingstoke, & still more all in the rain back again, because it rained harder; and soon after our return to Dean a sudden invitation & an own postchaise took us to Ash Park, to

33

dine tete a tete with Mr Holder, Mr Gauntlett & James Digweed; but our tete a tete was cruelly reduced by the non-attendance of the two latter. We had a very quiet evening, I beleive Mary found it dull, but I thought it very pleasant. To sit in idleness over a good fire in a well-proportioned room is a luxurious sensation. Sometimes we talked & sometimes we were quite silent; I said two or three amusing things, & Mr Holder made a few infamous puns. I have had a most affectionate letter from Buller; I was afraid he would oppress me by his felicity & his love for his wife, but this is not the case; he calls her simply Anna without any angelic embellishments, for which I respect & wish him happy—and throughout the whole of his letter indeed he seems more engrossed by his feelings towards our family, than towards her, which you know cannot give any one disgust. He is very pressing in his invitation to us all to come & see him at Colyton, & my father is very much inclined to go there next Summer. It is a circumstance that may considerably assist the Dawlish scheme. Buller has desired me to write again, to give him more particulars of us all. Mr Heathcote met with a genteel little accident the other day in hunting; he got off to lead his horse over a hedge or a house or a something, & his horse in his haste trod upon his leg, or rather ancle I beleive, & it is not certain whether the small bone is not broke. Harris[1] seems still in a poor way, from his bad habit of body; his hand bled again a little the other day, & Dr Littlehales has been with him lately. Martha has accepted Mary's invitation for Ld Portsmouth's Ball. He has not yet sent out his *own* invitations, but *that* does not signify; Martha comes, & a Ball there must be. I think it will

---

[1] Bigg-Wither.

be too early in her Mother's absence for me to return
with her. Mr Holder told Wm Portal a few days ago
that Edward objected to the narrowness of the path
which his plantation has left in one part of the Rookery.
Wm Portal has since examined it himself, acknowledges
it to be much too narrow, & promises to have it altered.
He wishes to avoid the necessity of removing the end
of his plantation with it's newly-planted quick &c, but
if a proper footpath cannot be made by poking away
the bank on the other side, he will not spare the former.
I have finished this on Sunday morning

am y^rs ever J A.

Sunday Evening. We have had a dreadful storm of
wind in the forepart of this day, which has done a
great deal of mischeif among our trees. I was sitting
alone in the dining room, when an odd kind of crash
startled me—in a moment afterwards it was repeated;
I then went to the window, which I reached just in
time to see the last of our two highly valued Elms
descend into the Sweep ! ! ! ! ! The other, which had
fallen I suppose in the first crash, & which was the
nearest to the pond, taking a more easterly direction
sunk amongst our screen of chesnuts and firs, knocking
down one spruce fir, beating off the head of another, &
stripping the two corner chesnuts of several branches,
in its fall. This is not all. One large Elm out of two on
the left hand side, as you enter what I call the Elm
walk, was likewise blown down, the Maypole bearing
the weathercock was broke in two, and what I regret
more than all the rest, is that all the three Elms which
grew in Hall's meadow & gave such ornament to it,
are gone. Two were blown down, & the other so much
injured that it cannot stand. I am happy to add

however that no greater Evil than the loss of Trees has
been the consequence of the Storm in this place, or in
our immediate neighbourhood. We greive therefore in
some comfort.

You spend your time just as quietly & comfortably
as I supposed you would. We have all seen & admired
Fanny's letter to her Aunt. The Endymion sailed on a
cruize last friday.

I hope it is true that Edward Taylor is to marry his
cousin Charlotte. Those beautiful dark Eyes will then
adorn another Generation at least in all their purity.

Mr Holder's paper tells us that sometime in last
August, Capt: Austen & the Petterell were very active
in securing a Turkish Ship (driven into a Port in
Cyprus by bad weather) from the French. He was
forced to burn her however. You will see the account
in the Sun I dare say.

26. *To Martha Lloyd, Wednesday 12 Nov.* ⟨1800⟩

Steventon Wednesday Eveng. Nov:r 12th

My dear Martha

I did not receive your note yesterday till after
Charlotte had left Deane, or I would have sent my
answer by her, instead of being the means, as I now
must be, of lessening the Elegance of your new Dress
for the Hurstbourn Ball by the value of 3d. You are
very good in wishing to see me at Ibthrop so soon, & I
am equally good in wishing to come to you; I beleive
our Merit in that respect is much upon a par, our Self-
denial mutually strong. Having paid this tribute to the
Virtue of both, I shall have done with Panegyric &
proceed to plain matter of fact. In about a fortnight's

time I hope to be with you; I have two reasons for not
being able to come before; I wish so to arrange my visit
as to spend some days with you after your Mother's
return, in the 1st place that I may have the pleasure of
seeing her, & in the 2d, that I may have a better chance
of bringing you back with me. Your promise in my
favour was not quite absolute, but if your Will is not
perverse, you & I will do all in our power to overcome
your scruples of conscience. I hope we shall meet next
week to talk all this over, till we have tired ourselves
with the very idea of my visit, before my visit begins.
Our invitations for the 19th are arrived, & very curiously
are they worded. Mary mentioned to you yesterday
poor Earle's unfortunate accident I dare say; he does
not seem to be going on very well; the two or three
last posts have brought rather less & less favourable
accounts of him. This morning's letter states the appre-
hensions of the Surgeon that the violent catchings of
his Patient have done material injury to the bone,
which from the first has appeared so nearly broken that
any particular irritation or sudden movement might
make the fracture certain. John Harwood is gone to
Gosport again to day. We have two families of friends
that are now in a most anxious state; for tho' by a note
from Catherine this morning there seems now to be a
revival of hope at Manydown, it's continuance may be
too reasonably doubted. Mr. Heathcote however who
has broken the small bone of his leg, is so good as to
be doing very well. It would be really too much to
have three people to care for!

Mary has heard from Cassandra to day; she is now
gone with Edward & Elizabeth to the Cages for two
or three Nights. You distress me cruelly by your request about Books; I cannot think of any to bring with

me, nor have I any idea of our wanting them. I come
to you to be talked to, not to read or hear reading. I can
do *that* at home; & indeed I am now laying in a stock
of intelligence to pour out on you as *my* share of Conversation. I am reading Henry's History of England,
which I will repeat to you in any manner you may
prefer, either in a loose, disultary, unconnected strain,
or dividing my recital as the Historian divides it himself, into seven parts, The Civil & Military—Religion
—Constitution—Learning & Learned Men—Arts &
Sciences—Commerce Coins & Shipping—& Manners;
—so that for every evening of the week there will be a
different subject; The friday's lot, Commerce, Coin &
Shipping, You will find the least entertaining; but the
next Eveng:'s portion will make amends. With such a
provision on my part, if you will do your's by repeat-
ing the French Grammar, & Mrs Stent will now & then
ejaculate some wonder about the Cocks & Hens, what
can we want? Farewell for a short time—You are to
dine here on tuesday to meet James Digweed, whom
you must wish to see before he goes into Kent. We all
unite in best Love, & I am

Y^r very affec^te JA.—

It is reported at Portsmouth that Sir T. Williams is
going to be married—It has been reported indeed
twenty times before, but Charles is inclined to give
some credit to it now, as they hardly ever see him on
board, & he looks very much like a Lover.
Thursday. The Harwoods have received a much better
account of Earle this morning; & Charles, from whom
I have just had a letter, has been assured by the
Hospital-Surgeon that the wound is in as favourable a
state as can be.

28. *To Cassandra Austen. Sunday* 30 *Nov.* 1800

Ibthrop Sunday Novr 30th

My dear Cassandra

Shall you expect to hear from me on Wednesday or not? I think you will, or I should not write, as the three days & half which have passed since my last letter was sent, have not produced many materials towards filling another sheet of paper. But like Mrs Hastings,[1] 'I do not despair'—& you perhaps like the faithful Maria may feel still more certain of the happy Event. I have been here ever since a quarter after three on thursday last, by the Shrewsbury Clock, which I am fortunately enabled absolutely to ascertain, because Mrs. Stent once lived at Shrewsbury, or at least at Tewksbury. I have the pleasure of thinking myself a very welcome Guest, & the pleasure of spending my time very pleasantly. Martha looks very well, & wants me to find out that she grows fat; but I cannot carry my complaisance farther than to beleive whatever she asserts on the subject. Mrs. Stent gives us quite as much of her company as we wish for, & rather more than she used to do; but perhaps not more than is to our advantage in the end, because it is too dirty even for such desperate walkers as Martha and I to get out of doors, & we are therefore confined to each other's society from morning till night, with very little variety of Books or Gowns. Three of the Miss Debaries called here the morning after my arrival, but I have not yet been able to return their civility;— You know it is not an uncommon circumstance in this parish to have the road from Ibthrop to the Parsonage much dirtier and more impracticable for walking than

---

[1] Probably Warren H.'s wife.

39

the road from the Parsonage to Ibthrop. I left my
Mother very well when I came away, & left her with
strict orders to continue so. My Journey was safe &
not unpleasant; I spent an hour in Andover, of which
Messrs Painter & Pridding had the larger part; twenty
minutes however fell to the lot of Mrs Poore & her
mother, whom I was glad to see in good looks & spirits.
The latter asked me more questions than I had very
well time to answer; the former I beleive is very big;
but I am by no means certain; she is either very big, or
not at all big, I forgot to be accurate in my observation
at the time, & tho' my thoughts are now more about
me on the subject, the power of exercising them to any
effect is much diminished. The two youngest boys only
were at home; I mounted the highly-extolled staircase
& went into the elegant Drawing room, which I fancy
is now Mrs Harrison's apartment; and in short did
everything that extraordinary Abilities can be supposed to compass in so short a space of time. The endless Debaries are of course very well acquainted with
the lady who is to marry Sir Thomas,[1] & all her family.
I pardon them however, as their description of her is
favourable. Mrs Wapshire is a widow, with several sons
& daughters, a good fortune, & a house in Salisbury;
where Miss Wapshire has been for many years a distinguished beauty. She is now seven or eight & twenty,
and tho' still handsome less handsome than she has
been. This promises better, than the bloom of seventeen; & in addition to this, they say that she has always
been remarkable for the propriety of her behaviour,
distinguishing her far above the general class of Town
Misses, & rendering her of course very unpopular
among them. I hope I have now gained the real truth,

[1] See note, p. 213.

& that my letters may in future go on without conveying any farther contradictions of what was last asserted
about Sir Thomas Williams and Miss Wapshire. I wish
I could be certain that her name were Emma; but her
being the Eldest daughter leaves that circumstance
doubtful. At Salisbury the match is considered as certain & as near at hand. Martha desires her best love, &
will be happy to welcome any letter from you to this
house, whether it be addressed to herself or to me—
and in fact, the difference of direction will not be
material. *She* is pleased with my Gown, & particularly
bids me to say that if you could see me in it for five
minutes, she is sure you would be eager to make up
your own. I have been obliged to mention this, but
have not failed to blush the whole time of my writing
it. Part of the money & time which I spent at Andover
were devoted to the purchase of some figured cambric
muslin for a frock for Edward—a circumstance from
which I derive two pleasing reflections; it has in the
first place opened to me a fresh source of self-con-
gratulation on being able to make so munificent a
present, & secondly it has been the means of informing
me that the very pretty manufacture in question may
be bought for 4s. 6d. p^r y^d—yard & half wide. Martha
has promised to return with me, & our plan is to have
a nice black frost for walking to Whitechurch, & there
throw ourselves into a postchaise, one upon the other,
our heads hanging out at one door, & our feet at the
opposite. If you have never heard that Miss Dawes has
been married these two months, I will mention it in my
next. Pray do not forget to go to the Canterbury Ball.
I shall despise you all most insufferably if you do. By
the bye, there will not be any Ball, because Delmar
lost so much by the Assemblies last winter that he has

protested against opening his rooms this year. I have charged my Myrmidons to send me an account of the Basingstoke Ball; I have placed my spies at different places that they may collect the more; & by so doing, by sending Miss Bigg to the Townhall itself, & posting my Mother at Steventon I hope to derive from their various observations a good general idea of the whole.

Monday. Martha has this moment received your letter—I hope there is nothing in it requiring an immediate answer as we are at dinner, & she has neither time to read nor I to write. Y^{rs} ever

J A.

29. *To Cassandra Austen. Saturday* 3 *Jan.* 1801

Steventon: Saturday Jan^{ry} 3^d.

My dear Cassandra

As you have by this time received my last letter, it is fit that I should begin another; & I begin with the hope, which is at present uppermost in my mind, that you often wore a white gown in the morning, at the time of all the gay party's being with you. Our visit at Ash Park last Wednesday, went off in a come-cá way; we met Mr. Lefroy & Tom Chute, played at cards & came home again. James & Mary dined here on the following day, & at night Henry set off in the Mail for London. He was as agreable as ever during his visit, & has not lost anything in Miss Lloyd's estimation. Yesterday, we were quite alone, only our four selves; but today the scene is agreeably varied by Mary's driving Martha to Basingstoke, & Martha's afterwards dining at Deane. My Mother looks forward with as much certainty as you can do, to our keeping two Maids—my father is the only one not in the secret.

We plan having a steady Cook, & a young giddy
Housemaid, with a sedate, middle aged Man, who is
to undertake the double office of Husband to the
former & sweetheart to the latter. No Children of
course to be allowed on either side. You feel more for
John Bond, than John Bond deserves; I am sorry to
lower his Character, but he is not ashamed to own
himself, that he has no doubt at all of getting a good
place, & that he had even an offer many years ago
from a Farmer Paine of taking him into his service
whenever he might quit my father's. There are three
parts of Bath which we have thought of as likely to
have Houses in them. Westgate Buildings, Charles
Street, & some of the short streets leading from Laura
Place or Pulteney St: Westgate Buildings, tho' quite
in the lower part of the Town are not badly situated
themselves; the street is broad, & has rather a good
appearance. Charles Street however I think is prefer-
able; the buildings are new, & it's nearness to Kings-
mead fields would be a pleasant circumstance. Perhaps
you may remember, or perhaps you may forget that
Charles Street leads from the Queen Square Chapel
to the two Green park-Streets. The Houses in the
streets near Laura Place I should expect to be above
our price. Gay Street would be too high, except only
the lower house on the left hand side as you ascend;
towards *that* my Mother has no disinclination; it used
to be lower rented than any other house in the row,
from some inferiority in the apartments. But above all
other's, her wishes are at present fixed on the corner
house in Chapel row, which opens into Prince's Street.
Her knowledge of it however is confined only to the
outside, & therefore she is equally uncertain of it's
being really desirable as of its being to be had. In the

meantime she assures you that she will do everything
in her power to avoid Trim St altho' you have not
expressed the fearful presentiment of it, which was
rather expected. We know that Mrs. Perrot will want
to get us into Axford Buildings, but we all unite in
particular dislike of that part of the Town, & therefore
hope to escape. Upon all these different situations, You
and Edward may confer together, & your opinion of
each will be expected with eagerness. As to our Pictures, the Battle peice, Mr. Nibbs, Sir Wm East, & all
the old heterogenous, miscellany, manuscript, Scrip-
toral peices dispersed over the House are to be given
to James. Your own Drawings will not cease to be your
own—& the two paintings on Tin will be at your disposal. My Mother says that the French agricultural
Prints in the best bed-room were given by Edward to
his two Sisters. Do you or he know anything about it?
She has written to my Aunt, & We are all impatient
for the answer. I do not know how to give up the idea
of our both going to Paragon in May; *Your* going I
consider as indispensably necessary, & I shall not like
being left behind; there is no place here or hereabouts
that I shall want to be staying at—& tho' to be sure
the keep of two will be more than of one, I will endeavour to make the difference less by disordering my
Stomach with Bath bunns; & as to the *trouble* of
accomodating us, whether there are one or two, it is
much the same. According to the first plan, my mother
& our two selves are to travel down together; & my
father follow us afterwards—in about a fortnight or
three weeks. We have promised to spend a couple of
days at Ibthrop in our way. We must all meet at Bath
you know before we set out for the Sea, & everything
considered I think the first plan as good as any. My

father & mother wisely aware of the difficulty of finding in all Bath such a bed as their own, have resolved
on taking it with them; All the beds indeed that we
shall want are to be removed, viz:—besides theirs, our
own two, the best for a spare one, & two for servants
—and these necessary articles will probably be the
only material ones that it ⟨wou⟩ld answer to send
down. I do not think it will be worth while to remove
any of our chests of Drawers—We shall be able to get
some of a much more commodious form, made of deal,
& painted to look very neat; & I flatter myself that for
little comforts of all kinds, our apartment will be one of
the most complete things of the sort all over Bath—
Bristol included. We have thought at times of removing the side-board, or a pembroke table, or some other
peice of furniture—but upon the whole it has ended
in thinking that the trouble & risk of the removal
would be more than the advantage of having them at
a place, where everything may be purchased. Pray
send your opinion. Martha has as good as promised to
come to us again in March. Her spirits are better than
they were. I have now attained the true art of letter-
writing, which we are always told, is to express on
paper exactly what one would say to the same person
by word of mouth; I have been talking to you almost
as fast as I could the whole of this letter. Your Christmas Gaieties are really quite surprising; I think they
would satisfy even Miss Walter herself. I hope the ten
shillings won by Miss Foote may make everything easy
between her & her cousin Frederick. So, Lady Bridges
in the delicate language of Coulson Wallop, is *in for it*!
I am very glad to hear of the Pearsons' good fortune.
It is a peice of promotion which I know they looked
forward to as very desirable some years ago, on Capt:

Lockyer's illness. It brings them a considerable increase of Income, & a better house. My Mother bargains for having no trouble at all in furnishing our house in Bath—& I have engaged for your willingly undertaking to do it all. I get more & more reconciled to the idea of our removal. We have lived long enough in this Neighbourhood, the Basingstoke Balls are certainly on the decline, there is something interesting in the bustle of going away, & the prospect of spending future summers by the Sea or in Wales is very delightful. For a time we shall now possess many of the advantages which I have often thought of with Envy in the wives of Sailors or Soldiers. It must not be generally known however that I am not sacrificing a great deal in quitting the Country—or I can expect to inspire no tenderness, no interest in those we leave behind. The threatened Act of Parliament does not seem to give any alarm.

My father is doing all in his power to encrease his Income by raising his Tythes &c., & I do not despair of getting very nearly six hundred a year. In what part of Bath do you mean to place your *Bees*? We are afraid of the South Parade's being too hot.

Monday. Martha desires her best Love, & says a great many kind things about spending some time with you in March—& depending on a large return from us both in the Autumn. Perhaps I may not write again before Sunday.

Yours affec^{ly}

J. A.

II. BATH

1801–5. *Twenty-five to Twenty-nine*

━━━

As we saw, we have letters of 1801 and 1805, only
one for the interval between those years. 35 and 36
show Jane and her parents staying with the Leigh-
Perrots (James L.-P. was Mrs. A.'s brother) in Paragon,
and house-hunting. They lived first at 4 Sidney Terrace (not in extant letters), then in Green Park Buildings, and after Mr. Austen's death at 25 Gay Street.

Life at Bath, where they made some acquaintances
but no friends, was varied each summer by excursions,
chiefly to the seaside: to Sidmouth (1801), Dawlish
(1802), perhaps Ramsgate (1803), Lyme (1804). It
may have been at Sidmouth that they met the man
whom Jane might have married but for his death not
long after. These rambles give us only one letter, 39
from Lyme. There is no evidence of writing, though
Lady Susan and *The Watsons* may belong to this
period.

35. *To Cassandra Austen. Tuesday 5 May* ⟨1801⟩

Paragon: Tuesday May 5

My dear Cassandra

I have the pleasure of writing from my *own* room up
two pair of stairs, with everything very comfortable
about me.

47

Our journey here was perfectly free from accident or event; we changed horses at the end of every stage, and paid at almost every turnpike. We had charming weather, hardly any dust, and were exceedingly agreeable, as we did not speak above once in three miles.

Between Luggershall and Everley we made our grand meal, and then with admiring astonishment perceived in what a magnificent manner our support had been provided for. We could not with the utmost exertion consume above the twentieth part of the beef. The cucumber will, I believe, be a very acceptable present, as my uncle talks of having inquired the price of one lately, when he was told a shilling.

We had a very neat chaise from Devizes; it looked almost as well as a gentleman's, at least as a very shabby gentleman's; in spite of this advantage, however, we were above three hours coming from thence to Paragon, and it was half after seven by your clocks before we entered the house.

Frank, whose black head was in waiting in the Hall window, received us very kindly; and his master and mistress did not show less cordiality. They both look very well, though my aunt has a violent cough. We drank tea as soon as we arrived, and so ends the account of our journey, which my mother bore without any fatigue.

How do you do to-day? I hope you improve in sleeping—I think you must, because *I* fall off; I have been awake ever since five and sooner; I fancy I had too much clothes over me; I thought I *should* by the feel of them before I went to bed, but I had not courage to alter them. I am warmer here without any fire than I have been lately with an excellent one.

Well, and so the good news is confirmed, and **Martha** triumphs. My uncle and aunt seemed quite surprised that you and my father were not coming sooner.

I have given the soap and the basket, and each have been kindly received. *One* thing only among all our concerns has not arrived in safety: when I got into the chaise at Devizes I discovered that your drawing ruler was broke in two; it is just at the top where the cross-piece is fastened on. I beg pardon.

There is to be only one more ball—next Monday is the day. The Chamberlaynes are still here. I begin to think better of Mrs. C——, and upon recollection believe she has rather a long chin than otherwise, as she remembers us in Gloucestershire when we were very charming young women.

The first view of Bath in fine weather does not answer my expectations; I think I see more distinctly through rain. The sun was got behind everything, and the appearance of the place from the top of Kingsdown was all vapour, shadow, smoke, and confusion.

I fancy we are to have a house in Seymour Street, or thereabouts. My uncle and aunt both like the situation. I was glad to hear the former talk of all the houses in New King Street as too small; it was my own idea of them. I had not been two minutes in the dining-room before he questioned me with all his accustomary eager interest about Frank and Charles, their views and intentions. I did my best to give information.

I am not without hopes of tempting Mrs. Lloyd to settle in Bath; meat is only 8*d*. per pound, butter 12*d*., and cheese 9½*d*. You must carefully conceal from her, however, the exorbitant price of fish: a salmon has been sold at 2*s*. 9*d*. per pound the whole fish. The Duchess of York's removal is expected to make that article more reasonable—and till it really appears so, say nothing about salmon.

Tuesday night. When my uncle went to take his second glass of water I walked with him, and in our morning's circuit we looked at two houses in Green Park Buildings, one of which pleased me very well. We walked all over it except into the garret; the dining-room is of a comfortable size, just as large as you like to fancy it; the second room about 14 ft. square. The apartment over the drawing-room pleased me particularly, because it is divided into two, the smaller one a very nice-sized dressing-room, which upon occasion might admit a bed. The aspect is south-east. The only doubt is about the dampness of the offices, of which there were symptoms.

Wednesday. Mrs. Mussell has got my gown, and I will endeavour to explain what her intentions are. It is to be a round gown, with a jacket and a frock front, like Cath. Bigg's, to open at the side. The jacket is all in one with the body, and comes as far as the pocket-holes—about half a quarter of a yard deep, I suppose, all the way round, cut off straight at the corners with a broad hem. No fulness appears either in the body or the flap; the back is quite plain in this form ⫙ , and the sides equally so. The front is sloped round to the bosom and drawn in, and there is to be a frill of the same to put on occasionally when all one's handker-chiefs are dirty—which frill *must* fall back. She is to put two breadths and a-half in the tail, and no gores—gores not being so much worn as they were. There is nothing new in the sleeves: they are to be plain, with a fulness of the same falling down and gathered up underneath, just like some of Martha's, or perhaps a little longer. Low in the back behind, and a belt of the same. I can think of nothing more, though I am afraid of not being particular enough.

My mother has ordered a new bonnet, and so have I; both white strip, trimmed with white ribbon. I find my straw bonnet looking very much like other people's, and quite as smart. Bonnets of cambric muslin on the plan of Lady Bridges' are a good deal worn, and some of them are very pretty; but I shall defer one of that sort till your arrival. Bath is getting so very empty that I am not afraid of doing too little. Black gauze cloaks are worn as much as anything. I shall write again in a day or two. Best love.

Yours ever, J. A..

We have had Mrs. Lillingstone and the Chamberlaynes to call on us. My mother was very much struck with the odd looks of the two latter; *I* have only seen *her*. Mrs. Busby drinks tea and plays at cribbage here to-morrow; and on Friday, I believe, we go to the Chamberlaynes'. Last night we walked by the Canal.

36. *To Cassandra Austen. Tuesday* 12 *May* ⟨1801⟩

Paragon Tuesday May 12th.

My dear Cassandra

My mother has heard from Mary[1] & I have heard from Frank; we therefore know something now of our concerns in distant quarters, & you I hope by some means or other are equally instructed, for I do not feel inclined to transcribe the letter of either. You know from Elizabeth I dare say that my father & Frank, deferring their visit to Kippington on account of Mr. M. Austen's absence are to be at Godmersham today;

---

[1] Mrs. J. A.; Frank did not marry his Mary till 1806.

& James I dare say has been over to Ibthrop by this
time to enquire particularly after Mrs. Lloyd's health,
& forestall whatever intelligence of the sale I might
attempt to give. Sixty-one guineas & a half for the
three cows gives one some support under the blow of
only Eleven Guineas for the Tables. Eight for my
Pianoforte, is about what I really expected to get; I am
more anxious to know the amount of my books, especially as they are said to have sold well.

My Adventures since I wrote last, have not been
very numerous; but such as they are, they are much at
your service. We met not a creature at Mrs. Lillingstone's, & yet were not so very stupid as I expected,
which I attribute to my wearing my new bonnet &
being in good looks. On Sunday we went to Church
twice, & after evening service walked a little in the
Crescent fields, but found it too cold to stay long.
Yesterday morning we looked into a house in Seymour
St: which there is reason to suppose will soon be
empty, and as we are assured from many quarters that
no inconvenience from the river is felt in those Buildings, we are at liberty to fix in them if we can; but this
house was not inviting; the largest room downstairs,
was not much more than fourteen feet square, with a
western aspect. In the evening I hope you honoured
my Toilette & Ball with a thought; I dressed myself as
well as I could, & had all my finery much admired at
home. By nine o'clock my Uncle, Aunt & I entered the
rooms & linked Miss Winstone on to us. Before tea, it
was rather a dull affair; but then the before tea did not
last long, for there was only one dance, danced by four
couple. Think of four couple, surrounded by about an
hundred people, dancing in the upper Rooms at Bath!
After tea we *cheered up*; the breaking up of private

parties sent some scores more to the Ball, & tho' it was shockingly & inhumanly thin for this place, there were people enough I suppose to have made five or six very pretty Basingstoke assemblies. I then got Mr. Evelyn to talk to, & Miss Twisleton to look at; and I am proud to say that I have a very good eye at an Adultress, for tho' repeatedly assured that another in the same party was the *She,* I fixed upon the right one from the first. A resemblance to Mrs. Leigh was my guide. She is not so pretty as I expected; her face has the same defect of baldness as her sister's, & her features not so handsome; she was highly rouged, & looked rather quietly & contentedly silly than anything else. Mrs. Badcock & two young Women were of the same party, except when Mrs. Badcock thought herself obliged to leave them to run round the room after her drunken Husband. His avoidance, & her pursuit, with the probable intoxication of both, was an amusing scene. The Evelyns returned our visit on saturday; we were very happy to meet, & all that; they are going tomorrow into Gloucestershire, to the Dolphins for ten days. Our acquaintance Mr. Woodward is just married to a Miss Rowe, a young lady rich in money & music. I thank you for your Sunday's letter, it is very long and very agreable. I fancy you know many more particulars of our sale than we do; we have heard the price of nothing but the Cows, Bacon, Hay, Hops, Tables, & my father's Chest of Drawers & Study Table. Mary is more minute in her account of their own Gains than in ours—probably being better informed in them. I will attend to Mrs. Lloyd's commission—& to her abhorrence of Musk when I write again. I have bestowed three calls of enquiry on the Mapletons, & I fancy very beneficial ones to Marianne, as I am always told that she is better. I have not seen any of them. Her complaint is a billious fever. I like my dark gown very much indeed, colour, make, & everything. I mean to have my new white one made up now, in case we should go to the rooms again next monday, which is to be really the last time.

Wednesday. Another stupid party last night; perhaps if larger they might be less intolerable, but here there were only just enough to make one card table, with six people to look on, & talk nonsense to each other. Ly Fust, Mrs. Busby & a Mrs. Owen sat down with my Uncle to Whist within five minutes after the three old *Toughs* came in, & there they sat with only the exchange of Adm: Stanhope for my Uncle till their chairs were announced. I cannot anyhow continue to find people agreable; I respect Mrs. Chamberlayne for doing her hair well, but cannot feel a more tender sentiment. Miss Langley is like any other short girl with a broad nose & wide mouth, fashionable dress, & exposed bosom. Adm: Stanhope is a gentlemanlike Man, but then his legs are too short, & his tail too long. Mrs. Stanhope could not come; I fancy she had a private appointment with Mr. Chamberlayne, whom I wished to see more than all the rest. My uncle has quite got the better of his lameness, or at least his walking with a stick is the only remains of it. He & I are soon to take the long-plann'd walk to the Cassoon —& on friday we are all to accompany Mrs. Chamberlayne & Miss Langley to Weston. My Mother had a letter yesterday from my father; it seems as if the W. Kent scheme were entirely given up. He talks of spending a fortnight at Godmersham & then returning to Town.

Y^{rs} ever   J. A.

Excepting a slight cold, my mother is very well; she has been quite free from feverish or billious complaints since her arrival here.

39. *To Cassandra Austen. Friday* 14 *Sept.* ⟨1804⟩

Lyme Friday Sept 14.

My dear Cassandra

I take the first sheet of this fine striped paper to thank you for your letter from Weymouth, and express my hopes of your being at Ibthrop before this time. I expect to hear that you reached it yesterday evening, being able to get as far as Blandford on Wednesday. Your account of Weymouth contains nothing which strikes me so forcibly as there being no ice in the town. For every other vexation I was in some measure prepared, and particularly for your disappointment in not seeing the Royal Family go on board on Tuesday, having already heard from Mr. Crawford that he had seen you in the very act of being too late, but for there being no ice what could prepare me? Weymouth is altogether a shocking place, I perceive, without recommendation of any kind, & worthy only of being frequented by the inhabitants of Gloucester. I am really very glad that we did not go there, & that Henry & Eliza saw nothing in it to make them feel differently. You found my letter at Andover, I hope, yesterday, and have now for many hours been satisfied that your kind anxiety on my behalf was as much thrown away as kind anxiety usually is. I continue quite well; in proof of which I have bathed again this morning. It was absolutely necessary that I should have the little fever and indisposition which I had: it has been all the fashion this week in Lyme. Miss Anna Cove was

confined for a day or two & her Mother thinks she
was saved only by a timely Emetic (prescribed by D^r
Robinson) from a serious illness & Miss Bonham has
been under Mr Carpenter's care for several days with
a sort of nervous fever, & tho' she is now well enough
to walk abroad she is still very tall & does not come
to the Rooms. We all of us attended them both on
Wednesday evening & last evening I suppose I must
say or Martha will think Mr Peter Debary slighted.
My mother had her pool of commerce each night &
divided the first with Le Chevalier, who was lucky
enough to divide the other with somebody else. I hope
he will always win enough to empower him to treat
himself with so great an indulgence as cards must be
to him. He enquired particularly after you, not being
aware of your departure. We are quite settled in our
Lodgings by this time as you may suppose, & everything goes on in the usual order. The servants behave
very well, & make no difficulties, tho' nothing certainly
can exceed the inconvenience of the offices, except the
general dirtiness of the house & furniture & all its
inhabitants. Hitherto the weather has been just what
we could wish—the continuance of the dry season is
very necessary to our comfort. I endeavour as far as I
can to supply your place & be useful, & keep things in
order. I detect dirt in the water-decanter as fast as I
can & give the Cook physic which she throws off her
stomach. I forget whether she used to do this, under
your administration. James is the delight of our lives,
he is quite an uncle Toby's annuity to us. My mother's
shoes were never so well blacked before, & our plate
never looked so clean. He waits extremely well, is
attentive, handy, quick and quiet, & in short has a
great many more than all the cardinal virtues (for the

cardinal virtues in themselves have been so often
possessed that they are no longer worth having) &
amongst the rest, that of wishing to go to Bath, as I
understand from Jenny. He has the laudable thirst I
fancy for travelling, which in poor James Selby[1] was
so much reprobated; & part of his disappointment in
not going with his master, arose from his wish of seeing London. My mother is at this moment reading a
letter from my aunt. Yours to Miss Irvine of which she
had had the perusal (which by the bye in your place
I should not like) has thrown them into a quandary
about Charles & his prospects. The case is that my
mother had previously told my aunt, without restric-
tion, that a sloop (which my aunt calls a Frigate) was
reserved in the East for Charles; whereas you had
replied to Miss Irvine's enquiries on the subject with
less explicitness & more caution. Never mind, let them
puzzle on together. As Charles will equally go to the
E. Indies, my uncle cannot be really uneasy, & my
aunt may do what she likes with her frigates. She talks
a great deal of the violent heat of the weather—we
know nothing of it here. My uncle has been suffering
a good deal lately; they mean however to go to Scarlets
about this time unless prevented by bad accounts of
Cook. The Coles have got their infamous plate upon
our door.[2] I dare say *that* makes a great part of the
massy plate so much talked of. The Irvines' house is
nearly completed. I believe they are to get into it on
Tuesday: my aunt owns it to have a comfortable appearance, & only 'hopes the kitchen may not be damp'.
I have not heard from Charles yet, which rather surprises me—some ingenious addition of his own to the

[1] In *Sir Charles Grandison.*
[2] In Sydney Place, which the Austens were soon to leave.

57

proper direction perhaps prevents my receiving his letter. I have written to Buller & I have written to Mr Pyne, on the subject of the broken lid; it was valued by Anning here we were told at five shillings, & as that appeared to us beyond the value of all the furniture in the room together, we have referred ourselves to the owner. The Ball last night was pleasant, but not full for Thursday. My father staid very contentedly till half-past nine (we went a little after eight), and then walked home with James and a lanthorn, though I believe the lanthorn was not lit, as the moon was up; but this lanthorn may sometimes be a great convenience to him. My mother and I staid about an hour later. Nobody asked me the two first dances; the two next I danced with Mr. Crawford, and had I chosen to stay longer might have danced with Mr. Granville, Mrs. Granville's son, whom my dear friend Miss Armstrong offered to introduce to me, or with a new odd-looking man who had been eyeing me for some time, and at last, without any introduction, asked me if I meant to dance again. I think he must be Irish by his ease, and because I imagine him to belong to the hon^{bl} Barnwalls, who are the son, and son's wife of an Irish viscount, bold queer-looking people, just fit to be quality at Lyme. Mrs. Fraser(?) & the Schuylers went away—I do not know where—last Tuesday for some days & when they return the Schuylers I understand are to remain here a very little while longer. I called yesterday morning (ought it not in strict propriety to be termed yester-morning?) on Miss Armstrong and was introduced to her father and mother. Like other young ladies she is considerably genteeler than her parents. Mrs. Armstrong sat darning a pair of stockings the whole of my visit. But I do not mention this at home, lest a warning should act as an example. We afterwards walked together for an hour on the Cobb; she is very converseable in a common way; I do not perceive wit or genius, but she has sense and some degree of taste, and her manners are very engaging. She seems to like people rather too easily. She thought the Downes pleasant etc etc. I have seen nothing of M^r & Mrs Manhood. My aunt mentions Mrs. Holder's being returned from Cheltenham so her summer ends before theirs begins. Hooper was heard of well at the Madeiras. Eliza would envy him. I hope Martha thinks you looking better than when she saw you in Bath. Jenny has fastened up my hair to-day in the same manner that she used to do up Miss Lloyd's—which makes us both very happy. I need not say that we are particularly anxious for your next letter to know how you find Mrs Lloyd & Martha. Say everything kind for us to the latter. The former I fear must be beyond any remembrance of or from the absent.

Y^{rs} affect^{ly}
J. A.

Friday Even^g. The bathing was so delightful this morning & Molly so pressing with me to enjoy myself that I believe I staid in rather too long, as since the middle of the day I have felt unreasonably tired. I shall be more careful another time, & shall not bathe to-morrow as I had before intended. Jenny & James are walked to Charmouth this afternoon. I am glad to have such an amusement for him, as I am very anxious for his being at once quiet & happy. He can read, & I must get him some books. Unfortunately he has read the 1st vol. of Robinson Crusoe. We have the Pinckards newspaper however which I shall take care to lend him.

40. *To Francis Austen. Monday 21 Jan.* 1805

Green Park B^gs Monday Jan^ry 21st

My dearest Frank

I have melancholy news to relate, & sincerely feel
for your feelings under the shock of it.—I wish I could
better prepare you for it. But having said so much,
your mind will already forestall the sort of event which
I have to communicate.—Our dear Father has closed
his virtuous & happy life, in a death almost as free
from suffering as his Children could have wished. He
was taken ill on Saturday morning, exactly in the same
way as heretofore, an oppression in the head, with
fever, violent tremulousness, & the greatest degree of
Feebleness. The same remedy of Cupping, which had
before been so successful, was immediately applied to
—but without such happy effects. The attack was
more violent, & at first he seemed scarcely at all
releived by the operation. Towards the Evening however he got better, had a tolerable night, & yesterday
morning was so greatly amended as to get up & join
us at breakfast as usual, & walk about with only the
help of a stick, & every symptom was then so favourable that when Bowen saw him at one, he felt sure of
his doing perfectly well. But as the day advanced, all
these comfortable appearances gradually changed; the
fever grew stronger than ever, & when Bowen saw
him at ten at night, he pronounc'd his situation to be
most alarming. At nine this morning he came again—
& by his desire a Physician was called in;—Dr. Gibbs
—But it was then absolutely a lost case—. Dr. Gibbs
said that nothing but a Miracle could save him, and
about twenty minutes after Ten he drew his last gasp.

Heavy as is the blow, we can already feel that a
thousand comforts remain to us to soften it. Next to
that of the consciousness of his worth & constant preparation for another World, is the remembrance of
his having suffered, comparatively speaking, nothing.
Being quite insensible of his own state, he was spared
all the pain of separation, & he went off almost in his
Sleep. My Mother bears the Shock as well as possible;
she was quite prepared for it, & feels all the blessing
of his being spared a long Illness. My Uncle & Aunt
have been with us, & shew us every imaginable kindness. And to-morrow we shall I dare say have the
comfort of James's presence, as an express has been
sent to him. We write also of course to Godmersham &
Brompton. Adieu my dearest Frank. The loss of such a
Parent must be felt, or we should be Brutes—. I wish
I could have given you better preparation—but it has
been impossible. Yours Ever affec^ly

J A.

41. *To Francis Austen. Tuesday* 22 *Jan.* ⟨1805⟩

Green Park B^gs Tuesday Even^g, Jan^ry 22^d

My dearest Frank

I wrote to you yesterday; but your letter to Cassandra
this morning, by which we learn the probability of your
being by this time at Portsmouth, obliges me to write
to you again, having unfortunately a communication
as necessary as painful to make to you. Your affectionate heart will be greatly wounded, & I wish the shock
could have been lessen'd by a better preparation; but
the Event has been sudden, & so must be the information of it. We have lost an Excellent Father. An illness

of only eight & forty hours carried him off yesterday morning between ten & eleven. He was seized on saturday with a return of the feverish complaint, which he had been subject to for the three last years; evidently a more violent attack from the first, as the applications which had before produced almost immediate releif, seemed for some time to afford him scarcely any. On Sunday however he was much better, so much so as to make Bowen quite easy, & give us every hope of his being well again in a few days. But these hopes gradually gave way as the day advanced, & when Bowen saw him at ten that night he was greatly alarmed. A Physician was called in yesterday morning, but he was at that time past all possibility of cure—& Dr. Gibbs and Mr. Bowen had scarcely left his room before he sunk into a Sleep from which he never woke. Everything I trust & beleive was done for him that was possible! It has been very sudden! within twenty four hours of his death he was walking with only the help of a stick, was even reading! We had however some hours of preparation, & when we understood his recovery to be hopeless, most fervently did we pray for the speedy release which ensued. To have seen him languishing long, struggling for Hours, would have been dreadful! & thank God! we were all spared from it. Except the restlessness & confusion of high Fever, he did not suffer—& he was mercifully spared from knowing that he was about to quit the Objects so beloved, so fondly cherished as his wife & Children ever were. His tenderness as a Father, who can do justice to? My Mother is tolerably well; she bears up with great fortitude, but I fear her health must suffer under such a shock. An express was sent for James, & he arrived here this morning before eight o'clock. The funeral is to be on Saturday, at Walcot Church. The Serenity of the Corpse is most delightful! It preserves the sweet benevolent smile which always distinguished him. They kindly press my Mother to remove to Steventon as soon as it is all over, but I do not beleive she will leave Bath at present. We must have this house for three months longer, & here we shall probably stay till the end of that time.

We all unite in Love, & I am affec^{ly} Yours

J A.

44. *To Cassandra Austen. Sunday 21 April* ⟨1805⟩

Gay St Sunday Evening, April 21st

My dear Cassandra

I am much obliged to you for writing to me again so soon; your letter yesterday was quite an unexpected pleasure. Poor Mrs Stent! it has been her lot to be always in the way; but we must be merciful, for perhaps in time we may come to be Mrs Stents ourselves, unequal to anything & unwelcome to everybody. We shall be very glad to see you whenever you can get away, but I have no expectation of your coming before the 10th or 11th of May. Your account of Martha is very comfortable indeed, & now we shall be in no fear of receiving a worse. This day, if she has gone to Church, must have been a trial of her feelings, but I hope it will be the last of any acuteness. James may not be a Man of Business, but as a 'Man of Letters' he is certainly very useful; he affords you a most convenient communication with the Newbury Post. You were very right in supposing I wore my crape sleeves to the Concert, I had them put in on the occasion; on my head I wore my crape & flowers, but I do not think it looked particularly well. My Aunt is in a great hurry to pay me for my Cap, but cannot find in her heart to give me good money. 'If I have any intention of going to the Grand Sydney-Garden Breakfast, if there is any party I wish to join, Perrot will take out a ticket for me.' Such an offer I shall of course decline; & all the service she will render me therefore, is to put it out of my power to go at all, whatever may occur to make it desirable. Yesterday was a busy day with me, or at least with my feet & my stockings; I was walking almost all day long; I went to Sydney Gardens soon after one, & did not return till four, & after dinner I walked to Weston. My morning engagement was with the Cookes, & our party consisted of George & Mary, a M^r & Miss Bendish who had been with us at the Concert, & the youngest Miss Whitby;—not Julia, we have done with her, she is very ill, but Mary; Mary Whitby's turn is actually come to be grown up & have a fine complexion & wear great square muslin shawls. I have not expressly enumerated myself among the party, but there I was, & my cousin George was very kind & talked sense to me every now & then in the intervals of his more animated fooleries with Miss Bendish, who is very young & rather handsome, & whose gracious manners, ready wit, & solid remarks put me somewhat in mind of my old acquaintance Lucy Lefroy. There was a monstrous deal of stupid quizzing, & commonplace nonsense talked, but scarcely any wit;—all that border'd on it, or on sense came from my Cousin George, whom altogether I like very well. Mr Bendish seems nothing more than a tall young man. I met Mr F. Bonham the other day, & almost his first salutation was 'So Miss Austen your cousin is come'. My Evening

Engagement & walk was with Miss Armstrong, who had called on me the day before, & gently upbraided me in her turn with change of manners to her since she had been in Bath, or at least of late. Unlucky me! that my notice should be of such consequence & my Manners so bad! She was so well-disposed, & so reasonable that I soon forgave her, & made this engagement with her in proof of it. She is really an agreable girl, so I think I may like her, & her great want of a companion at home, which may well make any tolerable acquaintance important to her, gives her another claim on my attention. I shall endeavour as much as possible to keep my Intimacies in their proper place, & prevent their clashing. I have been this morning with Miss Irvine; it is not in my power to return her evening-visits at present. I must pay her as I can. On tuesday we are to have a party. It came into my wise head that tho' my Mother did not go out of an evening, there was no reason against her seeing her friends at home, & that it would be as well to get over the Chamberlaynes visit now, as to delay it. I accordingly invited them this morning, Mrs C. fixed on tuesday, & I rather think they will all come; the possibility of it will deter us from asking M^r & Mrs L. P. to meet them. I asked Miss Irvine, but she declined it, as not feeling quite stout, & wishing to keep quiet;—but her Mother is to enliven our circle. Bickerton has been at home for the Easter Holidays, & returns tomorrow; he is a very sweet boy, both in manner & countenance. He seems to have the attentive, affectionate feelings of Fulwar-William—who by the bye is actually fourteen —what are we to do?—I have never seen Bickerton without his immediately enquiring whether I had heard from you—from 'Miss Cassandra', was his expression at first. As far as I can learn, the Family are very much pleased with Bath, & excessively overcome by the heat, or the cold, or whatever happens to be the weather. They go on with their Masters & Mistresses, & are to have a Miss; Amelia is to take lessons of Miss Sharpe. Among so many friends it will be well if I do not get into a scrape; & now here is Miss Blachford come. I should have gone distracted if the Bullers had staid. The Cookes leave Bath next week I believe, & my Cousin goes earlier. The papers announce the Marriage of the Rev. Edward Bather, Rector of some place in Shropshire to a Miss Emma Halifax—a wretch!—he does not deserve an Emma Halifax's maid Betty. Mr Hampson is here; this must interest Martha; I met him the other morning in his way (as he said) to Green Park B^gs; I trusted to his forgetting our number in Gay S^t when I gave it him, & so I conclude he has, as he has not yet called. Mrs Stanhope has let her house from Midsummer, so we shall get rid of them. She is lucky in disposing of it so soon, as there is an astonishing number of Houses at this time vacant in that end of the Town. Mrs Elliot is to quit hers at Michaelmas. I wonder whether Mr Hampson's friend Mr Saunders is any relation to the famous Saunders whose letters have been lately published! I am quite of your opinion as to the folly of concealing any longer our intended Partnership with Martha, & whenever there has of late been an enquiry on the subject I have always been sincere; & I have sent word of it to the Mediterranean in a letter to Frank. None of *our* nearest connections I think will be unprepared for it; & I do not know how to suppose that Martha's have not foreseen it. When I tell you that we have been visiting a Countess this morning, you will immediately with

great justice, but no truth, guess it to be Lady Roden.
No, it is Lady Leven, the mother of Ld Balgonie. On
receiving a message from Lord & Lady Leven thro' the
Mackays declaring their intention of waiting on us, we
thought it right to go to them. I hope we have not done
too much, but the friends & admirers of Charles must
be attended to. They seem very reasonable, good sort of
people, very civil, & full of his praise. We were shewn
at first into an empty Drawing-room, & presently in
came his Lordship, not knowing who we were, to
apologise for the servant's mistake, & tell a lie himself,
that Lady Leven was not within. He is a tall, gentlemanlike man, with spectacles, & rather deaf:—after
sitting with him ten minutes we walked away; but
Lady L. coming out of the Dining parlour as we passed
the door, we were obliged to attend her back to it, &
pay our visit over again. She is a stout woman, with
a very handsome face. By this means we had the
pleasure of hearing Charles's praises twice over;—
they think themselves excessively obliged to him, &
estimate him so highly as to wish Ld Balgonie when
he is quite recovered, to go out to him. The young
man is much better, & is gone for the confirmation of
his health, to Penzance. There is a pretty little Lady
Marianne of the party, to be shaken hands with &
asked if she remembers Mr Austen.

Monday. The Cookes' place seems of a sort to suit
Isaac, if he means to go to service again, & does not
object to change of Country. He will have a good soil,
& a good Mistress, & I suppose will not mind taking
physic now & then. The only doubt which occurs to
me is whether Mr Cooke may not be a disagreable,
fidgetty Master, especially in matters concerning the
Garden. Mr Mant has not yet paid my Mother the

remainder of her money, but she has very lately received his apology for it, with his hope of being able to close the account shortly. You told me some time ago that Tom Chute had had a fall from his horse, but I am waiting to know how it happened before I begin pitying him, as I cannot help suspecting it was in consequence of his taking orders; very likely as he was going to do Duty or returning from it.

Tuesday. I have not much more to add. My Uncle & Aunt drank tea with us last night, & in spite of my resolution to the contrary, I could not help putting forward to invite them again this Evening. I thought it was of the first consequence to avoid anything that might seem a slight to them. I shall be glad when it is over, & hope to have no necessity for having so many dear friends at once again. I shall write to Charles by the next Packet, unless you tell me in the meantime of your intending to do it. Beleive me if you chuse

Y^r affec^{te} Sister.

III. SOUTHAMPTON

1807–9: *Thirty-one to Thirty-three*

━━━━

THE widow and her daughters left Bath ('with what happy feelings of escape', JA wrote two years later) in July 1806; but they reached Southampton six months later. We have no letters between 47 (Aug. 1805, Goodnestone) and 48 (Jan. 1807, Southampton); but it is known that they visited their Leigh relations at Stoneleigh and Adlestrop. In 1807 they are in lodgings at Southampton, preparing to set up home in Castle Square; in September JA is at Chawton Manor. In 1808 she visits Henry at Brompton and Edward at Godmersham (52). In 1809 (63) they are still at Southampton but look forward to settling at Chawton. They left in April, but did not reach Chawton Cottage (as it was later called; it is really a substantial and roomy house) until July—a date commemorated annually by the Jane Austen Society.

48. *To Cassandra Austen. Wednesday 7 Jan.* ⟨1807⟩

Southampton: Wednesday January 7

My dear Cassandra

You were mistaken in supposing I should expect your letter on Sunday; I had no idea of hearing from you before Tuesday, and my pleasure yesterday was

69

therefore unhurt by any previous disappointment. I thank you for writing so much; you must really have sent me the value of two letters in one. We are extremely glad to hear that Elizabeth is so much better, and hope you will be sensible of still further amendment in her when you return from Canterbury.

Of your visit there I must now speak 'incessantly;' it surprises, but pleases me more, and I consider it as a very just and honourable distinction of you, and not less to the credit of Mrs. Knight. I have no doubt of your spending your time with her most pleasantly in quiet and rational conversation, and am so far from thinking her expectations of you will be deceived, that my only fear is of your being so agreeable, so much to her taste, as to make her wish to keep you with her for ever. If that should be the case, we must remove to Canterbury, which I should not like so well as Southampton.

When you receive this, our guests will be all gone or going; and I shall be left to the comfortable disposal of my time, to ease of mind from the torments of rice puddings and apple dumplings, and probably to regret that I did not take more pains to please them all.

Mrs. J. Austen has asked me to return with her to Steventon; I need not give my answer; and she has invited my mother to spend there the time of Mrs. F. A.'s confinement, which she seems half inclined to do.

A few days ago I had a letter from Miss Irvine, and as I was in her debt, you will guess it to be a remonstrance, not a very severe one, however; the first page is in her usual retrospective, jealous, inconsistent style, but the remainder is chatty and harmless. She supposes my silence may have proceeded from resentment of her not having written to inquire particularly after my hooping cough, &c. She is a funny one.

I have answered her letter, and have endeavoured to give something like the truth with as little incivility as I could, by placing my silence to the want of subject in the very quiet way in which we live. Phebe has repented, and stays. I have also written to Charles, and I answered Miss Buller's letter by return of post, as I intended to tell you in my last.

Two or three things I recollected when it was too late, that I might have told you; one is, that the Welbys have lost their eldest son by a putrid fever at Eton, and another that Tom Chute is going to settle in Norfolk.

You have scarcely ever mentioned Lizzy[1] since your being at Godmersham. I hope it is not because she is altered for the worse.

I cannot yet satisfy Fanny as to Mrs. Foote's baby's name, and I must not encourage her to expect a good one, as Captain Foote is a professed adversary to all but the plainest; he likes only Mary, Elizabeth, Anne, &c. Our best chance is of 'Caroline,' which in compliment to a sister seems the only exception.

He dined with us on Friday, and I fear will not soon venture again, for the strength of our dinner was a boiled leg of mutton, underdone even for James; and Captain Foote has a particular dislike of underdone mutton; but he was so good-humoured and pleasant that I did not much mind his being starved. He gives us all the most cordial invitation to his house in the country, saying just what the Williams[2] ought to say to make us welcome. Of them we have seen nothing since

---

[1] Edward's second daughter.
[2] Sir Thomas W. and his second wife.

71

you left us, and we hear that they are just gone to Bath again, to be out of the way of further alterations at Brooklands.

Mrs. F. A. has had a very agreeable letter from Mrs. Dickson, who was delighted with the purse, and desires her not to provide herself with a christening dress, which is exactly what her young correspondent wanted; and she means to defer making any of the caps as long as she can, in hope of having Mrs. D.'s present in time to be serviceable as a pattern. She desires me to tell you that the gowns were cut out before your letter arrived, but that they are long enough for Caroline. The *Beds*, as I believe they are called, have fallen to Frank's share to continue, and of course are cut out to admiration.

'Alphonsine' did not do. We were disgusted in twenty pages, as, independent of a bad translation, it has indelicacies which disgrace a pen hitherto so pure; and we changed it for the 'Female Quixotte,' which now makes our evening amusement; to me a very high one, as I find the work quite equal to what I remembered it. Mrs. F. A., to whom it is new, enjoys it as one could wish; the other Mary, I believe, has little pleasure from that or any other book.

My mother does not seem at all more disappointed than ourselves at the termination of the family treaty;[1] she thinks less of *that* just now than of the comfortable state of her own finances, which she finds on closing her year's accounts beyond her expectation, as she begins the new year with a balance of 30*l.* in her favour; and when she has written her answer to my aunt, which you know always hangs a little upon her mind, she will be above the world entirely. You will

[1] See note, p. 213.

have a great deal of unreserved discourse with Mrs. K.,[1] I dare say, upon this subject, as well as upon many other of our family matters. Abuse everybody but me.

Thursday. We expected James yesterday, but he did not come; if he comes at all now, his visit will be a very short one, as he must return to-morrow, that Ajax and the chair may be sent to Winchester on Saturday. Caroline's new pelisse depended upon her mother's being able or not to come so far in the chair; how the guinea that will be saved by the same means of return is to be spent I know not. Mrs. J. A. does not talk much of poverty now, though she has no hope of my brother's being able to buy another horse *next* summer.

Their scheme against Warwickshire continues, but I doubt the family's being at Stoneleigh so early as James says he must go, which is May.

My mother is afraid I have not been explicit enough on the subject of her wealth; she began 1806 with 68*l.*, she begins 1807 with 99*l.*, and this after 32*l.* purchase of stock. Frank too has been settling his accounts and making calculations, and each party feels quite equal to our present expenses; but much increase of house-rent would not do for either. Frank limits himself, I believe, to four hundred a year.

You will be surprised to hear that Jenny is not yet come back; we have heard nothing of her since her reaching Itchingswell, and can only suppose that she must be detained by illness in somebody or other, and that she has been each day expecting to be able to come on the morrow. I am glad I did not know beforehand that she was to be absent during the whole or almost the whole of our friends being with us, for though the inconvenience has not been nothing, I

[1] Knight.

should have feared still more. Our dinners have certainly suffered not a little by having only Molly's head and Molly's hands to conduct them; she fries better than she did, but not like Jenny.

We did *not* take our walk on Friday, it was too dirty, nor have we yet done it; we may perhaps do something like it to-day, as after seeing Frank skate, which he hopes to do in the meadows by the beech, we are to treat ourselves with a passage over the ferry. It is one of the pleasantest frosts I ever knew, so very quiet. I hope it will last some time longer for Frank's sake, who is quite anxious to get some skating; he tried yesterday, but it would not do.

Our acquaintance increase too fast. He was recognised lately by Admiral Bertie, and a few days since arrived the Admiral and his daughter Catherine to wait upon us. There was nothing to like or dislike in either. To the Berties are to be added the Lances, with whose cards we have been endowed, and whose visit Frank and I returned yesterday. They live about a mile and three-quarters from S. to the right of the new road to Portsmouth, and I believe their house is one of those which are to be seen almost anywhere among the woods on the other side of the Itchen. It is a handsome building, stands high, and in a very beautiful situation.

We found only Mrs. Lance at home, and whether she boasts any offspring besides a grand pianoforte did not appear. She was civil and chatty enough, and offered to introduce us to some acquaintance in Southampton, which we gratefully declined.

I suppose they must be acting by the orders of Mr. Lance of Netherton in this civility, as there seems no other reason for their coming near us. They will not come often, I dare say. They live in a handsome style and are rich, and she seemed to like to be rich, and we gave her to understand that we were far from being so; she will soon feel therefore that we are not worth her acquaintance.

You must have heard from Martha by this time. We have had no accounts of Kintbury since her letter to me.

Mrs. F. A. has had one fainting fit lately; it came on as usual after eating a hearty dinner, but did not last long.

I can recollect nothing more to say. When my letter is gone, I suppose I shall.

Yours affectionately,   J. A.

I have just asked Caroline if I should send her love to her godmama, to which she answered 'Yes.'

49. *To Cassandra Austen.* ⟨*Sunday*⟩ 8 *Feb.* 1807

Southampton Feb. 8th

My dearest Cassandra

My expectation of having nothing to say to you after the conclusion of my last, seems nearer Truth than I thought it would be, for I feel to have but little. I need not therefore be above acknowledging the receipt of yours this mornᵍ; or of replying to every part of it which is capable of an answer; & you may accordingly prepare for my ringing the Changes of the Glads & Sorrys for the rest of the page. Unluckily however I see nothing to be glad of, unless I make it a matter of Joy that Mrs. Wylmot has another son, & that Lᵈ Lucan has taken a Mistress, both of which Events are of course joyful to the Actors; but to be sorry I find many occasions, the first is that your return is to be delayed,

& whether I ever get beyond the first is doubtful. It is no use to lament. I never heard that even Queen Mary's Lamentation[1] did her any good, & I could not therefore expect benefit from mine. We are all sorry, & now that subject is exhausted. I heard from Martha yesterday: she spends this week with the Harwoods, goes afterwards with James & Mary for a few days to see Peter Debary & two of his sisters at Eversley—the Living of which he has gained on the death of Sir R. Cope—& means to be here on ye 24th, which will be Tuesday fortnight. I shall be truely glad if she can keep to her day, but dare not depend on it;—& am so apprehensive of farther detention that, if nothing else occurs to create it, I cannot help thinking she will marry Peter Debary. It vexed me that I could not get any fish for Kintbury while their family was large; but so it was, & till last Tuesday I could procure none. I then sent them four pair of small soals, & should be glad to be certain of their arriving in good time, but I have heard nothing about them since, & had rather hear nothing than Evil. They cost six shillings, & as they travelled in a Basket which came from Kintbury a few days before with Poultry &c, I insist upon treating you with the Booking *whatever it may be*, You are only Eighteen pence in my debt. Mrs. E. Leigh did not make the slightest allusion to my Uncle's Business,[2] as I remember telling you at the time, but you shall have it as often as you like. My Mother wrote to her a week ago. Martha's rug is just finished, & looks well, tho' not quite so well as I had hoped. I see no fault in the Border, but the Middle is dingy. My Mother desires me to say that she will knit one for you, as soon as you return to chuse the colours & pattern. I am sorry I have

[1] See note, p. 213. [2] See note, p. 213, on p. 72.

affronted you on the subject of Mr. Moore, but I do not
mean ever to like him; & as to pitying a young woman
merely because she cannot live in two places at the
same time, & at once enjoy the comforts of being
married & single, I shall not attempt it, even for
Harriet. You see I have a spirit, as well as yourself.
Frank & Mary cannot at all approve of your not being
at home in time to help them in their finishing purchases, & desire me to say that, if you are not, they
shall be as spiteful as possible & chuse everything in
the stile most likely to vex you, knives that will not cut,
glasses that will not hold, a sofa without a seat, & a
Bookcase without shelves. Our Garden is putting in
order, by a Man who bears a remarkably good character, has a very fine complexion & asks something less
than the first. The shrubs which border the gravel
walk he says are only sweetbriar & roses, & the latter
of an indifferent sort;—we mean to get a few of a
better kind therefore, & at my own particular desire
he procures us some Syringas. I could not do without
a Syringa, for the sake of Cowper's Line.[1] We talk also
of a Laburnam. The Border under the Terrace Wall,
is clearing away to receive Currants & Gooseberry
Bushes, & a spot is found very proper for raspberries.
The alterations & improvements within doors too ad-
vance very properly, & the offices will be made very
convenient indeed. Our Dressing-Table is constructing
on the spot, out of a large Kitchen Table belonging to
the House, for doing which we have the permission
of Mr. Husket Lord Lansdown's Painter,—domestic
Painter I sh^d call him, for he lives in the Castle.
Domestic Chaplains have given way to this more

---

[1] Laburnum, rich In streaming gold; syringa, iv'ry pure. *The Task*,
vi. 150.

necessary office, & I suppose whenever the Walls want no touching up, he is employed about my Lady's face. The morning was so wet that I was afraid we should not be able to see our little visitor, but Frank who alone could go to Church called for her after service, & she is now talking away at my side & examining the Treasures of my Writing-desk drawer;—very happy I beleive;—not at all shy of course. Her name is Catherine & her Sister's Caroline.[1] She is something like her Brother, & as short for her age, but not so well-looking. What is become of all the Shyness in the World? Moral as well as Natural Diseases disappear in the progress of time, & new ones take their place. Shyness and the Sweating Sickness have given way to Confidence & Paralytic complaints. I am sorry to hear of Mrs. Whitfield's encreasing Illness, & of poor Marianne Bridges's having suffered so much;—these are some of my sorrows,—& that Mrs. Deedes is to have another Child I suppose I may lament. The death of Mrs. W. K.[2] we had seen; I had no idea that any-body liked her, & therefore felt nothing for any Sur-vivor, but I am now feeling away on her Husband's account, and think he had better marry Miss Sharpe. I have this instant made my present, & have the pleasure of seeing it smiled over with genuine satisfac-tion. I am sure I may on this occasion call Kitty Foote, as Hastings[3] did H. Egerton, my 'very valuable Friend.' —*Even^g*.—Our little visitor has just left us, & left us highly pleased with her; she is a nice, natural, open-hearted, affectionate girl, with all the ready civility which one sees in the best Children in the present day;

[1] Captain Foote's children.
[2] Wyndham Knatchbull; the Knatchbulls and Knights were intimate.
[3] See note, p. 213.

so unlike anything that I was myself at her age, that I am often all astonishment & shame. Half her time here was spent at Spillikins, which I consider as a very valuable part of our Household furniture, & as not the least important Benefaction from the family of Knight to that of Austen. But I must tell you a story. Mary has for some time had notice from Mrs. Dickson of the intended arrival of a certain Miss Fowler in this place; —Miss F. is an intimate friend of Mrs. D. & a good deal known as such to Mary. On Thursday last she called here while we were out;—Mary found on our return her card with only her name on it, & she had left word that she w[d] call again. The particularity of this made us talk, & among other conjectures Frank said in joke 'I dare say she is staying with the Pearsons.' The connection of the names struck Mary, & she immediately recollected Miss Fowler's having been very intimate with persons so called;—and upon putting everything together we have scarcely a doubt of her being actually staying with the only Family in the place whom we cannot visit.[1] What a Contretems!— in the Language of France; What an unluckiness! in that of M[de] Duval[2]:—The Black Gentleman has certainly employed one of his menial imps to bring about this complete tho' trifling mischeif. Miss F. has never called again, but we are in daily expectation of it. Miss P. has of course given her a proper understanding of the Business; it is evident that Miss F. did not expect or wish to have the visit returned, & Frank is quite as much on his guard for his wife as we c[d] desire for her sake or our own. We shall rejoice in being so near Winchester when Edward[3] belongs to it, & can never

[1] See note, p. 213. [2] In *Evelina*.
[3] James Edward.

have our spare bed filled more to our satisfaction than by him. Does he leave Eltham at Easter? We are reading Clarentine, & are surprised to find how foolish it is. I remember liking it much less on a 2[d] reading than at the 1st & it does not bear a 3[d] at all. It is full of unnatural conduct & forced difficulties, without striking merit of any kind.

Miss Harrison is going into Devonshire to attend Mrs. Dusautoy as usual. Miss Jackson is married to young Mr. Gunthorpe, & is to be very unhappy. He swears, drinks, is cross, jealous, selfish & Brutal; the match makes *her* family miserable, & has occasioned *his* being disinherited. The Browns are added to our list of acquaintance; He commands the Sea Fencibles here under Sir Tho.[1] & was introduced at his own desire by the latter when we saw him last week. As yet the Gentlemen only have visited, as Mrs. B. is ill, but she is a nice looking woman & wears one of the prettiest straw Bonnets in the place.—*Monday*. The Garretbeds are made, & ours will be finished today. I had hoped it w[d] be finished on Saturday, but neither Mrs. Hall nor Jenny were able to give help enough for that; & I have as yet done very little & Mary nothing at all. This week we shall do more, & I sh[d] like to have all the 5 beds completed by the end of it. There will then be the Window-Curtains, sofa-cover, & a carpet to be altered. I should not be surprised if we were to be visited by James again this week; he gave us reason to expect him soon; & if they go to Eversley he cannot come next week.

I am sorry & angry that his Visits should not give one more pleasure; the company of so good & so clever a Man ought to be gratifying in itself; but his Chat

---

[1] Williams.

seems all forced, his Opinions on many points too much
copied from his Wife's, & his time here is spent I think
in walking about the House & banging the doors, or
ringing the bell for a glass of water.

There, I flatter myself I have constructed you a
smartish Letter, considering my want of Materials. But
like my dear Dr. Johnson I beleive I have dealt more
in Notions than Facts.[1]

I hope your Cough is gone & that you are otherwise
well. And remain with Love,

Y^{rs} affec^{tely}   J. A.

52. *To Cassandra Austen. Monday 20 June* 1808

Godmersham Monday June 20th.

My dear Cassandra

I will first talk of my visit to Canterbury, as Mrs.
J. A.'s letter to Anna cannot have given you every particular of it, which you are likely to wish for. I had a
most affectionate welcome from Harriot[2] & was happy
to see her looking almost as well as ever. She walked
with me to call on Mrs. Brydges, when Elizth & Louisa[3]
went to Mrs. Milles'; Mrs. B. was dressing & c^d not see
us, & we proceeded to the White Friars, where Mrs.
K.[4] was alone in her Drawing room, as gentle & kind
& friendly as usual. She enquired after every body,
especially my Mother & yourself. We were with her
a quarter of an hour before Eliz. & Louisa, hot from
Mrs. Baskerville's Shop, walked in; they were soon
followed by the Carriage, & another five minutes
brought Mr. Moore himself, just returned from his

---

[1] See note, p. 213.   [2] Moore, Elizabeth Austen's sister.
[3] Bridges, Elizabeth Austen's sister.   [4] Knight.

morn^g ride. Well!—& what do I think of Mr. Moore?
I will not pretend in one meeting to *dislike* him, whatever Mary may say, but I can honestly assure her that
I saw nothing in him to admire. His manners, as you
have always said, are gentlemanlike—but by no means
winning. He made one formal enquiry after you. I saw
their little girl, & very small & very pretty she is; her
features are as delicate as Mary Jane's,[1] with nice dark
eyes, & if she had Mary Jane's fine colour, she w^d be
quite complete. Harriot's fondness for her seems just
what is amiable & natural, & not foolish. I saw Caroline
also, & thought her very plain. Edward's plan for
Hampshire does not vary, he only improves it with the
kind intention of taking me on to Southampton, &
spending one whole day with you; & if it is found
practicable, Edward Junr[2] will be added to our party
for that one day also, which is to be Sunday ye 10th of
July. I hope you may have beds for them. We are
to begin our Journey on ye 8th & reach you late on
ye 9th. This morning brought me a letter from Mrs.
Knight, containing the usual Fee, & all the usual
Kindness. She asks me to spend a day or two with her
this week, to meet Mrs. C. Knatchbull, who with her
Husband comes to the W. Friars today—& I beleive
I shall go. I have consulted Edwd—& think it will be
arranged for Mrs. J. A.'s going with me one morn^g, my
staying the night, & Edward's driving me home the
next Even^g. Her very agreable present will make my
circumstances quite easy. I shall reserve half for my
Pelisse. I hope, by this early return I am sure of seeing
Catherine & Alethea;[3] & I propose that either with or
without them you & I & Martha shall have a snug

---

[1] Frank's daughter.
[2] Edward's Edward, then at Winchester. [3] Bigg.

fortnight while my Mother is at Steventon. We go on
very well here, Mary finds the Children less troublesome than she expected, & independent of *them*, there
is certainly not much to try the patience or hurt the
spirits at Godmersham. I initiated her yesterday into
the mysteries of Inman-ism. The poor old Lady is as
thin & chearful as ever, & very thankful for a new
acquaintance. I had called on her before with Eliz. &
Louisa. I find John Bridges grown very old & black,
but his manners are not altered; he is very pleasing,
& talks of Hampshire with great admiration. Pray let
Anna have the pleasure of knowing that she is remembered with kindness both by Mrs. Cooke & Miss
Sharpe. Her manners must be very much worsted by
your description of them, but I hope they will improve
by this visit. Mrs. Knight finishes her letter with 'Give
my best Love to Cassandra when you write to her.'
I shall like spending a day at the White Friars very
much. We breakfasted in the Library this morn^g for
the first time, & most of the party have been complain-
ing all day of the heat; but Louisa & I feel alike as to
weather, & are cool and comfortable.—Wednesday.
The Moores came yesterday in their Curricle between
one & two o'clock, & immediately after the noonshine
which succeeded their arrival, a party set off for Buck-
well to see the Pond dragged;—Mr. Moore, James,
Edward & James-Edward on horseback, John Bridges
driving Mary in his gig. The rest of us remained quietly
& comfortably at home. We had a very pleasant
Dinner, at the lower end of The table at least; the mer-
riment was cheifly between Edwd Louisa, Harriot &
myself. Mr. Moore did not talk so much as I expected,
& I understand from Fanny, that I did not see him
at all as he is in general; our being strangers made

him so much more silent & quiet. Had I had no reason
for observing what he said & did, I sh^d scarcely have
thought about him. His manners to her want Tenderness—& he was a little violent at last about the impos-
sibility of her going to Eastwell.—I cannot see any
unhappiness in her however; & as to kindheartedness
&c. she is quite unaltered. Mary was disappointed in
her beauty, & thought *him* very disagreable; James
admires *her*, & finds *him* conversible & pleasant. I sent
my answer by them to Mrs. Knight, my double accep-
tance of her note & her invitation, which I wrote without much effort; for I was rich—& the rich are always
respectable, whatever be their stile of writing. I am
to meet Harriot at dinner to-morrow; it is one of the
Audit days, and Mr. M. dines with the Dean, who is
just come to Canterbury. On Tuesday there is to be a
family meeting at Mrs. C. Milles's. Lady Bridges &
Louisa from Goodnestone, the Moores, & a party from
this House, Elizth John Bridges & myself. It will give
me pleasure to see Lady B.—she is now quite well.
Louisa goes home on friday, & John with her; but he
returns the next day. These are our engagements;
make the most of them. Mr. Waller is dead I see; I
cannot greive about it, nor perhaps can his Widow
very much. Edward began cutting S^tfoin on saturday
& I hope is likely to have favourable weather; the crop
is good. There has been a cold & sorethroat prevailing
very much in this House lately, the Children have
almost all been ill with it, & we were afraid Lizzy was
going to be very ill one day; she had specks & a great
deal of fever. It went off however, & they are all
pretty well now. I want to hear of your gathering
Strawberries, we have had them three times here.
I suppose you have been obliged to have in some white

wine, & must visit the Store Closet a little oftener than
when you were quite by yourselves. One begins really
to expect the St. Albans now, & I wish she may come
before Henry goes to Cheltenham, it will be so much
more convenient to him. He will be very glad if Frank
can come to him in London, as his own Time is likely
to be very precious, but does not depend on it. I shall
not forget Charles next week. So much did I write
before breakfast—& now to my agreable surprise I
have to acknowledge another Letter from you. I had
not the least notion of hearing before tomorrow, &
heard of Russell's being about to pass the Windows
without any anxiety. You are very amiable & very
clever to write such long Letters; every page of yours
has more lines than this, & every line more words than
the average of mine. I am quite ashamed—but you
have certainly more little events than we have. Mr.
Lyford supplies you with a great deal of interesting
Matter (Matter Intellectual, not physical)—but I have
nothing to say of Mr. Scudamore. And now, that is
such a sad stupid attempt at Wit, about Matter, that
nobody can smile at it, & I am quite out of heart. I am
sick of myself, & my bad pens.[1] I have no other complaint, however, my languor is entirely removed.
Ought I to be very much pleased with Marmion?—as
yet I am not. James reads it aloud in the Evenᵍ
the short Evenᵍ—beginning at about 10, & broken by
supper. Happy Mrs. Harrison & Miss Austen![2]—You
seem to be always calling on them. I am glad your
various civilities have turned out so well; & most
heartily wish you success & pleasure in your present
engagement. I shall think of you tonight as at Netley,

[1] *sic*; JA did not write *puns*.
[2] Cousins living at Southampton.

& tomorrow too, that I may be quite sure of being right—& therefore I guess you will not go to Netley at all. This is a sad story about Mrs. Powlett. I should not have suspected her of such a thing. She staid the Sacrament I remember, the last time that you & I did. A hint of it, with Initials, was in yesterday's Courier; and Mr. Moore guessed it to be Ld Sackville, beleiving there was no other Viscount S. in the peerage, & so it proved—Ld Viscount Seymour not being there. Yes, I enjoy my apartment very much, & always spend two or three hours in it after breakfast. The change from Brompton Quarters[1] to these is material as to Space. I catch myself going on to the Hall Chamber now & then. Little Caroline[2] looks very plain among her Cousins, and tho' she is not so headstrong or humoursome as they are, I do not think her at all more engaging. Her brother is to go with us to Canterbury tomorrow, & Fanny completes the party. I fancy Mrs. K. feels less interest in that branch of the family than any other. I dare say she will do her *duty* however, by the Boy. His Uncle Edward talks nonsense to him delightfully—more than he can always understand. The two Morrises are come to dine & spend the day with him. Mary wishes my Mother to buy whatever she thinks necessary for Anna's shifts;—& hopes to see her at Steventon soon after ye 9th of July, if that time is as convenient to my Mother as any other. I have hardly done justice to what she means on the subject, as her intention is that my Mother sh^d come at whatever time she likes best. They will be at home on ye 9th. I always come in for a morning visit from Crondale, & Mr. and Mrs. Filmer have just given me my due. He & I talked away gaily of Southampton, the Harrisons

---

[1] Henry at this time lived at B.   [2] Moore.

Wallers &c. Fanny sends her best Love to you all, &
will write to Anna very soon. Yours very affec^ly

Jane

I want some news from Paragon. I am almost sorry
that Rose Hill Cottage sh^d be so near suiting us, as it
does not quite.

58. *To Cassandra Austen. Saturday* 15 *Oct.* 1808

Castle Square: Saturday night October 15.

My dear Cassandra,

Your accounts make us as comfortable as we can
expect to be at such a time. Edward's loss[1] is terrible,
and must be felt as such, and these are too early days
indeed to think of moderation in grief, either in him
or his afflicted daughter, but soon we may hope that
our dear Fanny's sense of duty to that beloved father
will rouse her to exertion. For his sake, and as the most
acceptable proof of love to the spirit of her departed
mother, she will try to be tranquil and resigned. Does
she feel you to be a comfort to her, or is she too much
overpowered for anything but solitude?

Your account of Lizzy[2] is very interesting. Poor
child! One must hope the impression *will* be strong,
and yet one's heart aches for a dejected mind of eight
years old.

I suppose you see the corpse? How does it appear?
We are anxious to be assured that Edward will not
attend the funeral, but when it comes to the point I
think he must feel it impossible.

[1] Elizabeth A. died 10 Oct., soon after the birth of her eleventh
child.

[2] Edward's second daughter.

Your parcel shall set off on Monday, and I hope the shoes will fit; Martha and I both tried them on. I shall send you such of your mourning as I think most likely to be useful, reserving for myself your stockings and half the velvet, in which selfish arrangement I know I am doing what you wish.

I am to be in bombazeen and crape, according to what we are told is universal *here*, and which agrees with Martha's previous observation. My mourning, however, will not impoverish me, for by having my velvet pelisse fresh lined and made up, I am sure I shall have no occasion *this winter* for anything new of that sort. I take my cloak for the lining, and shall send yours on the chance of its doing something of the same for you, though I believe your pelisse is in better repair than mine. *One* Miss Baker makes my gown and the other my bonnet, which is to be silk covered with crape.

I have written to Edward Cooper, and hope he will not send one of his letters of cruel comfort to my poor brother; and yesterday I wrote to Alethea Bigg, in reply to a letter from her. She tells us in confidence that Catherine is to be married on Tuesday se'nnight. Mr. Hill is expected at Manydown in the course of the ensuing week.

We are desired by Mrs. Harrison and Miss Austen[1] to say everything proper for them to yourself and Edward on this sad occasion, especially that nothing but a wish of not giving additional trouble where so much is inevitable prevents their writing themselves to express their concern. They seem truly to feel concern.

I am glad you can say what you do of Mrs. Knight and of Goodnestone in general; it is a great relief to

---

[1] Sisters, cousins of our Austens.

me to know that the shock did not make any of them ill. But what a task was yours to announce it! *Now* **I** hope you are not overpowered with letter-writing, **as** Henry and John[1] can ease you of many of your correspondents.

Was Mr. Scudamore in the house at the time, was any application attempted, and is the seizure at all accounted for?

Sunday.—As Edward's letter to his son is not come here, we know that you must have been informed **as** early as Friday of the boys being at Steventon, which I am glad of.

Upon your letter to Dr. Goddard's[2] being forwarded to them, Mary wrote to ask whether my mother wished to have her grandsons sent to her. We decided on their remaining where they were, which I hope my brother will approve of. I am sure he will do us the justice of believing that in such a decision we sacrificed inclination to what we thought best.

I shall write by the coach to-morrow to Mrs. J. A., and to Edward,[3] about their mourning, though this day's post will probably bring directions to them on that subject from yourselves. I shall certainly make use of the opportunity of addressing our nephew[3] on the most serious of all concerns, as I naturally did in my letter to him before. The poor boys are, perhaps, more comfortable at Steventon than they could be here, but you will understand *my feelings* with respect to it.

To-morrow will be a dreadful day for you all. Mr.

[1] Henry is probably Austen, though there was a Henry Bridges. John is J. Bridges.

[2] The Headmaster of Winchester.

[3] James Edward; 'the poor boys' are the Godmersham boys, Edward and George.

Whitfield's will be a severe duty. Glad shall I be to hear that it is over.

That you are for ever in our thoughts you will not doubt. I see your mournful party in my mind's eye under every varying circumstance of the day; and in the evening especially figure to myself its sad gloom: the efforts to talk, the frequent summons to melancholy orders and cares, and poor Edward, restless in misery, going from one room to the other, and perhaps not seldom upstairs, to see all that remains of his Elizabeth. Dearest Fanny must now look upon herself as his prime source of comfort, his dearest friend; as the being who is gradually to supply to him, to the extent that is possible, what he has lost. This consideration will elevate and cheer her.

Adieu. You cannot write too often, as I said before. We are heartily rejoiced that the poor baby gives you no particular anxiety. Kiss dear Lizzy for us. Tell Fanny that I shall write in a day or two to Miss Sharpe.

My mother is not ill.

Yours most truly,   J. Austen

Tell Henry that a hamper of apples is gone to him from Kintbury, and that Mr. Fowle intended writing on Friday (supposing him in London) to beg that the charts, &c., may be consigned to the care of the Palmers. Mrs. Fowle has also written to Miss Palmer to beg she will send for them.

59. *To Cassandra Austen. Monday 24 Oct.* ⟨1808⟩

Castle Square: Monday October 24

My dear Cassandra,

Edward and George came to us soon after seven on Saturday, very well, but very cold, having by choice travelled on the outside, and with no great coat but what Mr. Wise, the coachman, good-naturedly spared them of his, as they sat by his side. They were so much chilled when they arrived, that I was afraid they must have taken cold; but it does not seem at all the case; I never saw them looking better.

They behave extremely well in every respect, showing quite as much feeling as one wishes to see, and on every occasion speaking of their father with the liveliest affection. His letter was read over by each of them yesterday, and with many tears; George sobbed aloud, Edward's tears do not flow so easily; but as far as I can judge they are both very properly impressed by what has happened. Miss Lloyd,[1] who is a more impartial judge than I can be, is exceedingly pleased with them.

George is almost a new acquaintance to me, and I find him in a different way as *engaging as Edward.*

We do not want amusement: bilbocatch, at which George is indefatigable, spillikins, paper ships, riddles, conundrums, and cards, with watching the flow and ebb of the river, and now and then a stroll out, keep us well employed; and we mean to avail ourselves of our kind papa's consideration, by not returning to Winchester till quite the evening of Wednesday.

Mrs. J. A. had not time to get them more than one suit of clothes; their others are making here, and though I do not believe Southampton is famous for tailoring, I hope it will prove itself better than Basingstoke. Edward has an old black coat, which will save *his* having a second new one; but I find that black pantaloons are considered by them as necessary, and of course one would not have them made uncomfortable by the want of what is usual on such occasions.

---

[1] Martha; JA is quoting the boys.

Fanny's letter was received with great pleasure yesterday, and her brother sends his thanks and will answer it soon. We all saw what she wrote, and were very much pleased with it.

To-morrow I hope to hear from you, and to-morrow we must think of poor Catherine.[1] To-day Lady Bridges is the heroine of our thoughts, and glad shall we be when we can fancy the meeting over. There will then be nothing so very bad for Edward to undergo.

The 'St. Albans,' I find, sailed on the very day of my letters reaching Yarmouth, so that we must not expect an answer at present; we scarcely feel, however, to be in suspense, or only enough to keep our plans[2] to ourselves. We have been obliged to explain them to our young visitors, in consequence of Fanny's letter, but we have not yet mentioned them to Steventon. We are all quite familiarised to the idea ourselves; my mother only wants Mrs. Seward to go out at Midsummer.

What sort of a kitchen garden is there? Mrs. J. A. expresses her fear of our settling in Kent, and, till this proposal was made, we began to look forward to it here; my mother was actually talking of a house at Wye. It will be best, however, as it is.

Anne has just given her mistress warning; she is going to be married; I wish she would stay her year.

On the subject of matrimony, I must notice a wedding in the Salisbury paper, which has amused me very much, Dr. Phillot to Lady Frances St. Lawrence. *She* wanted to have a husband I suppose, once in her life, and *he* a Lady Frances.

I hope your sorrowing party were at church yesterday, and have no longer *that* to dread. Martha was

---

[1] Bigg, who 25 Oct. became Mrs. Hill; 'poor', because H. was twenty-four years her senior; see p. 168.   [2] For Chawton.

kept at home by a *cold, but I went with my two
nephews, and I saw Edward was much affected by
the sermon, which, indeed, I could have supposed
purposely addressed*[1] to the afflicted, if the text had
not naturally come in the course of Dr. Mant's observations on the Litany: 'All that are in danger, necessity,
or tribulation,' was the subject of it. The weather did
not allow us afterwards to get farther than the quay,
where George was very happy as long as we could
stay, flying about from one side to the other, and skip-
ping on board a collier immediately.

In the evening we had the Psalms and Lessons, and
a sermon at home, to which they were very attentive;
but you will not expect to hear that they did not return
to conundrums the moment it *was over*. Their aunt[2]
has written pleasantly of them, which was more than
I hoped.

While I write now, George is most industriously
making and naming paper ships, at which he afterwards shoots with horse-chestnuts, brought from
Steventon on purpose; and Edward equally intent
over the 'Lake of Killarney,' twisting himself about
in one of our great chairs.

Tuesday.—Your close-written letter makes me quite
ashamed of my wide lines; you have sent me a great
deal of matter, most of it very welcome. As to your
lengthened stay, it is no more than I expected, and
what must be, but you cannot suppose I like it.

All that you say of Edward is truly comfortable; I
began to fear that when the bustle of the first week was
over, his spirits might for a time be more depressed;

[1] The underlining represented by italic is doubtless not JA's;
perhaps Fanny's, who owned the (untraced) original.
[2] Mrs. J. A.

and perhaps one must still expect something of the kind. If *you* escape a bilious attack, I shall wonder almost as much as rejoice. I am glad you mentioned where Catherine goes to-day; it is a good plan, but sensible people may generally be trusted to form such.

The day began cheerfully, but it is not likely to continue what it should, for them or for us. *We had a little water party* yesterday; I and my two nephews went from the Itchen Ferry up to Northam, where we landed, looked into the 74, and walked home, and it was so much enjoyed that I had intended to take them to Netley to-day; the tide is just right for our going immediately after noonshine, but I am afraid there will be rain; if we cannot get so far, however, we may perhaps go round from the ferry to the quay.

I had not proposed doing more than cross the Itchen yesterday, but it proved so pleasant, and so much to the satisfaction of all, that when we reached the middle of the stream we agreed to be rowed up the river; both the boys rowed great part of the way, and their questions and remarks, as well as their enjoyment, were very amusing; George's enquiries were endless, and his eagerness in everything reminds me often *of his Uncle Henry*.

Our evening was equally agreeable in its way: I introduced *speculation*, and it was so much approved that we hardly knew how to leave off.

Your idea of an early dinner to-morrow is exactly what we propose, for, after writing the first part of this letter, it came into my head that at this time of year we have not summer evenings. We shall watch the light to-day, that we may not give them a dark drive to-morrow.

They send their best love to papa and everybody,

94

with George's thanks for the letter brought by this post. Martha begs my brother may be assured of her interest in everything relating to him and his family, and of her sincerely partaking our pleasure in the receipt of every good account from Godmersham.

Of Chawton I think I can have nothing more to say, but that everything you say about it in the letter now before me will, I am sure, as soon as I am able to read it to her, make my mother consider the plan with more and more pleasure. We had formed the same views on H. Digweed's farm.

A very kind and feeling letter is arrived to-day from Kintbury. Mrs. Fowle's sympathy and solicitude on such an occasion you will be able to do justice to, and to express it as she wishes to my brother. Concerning *you*, she says: 'Cassandra will, I know, excuse my writing to her; it is not to save myself but *her* that I omit so doing. Give my best, my kindest love to her, and tell her I feel for her as I know she would for me on the same occasion, and that I most sincerely hope her health will not suffer.'

We have just had two hampers of apples from Kintbury, and the floor of our little garret is almost covered. Love to all.

Yours very affectionately,   J. A.

60. *To Cassandra Austen. Sunday* 20 *Nov.* ⟨1808⟩

Castle Square, Sunday Novr 21 (*sic*).—

Your letter my dear Cassandra, obliges me to write immediately, that you may have the earliest notice of Frank's intending if possible to go to Godmersham

exactly at the time now fixed for your visit to Goodnestone. He resolved almost directly on the receipt of
your former Letter, to try for an extension of his Leave
of absence that he might be able to go down to you for
two days, but charged me not to give you any notice
of it, on account of the uncertainty of success; Now
however, I must give it, & now perhaps he may be
giving it himself—for I am just in the hateful predica-
ment of being obliged to write what I know will some-
how or other be of no use.—He meant to ask for five
days more, & if they were granted, to go down by
Thursday-night's Mail & spend friday & saturday with
you; & he considered his chance of succeeding by no
means bad. I hope it will take place as he planned, &
that your arrangements with Goodnestone may admit
of suitable alteration. Your news of Edw: Bridges was
quite news, for I have had no letter from Wrotham.—
I wish him happy with all my heart, & hope his choice
may turn out according to his own expectations, &
beyond those of his Family—and I dare say it will.
Marriage is a great Improver—& in a similar situation
Harriet may be as amiable as Eleanor. As to Money,
that will come you may be sure, because they cannot
do without it. When you see him again, pray give him
our Congratulations & best wishes. This Match will
certainly set John & Lucy[1] going. There are six Bed-
chambers[2] at Chawton; Henry wrote to my Mother the
other day, & luckily mentioned the number—which is
just what we wanted to be assured of. He speaks also
of Garrets for store-places, one of which she immediately planned fitting up for Edward's Manservant—

---

[1] Their marriage, which did not happen, would have been a third
Bridges–Foote match.

[2] The Small House was not then called a cottage, which indeed it is
not.

& now perhaps it must be for our own—for she is already quite reconciled to our keeping one. The difficulty of doing without one, had been thought of before. His name shall be Robert, if you please. Before I can tell you of it, you will have heard that Miss Sawbridge is married. It took place I beleive on Thursday, Mrs. Fowle has for some time been in the secret, but the Neighbourhood in general were quite unsuspicious. Mr. Maxwell *was* tutor to the young Gregorys—consequently they must be one of the happiest Couple in the World, & either of them worthy of Envy—for *she* must be excessively in love, and he mounts from nothing, to a comfortable Home. Martha has heard him very highly spoken of. They continue for the present at Speen Hill. I have a Southampton Match to return for your Kentish one, Capt. G. Heathcote & Miss A. Lyell; I have it from Alethea—& like it, because I had made it before. Yes, the Stoneleigh business[1] is concluded, but it was not till yesterday that my Mother was regularly informed of it, tho' the news had reached us on Monday Even^g by way of Steventon. My Aunt says as little as may be on the subject by way of information, & nothing at all by way of satisfaction. She reflects on Mr. T. Leigh's dilatoriness, & looks about with great diligence & success for Inconvenience & Evil—among which she ingeniously places the danger of her new Housemaids catching cold on the outside of the Coach, when she goes down to Bath—for a carriage makes her sick. John Binns has been offered their place, but declines it—as she supposes, because he will not wear a Livery. Whatever be the cause, I like the effect. In spite of all my Mother's long and intimate knowledge of the Writer, she was not up to

[1] See note, p. 213, on p. 72.

the expectation of such a Letter as this; the discontentedness of it shocked & surprised her—but *I* see nothing in it out of Nature—tho' a sad nature.

She does not forget to wish for Chambers,[1] you may be sure. No particulars are given, not a word of arrears mentioned—tho' in her letter to James they were in a *general way* spoken of. The amount of them is a matter of conjecture, & to my Mother a most interesting one; she cannot fix any time for their beginning, with any satisfaction to herself, but Mrs. Leigh's death—& Henry's two Thousand pounds neither agrees with that period nor any other. I did not like to own, our previous information of what was intended last July— & have therefore only said that if we could see Henry we might hear many particulars, as I had understood that some confidential conversation had passed between him & Mr. T. L.[2] at Stoneleigh. We have been as quiet as usual since Frank & Mary left us; Mr. Criswick called on Martha that very morn^g in his way home again from Portsmouth, & we have had no visitor since. We called on the Miss Lyells one day, & heard a good account of Mr. Heathcote's canvass, the success of which of course exceeds his expectation. Alethea in her Letter hopes for *my interest*, which I conclude means Edward's—& I take this opportunity therefore of requesting that he will bring in Mr. Heathcote. Mr. Lance told us yesterday that Mr. H. had behaved very handsomely & waited on Mr. Thistlethwaite to say that if *he* (Mr. T.) would stand, *he* (Mr. H.) would not oppose him; but Mr. T. declined it, acknowledging himself still smarting under the payment of late Electioneering costs. The Mrs. Hulberts, we learn from

[1] Mrs. Leigh-Perrot had had a 'treasure' so named.
[2] Thomas Leigh.

98

Kintbury, come to Steventon this week, & bring Mary
Jane Fowle with them, in her way to Mrs. Nunes; she
returns at Christmas with her Brother. *Our* Brother we
may perhaps see in the course of a few days—& we
mean to take the opportunity of his help, to go one
night to the play. Martha ought to see the inside of
the Theatre once while she lives in Southampton, & I
think she will hardly wish to take a second veiw. The
Furniture of Bellevue is to be sold tomorrow, & we shall
take it in our usual walk if the Weather be favourable.
How could you have a wet day on Thursday?—with
us it was a Prince of days, the most delightful we have
had for weeks, soft, bright, with a brisk wind from the
south west;—everybody was out & talking of spring—
& Martha and I did not know how to turn back. on
Friday Even^g we had some very blowing weather—
from 6 to 9, I think we never heard it worse, even here.
And one night we had so much rain that it forced it's
way again into the store closet—& tho' the Evil was
comparatively slight, & the Mischief nothing, I had
some employment the next day in drying parcels &c.
I have now moved still more out of the way.

Martha sends her best Love, & thanks you for ad-
mitting her to the knowledge of the pros & cons about
Harriet Foote—she has an interest in all such matters.
I am also to say that she wants to see you. Mary Jane[1]
missed her papa & mama a good deal at first, but now
does very well without them. I am glad to hear of little
John's[2] being better; & hope your accounts of Mrs.
Knight will also improve. Adeiu. Remember me
affec^tely to everybody, & beleive me

Ever yours,   J A.

---

[1] When 'Frank and Mary left' (p. 98) they left their daughter
behind.   [2] Edward's sixth son.

63. *To Cassandra Austen. Tuesday* 10 *Jan.* ⟨1809⟩

Castle Square: Tuesday January 10

I am not surprised, my dear Cassandra, that you did not find my last letter very full of matter, and I wish this may not have the same deficiency; but we are doing nothing ourselves to write about, and I am therefore quite dependent upon the communioations of our friends, or my own wits.

This post brought me two interesting letters, yours and one from Bookham,[1] in answer to an enquiry of mine about your good godmother, of whom we had lately received a very alarming account from Paragon. Miss Arnold was the informant there, and she spoke of Mrs. E. L.[2] having been very dangerously ill, and attended by a physician from Oxford.

Your letter to Adlestrop may perhaps bring you information from the spot, but in case it should not, I must tell you that she is better; though Dr. Bourne cannot yet call her out of danger; such was the case last Wednesday, and Mrs. Cooke's having had no later account is a favourable sign. I am to hear again from the latter *next* week, but not *this*, if everything goes on well.

Her disorder is an inflammation on the lungs, arising from a severe chill, taken in church last Sunday three weeks; her mind all pious composure, as may be supposed. George Cooke was there when her illness began; his brother has now taken his place. Her age and feebleness considered, one's fears cannot but preponderate, though her amendment has already surpassed the expectation of the physician at the beginning. I am

---

[1] Mrs. Cooke.   [2] Elizabeth Leigh.

sorry to add that *Becky* is laid up with a complaint of the same kind.

I am very glad to have the time of your return at all fixed; we all rejoice in it, and it will not be later than I had expected. I dare not hope that Mary[1] and Miss Curling may be detained at Portsmouth so long or half so long; but it would be worth twopence to have it so.

The 'St. Albans' perhaps may soon be off to help bring home what may remain by this time of our poor army, whose state seems dreadfully critical. The 'Regency'[2] seems to have been heard of only here; my most political correspondents make no mention of it. Unlucky that I should have wasted so much reflection on the subject.

I can now answer your question to my mother more at large, and likewise more at small—with equal perspicuity and minuteness; for the very day of our leaving Southampton is fixed; and if the knowledge is of no *use* to Edward, I am sure it will give him pleasure. Easter Monday, April 3, is the day; we are to sleep that night at Alton, and be with our friends at Bookham the next, if they are then at home; there we remain till the following Monday, and on Tuesday, April 11, hope to be at Godmersham. If the Cookes are absent, we shall finish our journey on the 5th. These plans depend of course upon the weather, but I hope there will be no settled cold to delay us materially.

To make you amends for being at Bookham, it is in contemplation to spend a few days at Barton Lodge in our way *out* of Kent. The hint of such a visit is most affectionately welcomed by Mrs. Birch, in one of her odd pleasant letters lately, in which she speaks of *us* with the usual distinguished kindness, declaring that

---

[1] Mrs. F. A.   [2] The Regency became fact in 1810.

she shall not be at all satisfied unless a very *handsome* present is made us immediately from one quarter.[1]

Fanny's not coming with you is no more than we expected, and as we have not the hope of a bed for her, and shall see her so soon afterwards at Godmersham, we cannot wish it otherwise.

William[2] will be quite recovered, I trust, by the time you receive this. What a comfort his cross-stitch must have been! Pray tell him that I should like to see his work very much. I hope our answers this morning have given satisfaction; we had great pleasure in Uncle Deedes' packet; and pray let Marianne[2] know, in private, that I think she is quite right to work a rug for Uncle John's coffee urn, and that I am sure it must give great pleasure to herself now, and to him when he receives it.

The preference of Brag over Speculation does not greatly surprise me, I believe, because I feel the same myself; but it mortifies me deeply, because Speculation was under my patronage; and, after all, what is there so delightful in a pair royal of Braggers? It is but three nines or three knaves, or a mixture of them. When one comes to reason upon it, it cannot stand its ground against Speculation—of which I hope Edward is now convinced. Give my love to him if he is.

The letter from Paragon before mentioned was much like those which had preceded it, as to the felicity of its writer. They found their house so dirty and so damp that they were obliged to be a week at an inn. John Binns had behaved most unhandsomely and engaged himself elsewhere. They *have* a man, however, on the same footing, which my aunt does not like, and she finds both him and the new maid-

---

[1] The Leigh-Perrots ?   [2] Edward's children.

servant very, very inferior to Robert and Martha. Whether they mean to have any other domestics does not appear, nor whether they are to have a carriage while they are in Bath.

The Holders are as usual, though I believe it is not very usual for them to be happy, which they now are at a great rate, in Hooper's marriage. The Irvines are not mentioned.

The American lady[1] improved as we went on; but still the same faults in part recurred. We are now in Margiana, and like it very well indeed. We are just going to set off for Northumberland to be shut up in Widdrington Tower, where there must be two or three sets of victims already immured under a very fine villain.

Wednesday.—Your report of Eliza's[2] health gives me great pleasure, and the progress of the bank is a constant source of satisfaction. With such increasing profits, tell Henry that I hope he will not work poor High-diddle so hard as he used to do.

Has your newspaper given a sad story of a Mrs. Middleton, wife of a farmer in Yorkshire, her sister, and servant, being almost frozen to death in the late weather, her little child quite so? I hope this sister is not our friend Miss Woodd, and I rather think her brother-in-law had moved into Lincolnshire, but their name and station accord too well. Mrs. M. and the maid are said to be tolerably recovered, but the sister is likely to lose the use of her limbs.

Charles's rug will be finished to-day, and sent to-morrow to Frank, to be consigned by him to Mr.

---

[1] J. A. perhaps wrote *Lady*: Mrs. Grant's *Memoirs of an American Lady*.

[2] Mrs. Henry Austen.

Turner's care; and I am going to send Marmion out with it—very generous in me, I think.

As we have no letter from Adlestrop, we may suppose the good woman was alive on Monday, but I cannot help expecting bad news from thence or Bookham in a few days. Do you continue quite well?

Have you nothing to say of your little namesake? We join in love and many happy returns.[1]

Yours affectionately, J. Austen

The Manydown ball was a smaller thing than I expected, but it seems to have made Anna very happy. At *her* age it would not have done for *me*.

67. *To Crosbie & Co.* ⟨*Wednesday*⟩ 5 *April* 1809
(JA's copy)

Gentlemen

In the spring of the year 1803 a MS. Novel in 2 vol. entitled Susan[2] was sold to you by a Gentleman of the name of Seymour, & the purchase money £10. rec^d at the same time. Six years have since passed, & this work of which I am myself the Authoress, has never to the best of my knowledge, appeared in print, tho' an early publication was stipulated for at the time of sale. I can only account for such an extraordinary circumstance by supposing the MS. by some carelessness to have been lost; & if that was the case, am willing to supply you with another copy if you are disposed to avail yourselves of it, & will engage for no farther delay when it comes into your hands. It will not be in

---

[1] Of her birthday 9 January.
[2] *Northanger Abbey.*

my power from particular circumstances to command this copy before the Month of August, but then, if you accept my proposal, you may depend on receiving it. Be so good as to send me a Line in answer as soon as possible, as my stay in this place will not exceed a few days. Should no notice be taken of this address, I shall feel myself at liberty to secure the publication of my work, by applying elsewhere. I am Gentlemen &c. &c.

April 5. 1809.   M. A. D.

Direct to Mrs Ashton Dennis
Post Office, Southampton

67a. *From Richard Crosby.* ⟨*Saturday*⟩ 8 *April* 1809

Madam

We have to acknowledge the receipt of your letter of the 5th inst. It is true that at the time mentioned we purchased of Mr Seymour a MS. novel entitled *Susan* and paid him for it the sum of 10£ for which we have his stamped receipt as a full consideration, but there was not any time stipulated for its publication, neither are we bound to publish it, Should you or any-one else (*sic*) we shall take proceedings to stop the sale. The MS. shall be yours for the same as we paid for it

For R. Crosby & Co.

I am yours etc.

Richard Crosby

London
Ap 8 1809.

IV. CHAWTON

1809–17: *Thirty-four to Forty-one*

═══

HER years at Chawton, years of serenity and success, of growing confidence in her powers, and varied by happy visits in Kent and London, open characteristically with comic verse (68). Then a visit to Henry and Eliza in Sloane Street, *Sense and Sensibility* in the printer's hands. At Chawton again, we hear of plants in the garden (which the Jane Austen Society today is reproducing), of the sale of *Pride and Prejudice* (74.1), of the Chawton Book Society (78), of the arrival of the first copy of 'my own darling child' (*P. and P.*, 76, 77), and of the beginning of *Mansfield Park* (78.1). In the spring of 1813 she is in Sloane Street again, looking in the exhibition for portraits of Jane and Elizabeth (80). In November she is at Godmersham (91). In the spring of 1814 she is with Henry, now a widower in Henrietta Street, and he reads the MS. of *Mansfield Park* (92, 93). By the summer of 1814 *M. P.* is out, and she unbends to criticize her niece Anna's attempt at a novel: criticism that throws some light on her own views and methods (98, 100).

99.1, a recent discovery, has interesting remarks on religion and 'the Americans'. November begins a fascinating series of letters (103, 106, 140, 142) to Fanny Austen (Edward's daughter, now Knight) on the choice of a lover; there were two suitors, both rejected. The

winter of 1815 finds Jane with Henry in Hans Place,
where she extols his physician, Haden, and invites him
to amuse Fanny ('I *believe* at least they had *two*
chairs'). This visit was dignified by correspondence
with Clarke, the Regent's pompous chaplain, which
resulted in the dedication of *Emma* to the Prince and
in Jane's satirical *Plan of a Novel*.

In 1817 there are brief and tantalizing allusions to
Persuasion (published posthumously) and some account
of obscure ailments.

68. *To Francis Austen.* ⟨*Wednesday*⟩ 26 *July* 1809

Chawton, July 26.—1809.—

My dearest Frank, I wish you joy
Of Mary's safety with a Boy,
Whose birth has given little pain
Compared with that of Mary Jane.
May he a growing Blessing prove,
And well deserve his Parents' Love!
Endow'd with Art's & Nature's Good,
Thy name possessing with thy Blood,
In him, in all his ways, may we
Another Francis William see!
Thy infant days may he inherit,
Thy warmth, nay insolence of spirit;
We would not with one fault dispense
To weaken the resemblance.

May he revive thy Nursery sin,
Peeping as daringly within,
His curley Locks but just descried,
With, 'Bet, my be not come to bide.'

Fearless of danger, braving pain,
And threaten'd very oft in vain,
Still may one Terror daunt his soul,
One needful engine of Controul
Be found in this sublime array,
A neighbouring Donkey's aweful Bray.
So may his equal faults as Child,
Produce Maturity as mild!
His saucy words & fiery ways
In early Childhood's pettish days,
In Manhood, shew his Father's mind
Like him, considerate & kind;
All Gentleness to those around,
And eager only not to wound.

Then like his Father too, he must,
To his own former struggles just,
Feel his Deserts with honest Glow,
And all his self-improvement know.
A native fault may thus give birth
To the best blessing, conscious Worth.

As for ourselves, we're very well;
As unaffected prose will tell.
Cassandra's pen will paint our state,
The many comforts that await
Our Chawton home, how much we find
Already in it, to our mind;
And how convinced, that when complete
It will all other Houses beat
That ever have been made or mended,
With rooms concise, or rooms distended.
You'll find us very snug next year,
Perhaps with Charles & Fanny near,

For now it often does delight us
To fancy them just over-right us.

J. A.

69. *To Cassandra Austen.* **Thursday** 18 *April* 1811

Sloane St. Thursday April 18.

My dear Cassandra

I have so many little matters to tell you of, that I
cannot wait any longer before I begin to put them
down. I spent tuesday in Bentinck S^t; the Cookes
called here & took me back; & it was quite a Cooke
day, for the Miss Rolles paid a visit while I was there,
& Sam Arnold dropt in to tea. The badness of the
weather disconcerted an excellent plan of mine, that
of calling on Miss Beckford again, but from the middle
of the day it rained incessantly. Mary & I, after disposing of her Father & Mother, went to the Liverpool
Museum, & the British Gallery, & I had some amusement at each, tho' my preference for Men & Women,
always inclines me to attend more to the company than
the sight. Mrs. Cooke regrets very much that she did
not see you when you called, it was owing to some
blunder among the servants, for she did not know of
our visit till we were gone. She seems tolerably well;
but the nervous part of her Complaint I fear increases,
& makes her more and more unwilling to part with
Mary. I have proposed to the latter that she should go
to Chawton with me, on the supposition of my travelling the Guildford road—& *she*, I do beleive, would
be glad to do it, but perhaps it may be impossible;
unless a Brother can be at home at that time, it certainly must. George comes to them to day. I did not
see Theo' till late on Tuesday; he was gone to Ilford,

but he came back in time to shew his usual, nothing-meaning, harmless, heartless Civility. Henry, who had been confined the whole day to the Bank, took me in his way home; & after putting Life & Wit into the party for a quarter of an hour, put himself & his Sister into a Hackney coach. I bless my stars that I have done with tuesday!—But alas!—Wednesday was likewise a day of great doings, for Manon[1] & I took our walk to Grafton House, & I have a good deal to say on that subject. I am sorry to tell you that I am getting very extravagant & spending all my Money; & what is worse for *you*, I have been spending yours too; for in a Linendraper's shop to which I went for check'd muslin, & for which I was obliged to give seven shillings a yard, I was tempted by a pretty coloured muslin, and bought 10 y^ds of it, on the chance of your liking it; but at the same time if it sh^d not suit you, you must not think yourself at all obliged to take it; it is only 3/6 p^r y^d, & I sh^d not in the least mind keeping the whole. In texture, it is just what we prefer, but it's resemblance to green cruels I must own is not great, for the pattern is a small red spot. ⟨*One line cut out*⟩ & now I beleive I have done all my commissions, except Wedgwood. I liked my walk very much; it was shorter than I had expected, & the weather was delightful. We set off immediately after breakfast & must have reached Grafton House by ½ past 11, but when we entered the Shop, the whole Counter was thronged, & we waited *full* half an hour before we c^d be attended to. When we were served however, I was very well satisfied with my purchases, my Bugle Trimming at 2/4^d & 3 p^r silk stock^gs for a little less than 12./s a p^r. In my way back, who sh^d I meet but Mr. Moore, just come from

---

[1] Mrs. Henry Austen's maid?

Beckenham. I beleive he would have passed me, if I had not made him stop—but we were delighted to meet. I soon found however that he had nothing new to tell me, & then I let him go. Miss Burton has made me a very pretty little Bonnet—& now nothing can satisfy me but I must have a straw hat, of the riding hat shape, like Mrs. Tilson's; & a young woman in this Neighbourhood is actually making me one. I am really very shocking; but it will not be dear at a Guinea. Our Pelisses are 17/s. each—she charges only 8/ for the making, but the Buttons seem expensive;—*are* expensive, I might have said—for the fact is plain enough. We drank tea again yesterday with the Tilsons, & met the Smiths. I find all these little parties very pleasant. I like Mr. S. Miss Beaty is good-humour itself, & does not seem much besides. We spend tomorrow even^g with them, & are to meet the Col^n & Mrs. *Cantelo* Smith, you have been used to hear of; & if she is in good humour, are likely to have excellent singing. To night I might have been at the Play, Henry had kindly planned our going together to the Lyceum, but I have a cold which I sh^d not like to make worse before Saturday; so I stay within, all this day. Eliza is walking out by herself. She has plenty of business on her hands just now—for the day of the party is settled, & drawing near: above 80 people are invited for next tuesday Even^g & there is to be some very good Music, 5 professionals, 3 of them Glee singers, besides Amateurs. Fanny will listen to this. One of the Hirelings, is a Capital on the Harp, from which I expect great pleasure. The foundation of the party was a dinner to Henry Egerton & Henry Walter—but the latter leaves Town the day before. I am sorry—as I wished *her* prejudice to be done away—but sh^d have been more sorry if there had been no invitation. I am a wretch, to be so occupied with all these Things, as to seem to have no Thoughts to give to people & circumstances which really supply a far more lasting interest—the Society in which You are—but I do think of you all I assure you, & want to know all about everybody, & especially about your visit to the W. Friars[1]; 'mais le moyen' not to be occupied by one's own concerns?

Saturday. Frank is superseded in the Caledonia. Henry brought us this news yesterday from Mr. Daysh &—he heard at the same time that Charles may be in England in the course of a month. Sir Edwd Pellew succeeds Lord Gambier in his command, & some captain of his, succeeds Frank; & I beleive the order is already gone out. Henry means to enquire farther to day; he wrote to Mary on the occasion. This is something to think of. Henry is convinced that he will have the offer of something else, but does not think it will be at all incumbent on him to accept it; & then follows, what will he do? & where will he live?—I hope to hear from you today. How are you, as to Health, strength, Looks, stomach &c.? I had a very comfortable account from Chawton yesterday. If the weather permits, Eliza & I walk into London this morn^g. *She* is in want of chimney lights for Tuesday; & *I*, of an ounce of darning cotton. She has resolved not to venture to the Play tonight. The D'Entraigues & Comte Julien cannot come to the Party—which was at first a greif, but she has since supplied herself so well with Performers that it is of no consequence; their not coming has produced our going to them tomorrow Even^g—which I like the idea of. It will be amusing to see the ways of a French circle. I wrote to Mrs. Hill a

[1] Mrs. Knight, of White Friars, Canterbury.

few days ago, & have received a most kind & satisfactory answer; my time, the first week in May, exactly suits her; & therefore I consider my Goings as tolerably fixed. I shall leave Sloane St. on the 1st or 2d & be ready for James on ye 9th; & if his plan alters, I can take care of myself. I have explained my veiws here, & everything is smooth & pleasant; & Eliza talks kindly of conveying me to Streatham.[1] We met the Tilsons yesterday Eveng—but the singing Smiths sent an excuse—which put our Mrs. Smith out of humour.

We are come back, after a good dose of Walking & Coaching, & I have the pleasure of your letter. I wish I had James's verses, but they were left at Chawton. When I return thither, if Mrs. K. will give me leave, I will send them to her. Our first object to day was Henrietta St. to consult with Henry, in consequence of a very unlucky change of the play for this very night —Hamlet instead of King John—& we are to go on Monday to Macbeth, instead, but it is a disappointment to us both.

Love to all.

Yours affec:ly   Jane

70. *To Cassandra Austen. Thursday* 25 *April* ⟨1811⟩

Sloane St Thursday April 25

My dearest Cassandra

I can return the compliment by thanking you for the unexpected pleasure of *your* Letter yesterday, & as I like unexpected pleasure, it made me very happy; And indeed, you need not apologise for your Letter in any respect, for it is all very fine, but not *too* fine I hope to

---

[1] Mrs. Hill, *née* Bigg.

be written again, or something like it. I think Edward will not suffer much longer from heat; by the look of Things this morn^g I suspect the weather is rising into the balsamic Northeast. It has been hot here, as you may suppose, since it was so hot with you, but I have not suffered from it at all, nor felt it in such a degree as to make me imagine it would be anything in the country. Everybody has talked of the heat, but I set it all down to London. I give you joy of our new nephew, & hope if he ever comes to be hanged, it will not be till we are too old to care about it. It is a great comfort to have it so safely & speedily over. The Miss Curlings must be hard worked in writing so many Letters, but the novelty of it may recommend it to *them*;—mine was from Miss Eliza, & she says that my Brother[1] may arrive today.—No indeed, I am never too busy to think of S & S.[2] I can no more forget it, than a mother can forget her sucking child; & I am much obliged to you for your enquiries. I have had two sheets to correct, but the last only brings us to W.s[3] first appearance. Mrs K. regrets in the most flattering manner that she must wait *till* May, but I have scarcely a hope of its being out in June. Henry does not neglect it; he *has* hurried the Printer, & says he will see him again today. It will not stand still during his absence, it will be sent to Eliza. The *Incomes* remain as they were, but I will get them altered if I can.[4] I am very much gratified by Mrs K.s interest in it; & whatever may be the event of it as to my credit with her, sincerely wish her curiosity could be satisfied sooner than is now probable. I think she will like my Elinor, but cannot build on any thing

[1] Frank. [2] *Sense and Sensibility.*
[3] Willoughby.
[4] 'The Incomes' were altered in the second edition; see p. 383 in my edition.

else. Our party went off extremely well. There were
many solicitudes; alarms & vexations beforehand of
course, but at last everything was quite right. The
rooms were dressed up with flowers &c, & looked very
pretty. A glass for the Mantlepiece was lent, by the
Man who is making their own. Mr Egerton & M^r
Walter came at 1/2 past 5, & the festivities began
with a p^r of very fine Soals. Yes, Mr Walter—for he
postponed his leaving London on purpose—which did
not give much pleasure at the time, any more than the
circumstance from which it rose, his calling on Sunday
& being asked by Henry to take the family dinner on
that day, which he did—but it is all smooth'd over
now; & she likes him very well. At 1/2 past 7 arrived
the Musicians in two Hackney coaches, & by 8 the
lordly company began to appear. Among the earliest
were George & Mary Cooke, & I spent the greatest
part of the even^g very pleasantly with them. The
Draw^g room being soon hotter than we liked, we
placed ourselves in the connecting Passage, which was
comparatively cool, & gave us all the advantage of the
Music at a pleasant distance, as well as that of the first
veiw of every new comer. I was quite surrounded by
acquaintance, especially Gentlemen; & what with M^r
Hampson, Mr Seymour, Mr W. Knatchbull, M^r
Guillemarde, Mr Cure, a Capt Simpson, brother to *the*
Capt Simpson, besides Mr Walter & Mr Egerton, in
addition to the Cookes & Miss Beckford & Miss
Middleton, I had quite as much upon my hands as I
could do. Poor Miss B. has been suffering again from
her old complaint, & looks thinner than ever. She
certainly goes to Cheltenham the beginning of June.
We were all delight & cordiality of course. Miss M.
seems very happy, but has not beauty enough to figure

in London. Including everybody we were 66—which was considerably more than Eliza had expected, & quite enough to fill the Back Draw^g room, & leave a few to be scattered about in the other, & in the passage. The Music was extremely good. It opened (tell Fanny, with 'Poike pe Parp pin praise pof Prapela'[1]—& of the other Glees I remember, 'In Peace Love tunes,' 'Rosabelle,' 'The red cross Knight,' & 'Poor Insect.' Between the Songs were Lessons on the Harp, or Harp & Piano Forte together—& the Harp Player was Wiepart, whose name seems famous, tho' new to me. There was one female singer, a short Miss Davis all in blue, bringing up for the Public Line, whose voice was said to be very fine indeed; & all the Performers gave great satisfaction by doing what they were paid for, & giving themselves no airs. No amateur could be persuaded to do anything. The House was not clear till after 12. If you wish to hear more of it, you must put your questions, but I seem rather to have exhausted than spared the subject. This said Capt. Simpson told us, on the authority of some other Captn just arrived from Halifax, that Charles was bringing the Cleopatra home, & that she was probably by this time in the Channel—but as Capt. S. was certainly in liquor, we must not quite depend on it. It must give one a sort of expectation however, & will prevent my writing to him any more. I would rather he sh^d not reach England till I am at home, & the Steventon party gone. My Mother & Martha both write with great satisfaction of Anna's behaviour. She is quite an Anna with variations—but she cannot have reached her last, for that is always the most flourishing &

---

[1] 'Strike the harp in praise of Bragela'—adapted to a Godmersham nonsence language.

shewey—she is at about her 3ᵈ or 4ᵗʰ which are generally simple & pretty. Your Lilacs are in leaf, *ours* are in bloom. The Horse chesnuts are quite out, & the Elms almost. I had a pleasant walk in Kensington Gˢ on Sunday with Henry, Mʳ Smith & Mʳ Tilson— everything was fresh & beautiful. We *did* go to the play after all on Saturday, we went to the Lyceum, & saw the Hypocrite, an old play taken from Moliere's *Tartuffe*, & were well entertained. Dowton & Mathews were the good actors. Mrs Edwin was the Heroine—& her performance is just what it used to be. I have no chance of seeing Mʳˢ Siddons. She *did* act on Monday, but as Henry was told by the Boxkeeper that he did not think she would, the places, & all thought of it, were given up. I should particularly have liked seeing her in Constance, & could swear at her with little effort for disappointing me. Henry has been to the Water-colour Exhibition, which open'd on Monday, & is to meet us there again some mornᵍ. If Eliza cannot go (& she has a cold at present) Miss Beaty will be invited to be my companion. Henry leaves Town on Sunday afternoon—but he means to write soon himself to Edward—& will tell his own plans. The Tea is this moment setting out. Do not have your colᵈ muslin unless you really want it, because I am afraid I cᵈ not send it to the Coach without giving trouble here. Eliza caught her cold on Sunday in our way to the D'Entraigues; the Horses actually gibbed on this side of Hyde Park Gate—a load of fresh gravel made it a formidable Hill to them, and they refused the collar; I believe there was a sore shoulder to irritate. Eliza was frightened, & we got out—& were detained in the Evenᵍ air several minutes. The cold is in her chest— but she takes care of herself, & I hope it may not last

117

long. This engagement prevented Mr Walter's staying late—he had his coffee & went away. Eliza enjoyed her eveng very much & means to cultivate the acquaintance—& I see nothing to dislike in them, but their taking quantities of snuff. Monsieur the old Count, is a very fine looking man, with quiet manners, good enough for an Englishman—& I believe is a Man of great Information & Taste. He has some fine Paintings, which delighted Henry as much as the Son's music gratified Eliza—& among them, a Miniature of Philip 5. of Spain, Louis 14.s Grandson, which exactly suited *my* capacity. Count Julien's performance is very wonderful. We met only Mrs Latouche & Miss East—& we are just now engaged to spend next Sunday Eveng at Mrs L.s—& to meet the D'Entraigues; but M. le Comte must do without Henry. If he wd but speak english, *I* would take to him. Have you ever mentioned the leaving off Tea to Mrs K.? Eliza has just spoken of it again. The Benefit *she* has found from it in sleeping, has been very great. I shall write soon to Catherine[1] to fix my day, which will be Thursday. We have no engagements but for Sunday. Eliza's cold makes quiet adviseable. Her party is mentioned in this morning's paper. I am sorry to hear of poor Fanny's state. From *that* quarter I suppose is to be the alloy of her happiness.—I *will* have no more to say.

Yrs affecly

J. A.

Give my Love particularly to my God-daughter.[2]

---

[1] Hill, *née* Bigg.
[2] Edward's d. Louisa.

72. *To Cassandra Austen. Wednesday* 29 *May* 1811

Chawton: Wednesday May 29

It was a mistake of mine, my dear Cassandra, to talk of a tenth child at Hamstall.[1] I had forgot there were but eight already.

Your enquiry after my uncle and aunt were most happily timed, for the very same post brought an account of them. They are again at Gloucester House[2] enjoying fresh air, which they seem to have felt the want of in Bath, and are tolerably well, but not more than tolerable. My aunt does not enter into particulars, but she does not write in spirits, and we imagine that she has never entirely got the better of her disorder in the winter. Mrs. Welby takes her out airing in her barouche, which gives her a headache—a comfortable proof, I suppose, of the uselessness of the new carriage when they have got it.

You certainly must have heard before I can tell you that Col. Orde has married our cousin,[3] Margt. Beckford, the Marchess. of Douglas's sister. The papers say that her father disinherits her, but I think too well of an Orde to suppose that she has not a handsome independence of her own.

The chicken are all alive and fit for the table, but we save them for something grand. Some of the flower seeds are coming up very well, but your mignonette makes a wretched appearance. Miss Benn has been equally unlucky as to hers. She had seed from four different people, and none of it comes up. Our young piony at the foot of the fir-tree has just blown and looks very handsome, and the whole of the shrubbery

[1] Coopers.   [3] At Weymouth.
[2] See note, p. 213.

119

border will soon be very gay with pinks and sweet-williams, in addition to the columbines already in bloom. The syringas, too, are coming out. We are likely to have a great crop of Orleans plumbs, but not many greengages—on the standard scarcely any, three or four dozen, perhaps, against the wall. I believe I told you differently when I first came home, but I can now judge better than I could then.

I have had a medley and satisfactory letter this morning from the husband and wife at Cowes; and, in consequence of what is related of their plans, we have been talking over the possibility of inviting them here in their way from Steventon, which is what one should wish to do, and is, I daresay, what they expect; but, supposing Martha to be at home, it does not seem a very easy thing to accommodate so large a party. My mother offers to give up her room to Frank and Mary, but there will then be only the best for two maids and three children.

They go to Steventon about the 22nd, and I *guess*—for it is quite a guess—will stay there from a fortnight to three weeks.

I must not venture to press Miss Sharpe's coming at present; we may hardly be at liberty before August.

Poor John Bridges! we are very sorry for his situation and for the distress of the family.[1] Lady B. is in *one way* severely tried. And our own dear brother suffers a great deal, I dare say, on the occasion.

I have not much to say of ourselves. Anna is nursing a cold caught in the arbour at Faringdon, that she may be able to keep her engagement to Maria M.[2] this evening, when I suppose she will make it worse.

---

[1] In the death of Marianne Bridges.
[2] Middleton.

She did not return from Faringdon till Sunday,
when H. B.[1] walked home with her, and drank tea
here. She was with the Prowtings almost all Monday.
She went to learn to make feather trimmings of Miss
Anna, and they kept her to dinner, which was rather
lucky, as we were called upon to meet Mrs. and Miss
Terry the same evening at the Digweeds; and, though
Anna was of course invited too, I think it always safest
to keep her away from the family lest she should be
doing too little or too much.

Mrs. Terry, Mary, and Robert, with my aunt[2]
Harding and her daughter, came from Dummer for
a day and a night—all very agreeable and very much
delighted with the new house and with Chawton in
general.

We sat upstairs and had thunder and lightning as
usual. I never knew such a spring for thunder-storms as
it has been. Thank God! we have had no bad ones here.
I thought myself in luck to have my uncomfortable
feelings shared by the mistress of the house, as that
procured blinds and candles. It had been excessively
hot the whole day. Mrs. Harding is a good-looking
woman, but not much like Mrs. Toke, inasmuch as she
is very brown and has scarcely any teeth; she seems to
have some of Mrs. Toke's civility but does not profess
being so silly. Miss H. is an elegant, pleasing, pretty-
looking girl, about nineteen, I suppose, or nineteen
and a half, or nineteen and a quarter, with flowers in
her head and music at her finger ends. She plays very
well indeed. I have seldom heard anybody with more
pleasure. They were at Godington four or five years
ago. My[2] cousin, Flora Long, was there last year.

[1] Harriet Benn.
[2] See note, p. 213.

My[1] name is Diana. How does Fanny like it? What a change in the weather! We have a fire again now.

Harriet Benn sleeps at the Great House to-night and spends to-morrow with us; and the plan is that we should all walk with her to drink tea at Faringdon, for her mother is now recovered, but the state of the weather is not very promising at present.

Miss Benn has been returned to her cottage since the beginning of last week, and has now just got another girl; she comes from Alton. For many days Miss B. had nobody with her but her niece Elizabeth, who was delighted to be her visitor and her maid. They both dined here on Saturday while Anna was at Faringdon; and last night an accidental meeting and a sudden impulse produced Miss Benn and Maria Middleton at our tea-table.

If you have not heard it is very fit you should, that Mr. Harrison has had the living of Fareham given him by the Bishop, and is going to reside there; and now it is said that Mr. Peach (beautiful wiseacre) wants to have the curacy of Overton, and, if he *does* leave Wootton, James Digweed wishes to go there. Fare you well.

Yours affectionately,   Jane Austen

The chimneys at the Great House are done. Mr. Prowting has opened a gravel pit, very conveniently for my mother, just at the mouth of the approach to his house; but it looks a little as if he meant to catch all his company. Tolerable gravel.

---

[1] See note p. 213. I do not know Miss H.'s name; her mother was Dyonisia.

74.1. *To Martha Lloyd. Sunday* 29 *Nov.* ⟨1812⟩

Chawton Sunday Novr 29th

My dear Martha

I shall take care not to count the lines of your *last*
Letter; you have obliged me to eat humble-pie indeed;
I am really obliged to you however, & though it is in
general much pleasanter to reproach than to be grateful, I do not mind it now. We shall be glad to hear,
whenever you can write, & can well imagine that time
for writing must be wanting in such an arduous, busy,
useful office as you fill at present. You are made for
doing good, & have quite as great a turn for it I think
as for physicking little Children. The mental Physick
which you have been lately applying bears a stamp
beyond all common Charity, & I hope a Blessing will
continue to attend it. I am glad you are well & trust
you are sure of being so, while you are employed in
such a way; I must hope however that your health may
eer long stand the trial of a more common-place course
of days, & that you will be able to leave Barton when
Mrs D. D.[1] arrives there. There was no ready-made
Cloak at Alton that would do, but Coleby has under-
taken to supply one in a few days; it is to be Grey
Woollen & cost ten shillings. I hope you like the *sim*
of it. Sally knows your kind intentions & has received
your message, & in return for it all, she & I have between us made out that she sends her Duty & thanks
you for your goodness & means to be a good girl if I
please. I have forgot to enquire as to her wanting anything particularly, but there is no *apparent* deficiency,
she looks very neat & tidy. The Calico for her Mother

[1] Deans Dundas.

shall be bought soon. We have been quite alone,
except Miss Benn, since 12 o'clock on wednesday,
when Edward & his Harem[1] drove from the door; &
we have since heard of their safe arrival & happiness at
Winchester. Lizzy was much obliged to you for your
message, but *she* has the little room. Her Father having
his choice & being used to a very large Bed chamber
at home, would of course prefer the ample space of
yours. The visit was a very pleasant one I really beleive
on each side; they were certainly very sorry to go
away, but a little of that sorrow must be attributed to
a disinclination for what was before them. They have
had favourable weather however, & I hope Steventon
may have been better than they expected. We have
reason to suppose the change of name has taken place,
as we have to forward a Letter to Edward Knight
Esq[re] from the Lawyer who has the management of
the business. I must learn to make a better K. Our next
visitor is likely to be William from Eltham in his way
to Winchester, as D[r] Gabell[2] chuses he should come
then before the Holidays, though it can be only for a
week. If M[rs] Barker has any farther curiosity about the
Miss Webbs let her know that we are going to invite
them for Tuesday even[g]—also Capt. & M[rs] Clement
& Miss Benn, & that M[rs] Digweed is already secured.
'But why not M[r] Digweed?' M[rs] Barker will immediately say. To that you may answer that M[r] D. is
going on tuesday to Steventon to shoot rabbits. The
4 lines on Miss W.[3] which I sent you were all my own,
but James afterwards suggested what I thought a great

[1] Edward Austen, now Knight, had been staying with his mother
and with him a number of children, his 'and others'. The 'Great House'
was let to the Middletons.
[2] Headmaster of Winchester.
[3] Wallop; see note, p. 214.

improvement & as it stands in the Steventon **Edition**.
P. & P.[1] is sold. Egerton gives £110 for it. I would
rather have had £150, but we could not both be
pleased, & I am not at all surprised that he should not
chuse to hazard so much. It's being sold will I hope be
a great saving of Trouble to Henry, & therefore must
be welcome to me. The Money is to be paid at the end
of the twelvemonth. You have sometimes expressed a
wish of making Miss Benn some present; Cassandra &
I think that something of the Shawl kind to wear over
her Shoulders within doors in very cold weather might
be useful, but it must not be very handsome or she
would not use it. Her long Fur tippet is almost worn
out. If you do not return in time to send the Turkey
yourself, we must trouble you for Mr Morton's direction again, as we should be quite as much at a loss as
ever. It becomes now a sort of vanity in us not to know
Mr Morton's direction with any certainty. We are just
beginning to be engaged in another Christmas Duty,
& next to eating Turkies, a very pleasant one, laying
out Edward's money for the Poor; & the Sum that
passes through our hands this year is considerable,
as Mrs Knight left £20 to the Parish. Your nephew
William's[2] state seems very alarming. Mary Jane,[2] from
whom I heard the other day, writes of him as very
uneasy; I hope his Father & Mother are so too. When
you see Miss Murden, give her our Love & Good
wishes, & say that we are very sorry to hear of her so
often as an Invalid. Poor Mrs Stent I hope will not be
much longer a distress to anybody. All of you that are
well enough to look, are now passing your Judgements
I suppose on Mrs John Butler; & 'is she pretty? or is

---

[1] See note, p. 214.
[2] Fowle; their mother was Martha's sister.

she not?' is the knotty question. Happy Woman! to stand the gaze of a neighbourhood as the Bride of such a pink-faced, simple young Man!

Monday. A wettish day, bad for Steventon. Mary Deedes I think must be liked there, she is so perfectly unaffected & sweet tempered, & tho' as ready to be pleased as Fanny Cage, deals less in superlatives & rapture.—Pray give our best comp^ts to Mrs Dundas & tell her that we hope soon to hear of her complete recovery.—Yours affect:^y

J. Austen

75. *To Cassandra Austen. Sunday 24 Jan.* 1813

Chawton Sunday even^g Jan 24

My dear Cassandra

This is exactly the weather we could wish for, if you are but well enough to enjoy it. I shall be glad to hear that you are not confined to the house by an increase of cold. Mr Digweed has used us basely. Handsome is as handsome does, he is therefore a very ill-looking man. I hope you have sent off a letter to me by this day's post, unless you are tempted to wait till to-morrow by one of Mr Chute's franks. We have had no letter since you went away, & no visitor except Miss Benn, who dined with us on Friday; but we have received the half of an excellent Stilton cheese—we presume from Henry. My mother is very well & finds great amusement in the glove-knitting, when this pair is finished she means to knit another, & at present wants no other work. We quite run over with books. *She* has got Sir John Carr's Travels in Spain from Miss B. & *I* am reading a Society octavo,[1] an Essay on the

---

[1] Circulated by the Chawton Reading Society.

Military Police & Institutions of the British Empire by
Capt Pasley of the Engineers, a book which I protested
against at first, but which upon trial I find delightfully
written & highly entertaining. I am as much in love
with the author as ever I was with Clarkson or
Buchanan, or even the two Mr Smiths of the city—
the first soldier I ever sighed for—but he does write
with extraordinary force & spirit. Yesterday moreover
brought us Mrs Grant's letters[1] with Mr White's comp^ts.
But I have disposed of them, comp^ts & all, for the first
fortnight to Miss Papillon—& among so many readers
or retainers of books as we have in Chawton I daresay
there will be no difficulty in getting rid of them for
another fortnight if necessary. I learn from Sir J. Carr
that there is no Government House at Gibraltar.[2] I
must alter it to the Commissioner's. Our party on
Wednesday was not unagreeable, tho' as usual we
wanted a better Master of the House, one less anxious
& fidgetty & more conversible. In consequence of a
civil note that morning from Mrs Clement, I went with
her & her husband in their Tax-cart—civility on both
sides; *I* would rather have walked, & no doubt *they*
must have wished I had. I ran home with my own dear
Thomas at night in great luxury. Thomas was very
useful. We were eleven altogether, as you will find on
computation adding Miss Benn & two strange gentlemen, a Mr Twyford curate of G^t Worldham, who is
living in Alton, & his friend Mr Wilkes. I don't know
that Mr T. is anything except very dark-complexioned,
but Mr W. was a useful addition, being an easy, talking, pleasantish young man—a *very* young man, hardly
20 perhaps. He is of St John's Cambridge & spoke very

---

[1] *Letter from the Mountains.*
[2] In *Mansfield Park.*

127

highly of H. Walter as a schollar. he said he was considered as the best classick in the University. How
such a report would have interested my father! I could
see nothing very promising between Mr P.¹ & Miss
P. T.² She placed herself on one side of him at first,
but Miss Benn obliged her to move up higher; & she
had an empty plate, & even asked him to give her
some mutton twice without being attended to for some
time. There might be design in this, to be sure, on his
side; he might think an empty stomach the most
favourable for love. Upon Mrs Digweed's mentioning
that she had sent the Rejected Addresses to Mr Hinton,
I began talking to her a little about them, & expressed
my hope of their having amused her. Her answer was
'Oh dear yes, very much, very droll indeed—the opening of the House, & the striking up of the Fiddles!'
What she meant poor woman, who shall say? I sought
no farther. The Papillons have now got the book, & like
it very much; their neice Eleanor has recommended
it most warmly to them. *She* looks like a rejected
addresser. As soon as a whist party was formed, & a
round table threatened, I made my mother an excuse
& came away, leaving just as many for *their* round
table as there were at Mrs Grants.³ I wish they might
be as agreeable a set. It was past 10 when I got home,
so I was not ashamed of my dutiful delicacy. The
Coulthards were talked of you may be sure, no end of
them. Miss Terry had heard they were going to rent
Mr Bramston's house at Oakley, & Mrs Clement that
they were going to live at Streatham. Mrs Digweed &
I agreed that the house at Oakley could not possibly

---

¹ Papillon, the host.
² Presumably the Miss Terry *infra*.
³ That is six, as at Mansfield Parsonage.

be large enough for them, & now we find they have
really taken it. Mr Gauntlett is thought very agreeable
—& there are *no* children at all. The Miss Sibleys
want to establish a Book Society in their side of the
country, like ours. What can be a stronger proof of that
superiority in ours over the Steventon & Manydown
society, which I have always foreseen & felt? No
emulation of the kind was ever inspired by *their* proceedings. No such wish of the Miss Sibleys was ever
heard in the course of the many years of that Society's
existence. And what are their Biglands & their Barrows,
their Macartneys & Mackenzies to Capt Pasley's Essay
on the Military police of the British Empire, & the
rejected addresses? I have walked once to Alton, &
yesterday Miss Papillon & I walked together to call on
the Garnets. She invited herself very pleasantly to be
my companion, when I went to propose to her the indulgence of accommodating us about the Letters from
the Mountains. *I* had a very agreeable walk, & if *she*
had not, more shame for her, for I was quite as entertaining as she was. Dame G. is pretty well, & we
found her surrounded by her well-behaved, healthy,
large-eyed children. I took her an old shift, & promised
her a set of our Linen, & my companion left some of
her Bank Stock with her. Tuesday has done its duty &
I have had the pleasure of reading a very comfortable
letter. It contains so much that I feel obliged to write
down the whole of this page, & perhaps something in
a cover. When my parcel is finished I shall walk with
it to Alton. I believe Miss Benn will go with me. She
spent yesterday evening with us. As I know Mary is
interested in her not being neglected by her neighbours, pray tell her that Miss B dined last Wednesday
at Mr Papillon's—on Thursday with Capt & M^rs

Clement—friday here, Saturday with Mrs Digweed, & Sunday with the Papillons again. I had fancied that Martha w^d be at Barton from last Saturday, but am best pleased to be mistaken. I hope she is now quite well. Tell her that I hunt away the rogues every night from under her bed, they feel the difference of her being gone. Miss Benn wore her new shawl last night, sat in it the whole evening, & seemed to enjoy it very much.

'A very sloppy lane' last Friday. What an odd sort of country you must be in! I cannot at all understand it! It was just greasy here on Friday in consequence of the little snow that had fallen in the night. Perhaps it *was* cold on Wednesday, yes I believe it certainly was, but nothing terrible. Upon the whole the weather for winter weather is delightful, the walking excellent. I cannot imagine what sort of a place Steventon can be! My mother sends her love to Mary, with thanks for her kind intentions & enquiries as to the Pork & will prefer receiving her share from the two *last* Pigs: she has great pleasure in sending her a pair of garters, & is very glad that she had them ready knit. Her letter to Anna is to be forwarded if any opportunity offers, otherwise it may wait for her return. Mrs Leigh's letter came this morning, we are glad to hear anything so tolerable of Scarlets.[1] Poor Charles & his frigate—But there could be no chance of his having one, while it was thought such a certainty. I can hardly believe Brother Michael's news. We have no such idea in Chawton at least. Mrs Bramston is the sort of woman I detest. Mr Cottrell is worth ten of her. It is better to be given the lie direct than to excite no interest. . . .

---

[1] The Leigh-Perrots.

76. *To Cassandra Austen. Friday* 29 *Jan.* ⟨1813⟩

Chawton Friday Jany 29

I hope you received my little parcel by J. Bond on
Wednesday evening my dear Cassandra, & that you
will be ready to hear from me again on Sunday, for
I feel that I must write to you to-day. Your parcel
is safely arrived & everything shall be delivered as it
ought. Thank you for your note. As you had not heard
from me at that time it was very good in you to write,
but I shall not be so much your debtor soon. I want
to tell you that I have got my own darling child[1] from
London; on Wednesday I received one copy sent down
by Falknor with three lines from Henry to say that he
had given another to Charles, & sent a 3^d by the coach
to Godmersham—just the two sets which I was least
eager for the disposal of. I wrote to him immediately
to beg for my two other sets, unless he would take the
trouble of forwarding them at once to Steventon &
Portsmouth—not having an idea of his leaving Town
before to-day; by your account however he was gone
before my letter was written. The only evil is the delay:
nothing more can be done till his return—Tell James
& Mary so with my love. For *your* sake I am as well
pleased that it should be so, as it might be unpleasant
to you to be in the neighbourhood at the first burst of
the business. The Advertisement is in our paper to-day
for the first time 18^s. He shall ask £1. 1. for my two
next & £1. 8 for my stupidest of all. I shall write to
Frank that he may not think himself neglected. Miss
Benn dined with us on the very day of the books
coming & in the evening we set fairly at it, and read
half the first vol. to her, prefacing that, having intelli-

[1] *Pride and Prejudice.*

131

gence from Henry that such a work would soon appear,
we had desired him to send it whenever it came out,
and I believe it passed with her unsuspected. She was
amused, poor soul! *That* she could not help, you know,
with two such people to lead the way, but she really
does seem to admire Elizabeth. I must confess that I
think her as delightful a creature as ever appeared in
print, and how I shall be able to tolerate those who do
not like *her* at least I do not know. There are a few
typical errors; and a 'said he,' or a 'said she,' would
sometimes make the dialogue more immediately clear;
but

> I do not write for such dull elves
> As have not a great deal of ingenuity themselves.[1]

The second volume is shorter than I could wish, but
the difference is not so much in reality as in look, there
being a larger proportion of narrative in that part.
I have lop't and crop't so successfully, however, that
I imagine it must be rather shorter than S. & S.
altogether. Now I will try to write of something else, &
it shall be a complete change of subject—ordination[2]
—I am glad to find your enquiries have ended so well.
If you could discover whether Northamptonshire is a
country of Hedgerows I should be glad again. We
admire your Charades excessively—but as yet have
guessed only the 1st. The others seem very difficult.
There is so much beauty in the versification however,
that the finding them out is but a secondary pleasure.
I grant you that *this is* a cold day, & am sorry to think
how cold you will be through the process of your visit
at Manydown. I hope you will wear your China crape.
Poor wretch! I can see you shivering away with your

---

[1] A parody of *Marmion*.   [2] See note, p. 213.

miserable feeling feet. What a vile character Mr Digweed turns out, quite beyond anything & everything[1]
—instead of going to Steventon, they are to have a
dinner-party next Tuesday! I am sorry to say that I
c^d not eat a mince-pie at Mr Papillon's; I was rather
headachey that day & could not venture on anything
sweet except jelly, but *that* was excellent. There were
no stewed pears—but Miss Benn had some almonds &
raisins. By the bye she desired to be kindly remembered to you when I wrote last & I forgot it. Betsy
sends her duty to you & hopes you are well—& her
love to Miss Caroline & hopes she has got rid of
her cough. It was such a pleasure to her to think her
oranges were so well timed that I daresay she was
rather glad to hear of the cough. Since I wrote this
letter we have been visited by Mrs Digweed, her sister
& Miss Benn. I gave Mrs D. her little parcel which she
opened here, & seemed much pleased with—and she
desired me to make her best thanks etc. to Miss Lloyd
for it. Martha may guess how full of wonder & gratitude she was.

77. *To Cassandra Austen. Thursday* 4 *Feb.* ⟨1813⟩

Chawton, Thursday Feby 4

My dear Cassandra

Your letter was truly welcome, and I am much
obliged to you all for your praise; it came at a right
time, for I had had some fits of disgust. Our second
evening's reading to Miss Benn had not pleased me so
well, but I believe something must be attributed to my
mother's too rapid way of getting on: and though she
perfectly understands the characters herself, she can-

[1] J A quotes Mrs. Digweed.

not speak as they ought. Upon the whole, however, I am quite vain enough and well satisfied enough. The work is rather too light, and bright, and sparkling; it wants shade; it wants to be stretched out here and there with a long chapter of sense, if it could be had; if not, of solemn specious nonsense, about something unconnected with the story; an essay on writing, a critique on Walter Scott, or the history of Buonaparté, or anything that would form a contrast, and bring the reader with increased delight to the playfulness and epigrammatism of the general style. I doubt your quite agreeing with me here. I know your starched notions. The caution observed at Steventon with regard to the possession of the book is an agreeable surprise to me, & I heartily wish it may be the means of saving you from everything unpleasant—but you must be prepared for the neighbourhood being perhaps already informed of there being such a Work in the World & in the Chawton World! Dummer will do that you know. It was spoken of here one morning when M\ :sup:rs D.[1] called with Miss Benn. The greatest blunder in the printing that I have met with is in page 220, v. 3, where two speeches are made into one.[2] There might as well have been no suppers at Longbourn; but I suppose it was the remains of Mrs. Bennett's old Meryton habits. I am sorry for your disappointment about Manydown & fear this week must be a heavy one. As far as one may venture to judge at a distance of 20 miles, you must miss Martha. For *her* sake I was glad to hear of her going as I suppose she must have been growing anxious & wanting to be again in scenes of agitation & exertion. She had a lovely day for her

[1] Digweed.
[2] p. 343 in my edition of *Pride and Prejudice*.

journey. I walked to Alton, & dirt excepted found it delightful, it seemed like an old Feby come back again. Before I set out we were visited by Mrs Edwards, & while I was gone Miss Beckford & Maria, & Miss Woolls & Harriet B.[1] called, all of whom my Mother was glad to see, & I very glad to escape. John M.[2] is sailed & now Miss B thinks his father will really try for a house, & has hopes herself of avoiding Southampton, this is as it was repeated to me—& I can tell the Miss Williamses that Miss Beckford has no intention of inviting them to Chawton. Well done you—I thought of you at Manydown in the Drawing-room, & in your China crape, therefore you were in the Breakfast parlour in your brown Bombasin; if I thought of you *so*, you would have been in the Kitchen in your morning stuff. I feel that I have never mentioned the Harwoods[3] in my letters to you, which is shocking enough, but we are sincerely glad to hear all the good of them you send us. There is no chance I suppose, no danger of poor Mrs H.'s being persuaded to come to Chawton at present. I hope John H will not have more debts brought in than he likes. I am pleased with M. T.'s[4] being to dine at Steventon, it may enable you to be yet more decided with Fanny, & help to settle her faith. Thomas was married on Saturday, the wedding was kept at Neatham, & that is all I know about it. Browning is quite a new broom, & at present has no fault. He had lost some of his knowledge of waiting, & is I think rather slow, but he is not noisy, & not at all above being taught. The Back-gate is regularly locked. I did not forget Henry's fee to Thomas. I had a letter from

---

[1] Benn.   [2] Middleton.
[3] John H. of Deane had died leaving unsuspected debts.
[4] Perhaps Michael Terry, Rector of Dummer.

Henry yesterday, written on Sunday from Oxford, mine had been forwarded to him. Edward's[1] information therefore was correct. He says that copies were sent to S. & P.[2] at the same time with the others. He has some thoughts of going to Addlestrop.

78.1. *To Martha Lloyd. Tuesday* 16 *Feb.* ⟨1813⟩[3]

Chawton Tuesday Feb: 16.

My dear Martha

Your long Letter was valued as it ought, & as I think it fully entitled to a second from me, I am going to answer it now in an handsome manner before Cassandra's return; after which event, as I shall have the benefit of all your Letters to her I claim nothing more. I have great pleasure in what you communicate of Anna, & sincerely rejoice in Miss Murden's amendment; & only wish there were more stability in the Character of their two constitutions. I will not say anything of the weather we have lately had, for if you were not aware of it 's being terrible, it would be cruel to put it in your head. My Mother slept through a good deal of Sunday, but still it was impossible not to be disordered by such a sky, & even yesterday she was but poorly. She is pretty well again today, & I am in hopes may not be much longer a Prisoner. We are going to be all alive from this forenoon to tomorrow afternoon; it will be over when you receive this, & you may think of me as one not sorry that it is so. George, Henry & William[4] will soon be here & are to stay the night—and tomorrow the 2 Deedes' & Henry Bridges

---

[1] James Edward.
[2] Steventon and (Frank) Portsmouth.
[3] See note, p. 214.
[4] Edward's boys.

will be added to our party; we shall then have an early dinner & dispatch them all to Winchester. We have no late account from Sloane S^t & therefore conclude that everything is going on in one regular progress, without any striking change. Henry was to be in Town again last Tuesday. I have a Letter from Frank; they are all at Deal again, established once more in fresh Lodgings. I think they must soon have lodged in every house in the Town. We read of the Pyramus being returned into Port, with interest—& fear Mrs D.D.[1] will be regretting that she came away so soon. There is no being up to the tricks of the Sea. Your friend has her little Boys about her I imagine. I hope their Sister enjoyed the Ball at Lady Keith—tho' I do not know that I do much hope it, for it might be quite as well to have her shy & uncomfortable in such a croud of Strangers.

I am obliged to you for your enquiries about Northamptonshire,[2] but do not wish you to renew them, as I am sure of getting the intelligence I want from Henry, to whom I can apply at some convenient moment 'sans peur et sans reproche'. I suppose all the World is sitting in Judgement upon the Princess of Wales's Letter. Poor woman, I shall support her as long as I can, because she *is* a Woman, & because I hate her Husband—but I can hardly forgive her for calling herself 'attached & affectionate' to a Man whom she must detest—& the intimacy said to subsist between her & Lady Oxford is bad—I do not know what to do about it; but if I must give up the Princess, I am resolved at least always to think that she would have been respectable, if the Prince had behaved only tolerably by her at first.

Old Philmore is got pretty well, well enough to warn

[1] Deans Dundas.   [2] See note, p. 213, on p. 132.

Miss Benn out of her House. His son is to come into it. Poor Creature! You may imagine how full of cares she must be, & how anxious all Chawton will feel to get her decently settled somewhere.—She will have 3 months before her. & if anything else can be met with, she will be glad enough to be driven from her present wretched abode; it has been terrible for her during the late storms of wind & rain. Cassandra has been rather out of luck at Manydown—but that is a House, in which one is tolerably independent of weather. The Prowtings perhaps come down on Thursday or Saturday, but the accounts of *him* do not improve. Now I think I may in *Quantity* have deserved your Letter. My ideas of Justice in Epistolary Matters are you know very strict.—with Love from my Mother, I remain. Yʳˢ very affecˡʸ

J. Austen

Poor John Harwood![1] One is really obliged to engage in Pity again on his account—& when there is a lack of money, one is on pretty sure grounds. So after all, Charles, that thick-headed Charles is the best off of the Family. I rather grudge him his 2,500£.— My Mother is very decided in *selling* Deane—and if it is *not* sold, I think it will be clear that the Proprietor can have no plan of marrying.

80. *To Cassandra Austen. Monday* 24 *May* ⟨1813⟩

Sloane Sᵗ Monday May 24.

My dearest Cassandra

I am very much obliged to you for writing to me. You must have hated it after a worrying morning.

[1] See p. 135.

Your Letter came just in time to save my going to
Remnants, & fit me for Christian's, where I bought
Fanny's dimity. I went the day before (Friday) to
Laytons as I proposed, & got my Mother's gown 7 y^{ds}
at 6/6. I then walked into No. 10,[1] which is all dirt &
confusion, but in a very promising way, & after being
present at the opening of a new account to my great
amusement, Henry & I went to the Exhibition in
Spring Gardens. It is not thought a good collection,
but I was very well pleased—particularly (pray tell
Fanny) with a small portrait of Mrs. Bingley,[2] excessively like her. I went in hopes of seeing one of her
Sister, but there was no Mrs. Darcy;[2]—perhaps however, I may find her in the Great Exhibition[3] which we
shall go to, if we have time;—I have no chance of her
in the collection of Sir Joshua Reynolds's[4] Paintings
which is now shewing in Pall Mall, & which we are
also to visit. Mrs. Bingley's is exactly herself, size,
shaped face, features & sweetness; there never was a
greater likeness. She is dressed in a white gown, with
green ornaments, which convinces me of what I had
always supposed, that green was a favourite colour
with her. I dare say Mrs. D. will be in Yellow. Friday
was our worst day as to weather, we were out in a very
long & very heavy storm of hail, & there had been
others before, but I heard no Thunder. Saturday was a
good deal better, dry & cold. I gave 2/6 for the Dimity;
I do not boast of any Bargains, but think both the
Sarsenet & Dimity good of their sort. I have bought
your Locket, but was obliged to give 18^s for it—which

[1] Henrietta St.
[2] The Jane and Elizabeth of *Pride and Prejudice*; this exhibition was
that of the Society of Painters.
[3] That of the British Academy in Somerset Place.
[4] The British Institution was showing '130 of his performances'.

must be rather more than you intended; it is neat & plain, set in gold. ⟨*Four or five words cut out.*⟩ We were to have gone to the Somerset House Exhibition on Saturday, but when I reached Henrietta Street Mr. Hampson was wanted there, & Mr. Tilson & I were obliged to drive about Town after him, & by the time we had done, it was too late for anything but Home. We never found him after all. I have been interrupted by Mrs. Tilson. Poor Woman! She is in danger of not being able to attend Lady Drummond Smith's Party tonight. Miss Burdett was to have taken her, & now Miss Burdett has a cough & will not go. My cousin *Caroline*[1] is her sole dependance. The events of Yesterday were, our going to Belgrave Chapel in the morn^g, our being prevented by the rain from going to even^g service at St James, Mr. Hampson's calling, Messrs Barlow & Phillips dining here, & Mr. & Mrs. Tilson's coming in the even^g a l'ordinaire. *She* drank tea with us both Thursday & Saturday, *he* dined out each day, & on friday we were with them, & they wish us to go to them tomorrow even^g to meet Miss Burdett, but I do not know how it will end. Henry talks of a drive to Hampstead, which may interfere with it. I should like to see Miss Burdett very well, but that I am rather frightened by hearing that she wishes to be introduced to *me*. If I *am* a wild Beast,[2] I cannot help it. It is not my own fault. There is no change in our plan of leaving London, but we shall not be with you before Tuesday. Henry thinks Monday would appear too early a day. There is no danger of our being induced to stay longer.

I have not quite determined how I shall manage about my Cloathes, perhaps there may be only my

---

[1] See note, p. 213, on p. 119; Caro*line* is Mrs. Tilson's pronunciation.
[2] i.e. 'lionized'.

Trunk to send by the Coach, or there may be a Band-box with it. I have taken your gentle hint & written to Mrs. Hill. The Hoblyns want us to dine with them, but we have refused. When Henry returns he will be dining out a great deal I dare say; as he will then be alone, it will be more desirable; he will be more welcome at every Table, & every Invitation more welcome to him. He will not want either of us again till he is settled in Henrietta St. This is my present persuasion. And he will not be settled there, really settled, till late in the Autumn; 'he will not be come to bide,'[1] till after September. There is a Gentleman in treaty for this house. Gentleman himself is in the Country, but Gentleman's friend came to see it the other day & seemed pleased on the whole. Gentleman would rather prefer an increased rent to parting with five hundred Gs at once; & if that is the only difficulty, it will not be minded. Henry is indifferent as to the which. Get us the best weather you can for Wednesday, Thursday, & Friday. We are to go to Windsor in our way to Henley, which will be a great delight. We shall be leaving Sloane St. about 12, two or three hours after Charles's party have begun their Journey. You will miss them, but the comfort of getting back into your own room will be great! & then the Tea & Sugar!

I fear Miss Clewes is not better, or you wd have mentioned it. I shall not write again unless I have any unexpected communication or opportunity to tempt me. I enclose Mr. Herington's Bill & receipt.

I am very much obliged to Fanny for her Letter; it made me laugh heartily; but I cannot pretend to answer it. Even had I more time, I should not feel at all sure of the sort of Letter that Miss D.[2] would write.

---

[1] See p. 107.   [2] Georgiana Darcy in *Pride and Prejudice*.

I hope Miss Benn is got quite well again & will have a comfortable Dinner with you today. *Monday even^g*.— We have been both to the Exhibition & Sir J. Reynolds', and I am disappointed, for there was nothing like Mrs. D. at either. I can only imagine that Mr. D. prizes any Picture of her too much to like it should be exposed to the public eye. I can imagine he w^d have that sort of feeling—that mixture of Love, Pride & Delicacy. Setting aside this disappointment, I had great amusement among the Pictures; & the Driving about, the Carriage being open, was very pleasant. I liked my solitary elegance very much, & was ready to laugh all the time, at my being where I was. I could not but feel that I had naturally small right to be parading about London in a Barouche. Henry desires Edward may know that he has just bought 3 dozen of Claret for him (Cheap) & ordered it to be sent down to Chawton. I should not wonder if we got no farther than Reading on Thursday even^g—& so, reach Steventon only to a reasonable Dinner hour the next day; but whatever I may write or you may imagine we know it will be something different. I shall be quiet tomorrow morn^g; all my business is done, & I shall only call again upon Mrs. Hoblyn, &c.—Love to your much ⟨? redu⟩ced Party. —Y^rs affec^ly

J. Austen

81. *To Francis Austen.* ⟨*Saturday*⟩ 3 *July* 1813

Chawton July 3, 1813

My dearest Frank

Behold me going to write you as handsome a Letter as I can. Wish me good luck. We have had the pleasure of hearing of you lately through Mary, who sent us

some of the particulars of Yours of June 18th (I think)
written off Rugen, & we enter into the delight of your
having so good a Pilot. Why are you like Queen Elizth?
—Because you know how to chuse wise Ministers.
Does not this prove you as great a Captain as she was
a Queen? This may serve as a riddle for you to put
forth among your Officers, by way of increasing your
proper consequence. It must be real enjoyment to you,
since you are obliged to leave England, to be where
you are, seeing something of a new Country, & one
that has been so distinguished as Sweden. You must
have great pleasure in it.—I hope you may have gone
to Carlscroon. Your Profession has it's douceurs to
recompense for some of it's Privations; to an enquiring
& observing Mind like yours, such douceurs must be
considerable. Gustavus-Vasa, & Charles 12th, & Chris-
tina, & Linneus—do their Ghosts rise up before you?
I have a great respect for former Sweden. So zealous
as it was for Protestantism! And I have always fancied
it more like England than many Countries; & according to the Map, many of the names have a strong
resemblance to the English. July begins unpleasantly
with us, cold & showery, but it is often a baddish
month. We had some fine dry weather preceding it,
which was very acceptable to the Holders of Hay &
the Masters of Meadows. In general it must have been
a good haymaking Season. Edward has got in all his,
in excellent order; I speak only of Chawton; but here
he has had better luck than Mr. Middleton ever had in
the 5 years that he was Tenant. Good encouragement
for him to come again; & I really hope he will do so
another Year. The pleasure to us of having them here
is so great, that if we were not the best creatures in the
World we should not deserve it. We go on in the most

comfortable way, very frequently dining together, & always meeting in some part of every day. Edward is very well & enjoys himself as thoroughly as any Hampshire born Austen can desire. Chawton is not thrown away upon him. He talks of making a new Garden;[1] the present is a bad one & ill situated, near Mr. Papillon's; he means to have the new, at the top of the Lawn behind his own house. We like to have him proving & strengthening his attachment to the place by making it better. He will soon have all his Children about him, Edward, George & Charles are collected already, and another week brings Henry & William. It is the custom at Winchester for Georges to come away a fortnight before the Holidays, when they are not to return any more; for fear they should overstudy themselves just at last, I suppose. Really it is a piece of dishonourable accomodation to the Master. We are in hopes of another visit from our own true, lawful Henry very soon, he is to be *our* Guest this time. He is quite well I am happy to say, & does not leave it to *my* pen I am sure to communicate to you the joyful news of his being Deputy Receiver[2] no longer. It is a promotion which he thoroughly enjoys; as well he may;—the work of his own mind. He sends you all his own plans of course. The scheme for Scotland we think an excellent one both for himself & his nephew.[3] Upon the whole his Spirits are very much recovered. If I may so express myself, his Mind is not a Mind for affliction. He is too Busy, too active, too sanguine. Sincerely as he was attached to poor Eliza moreover, & excellently as he behaved to her, he was always so used to be away

[1] A walled garden behind the house replaced one in 'the church meadow'.

[2] He was now Receiver-General.

[3] Edward's Edward.

144

from her at times, that her Loss is not felt as that of many a beloved wife might be, especially when all the circumstances of her long and dreadful Illness are taken into the account. He very long knew that she must die, & it was indeed a release at last. Our mourning for her is not over, or we should now be putting it on again for Mr. Thoˢ Leigh—the respectable, worthy, clever, agreable Mᵣ Tho. Leigh, who has just closed a good life at the age of 79, & must have died the possessor of one of the finest Estates in England & of more worthless Nephews and Neices than any other private Man in the United Kingdoms. We are very anxious to know who will have the Living of Adlestrop, & where his excellent sister[1] will find a home for the remainder of her days. As yet she bears his Loss with fortitude, but she has always seemed so wrapt up in him, that I fear she must feel it very dreadfully when the fever of Business is over. There is another female sufferer on the occasion to be pitied. Poor Mrs. L. P.[2]—who would now have been Mistress of Stonleigh had there been none of that vile compromise, which in good truth has never been allowed to be of much use to them. It will be a hard trial. Charles's little girls were with us about a month, & had so endeared themselves that we were quite sorry to have them go. We have the pleasure however of hearing that they are thought very much improved at home— Harriet in health, Cassy in manners. The latter *ought* to be a very nice Child—Nature has done enough for her—but Method has been wanting: we thought her very much improved ourselves, but to have Papa & Mama think her so too, was very essential to our

---

[1] 'Mrs. E. Leigh'.
[2] Leigh-Perrot; for the compromise see note, p. 213, on p. 72.

contentment. She will really be a very pleasing Child,
if they will only exert themselves a little. Harriet is a
truely sweet-tempered little Darling. They are now all
at Southend together. Why do I mention *that*?—As if
Charles did not write himself. I hate to be spending
my time so needlessly, encroaching too upon the rights
of others. I wonder whether you happened to see Mr.
Blackhall's[1] marriage in the Papers last Jany. *We* did.
He was married at Clifton to a Miss Lewis, whose
Father had been late of Antigua. I should very much
like to know what sort of a Woman she is. He was a
piece of Perfection, noisy Perfection himself which I
always recollect with regard. We had noticed a few
months before his succeeding to a College Living, the
very Living which we remembered his talking of &
wishing for; an exceeding good one, Great Cadbury in
Somersetshire. I would wish Miss Lewis to be of a
silent turn & rather ignorant, but naturally intelligent
& wishing to learn; fond of cold veal pies, green tea in
the afternoon, & a green window blind at night.

You will be glad to hear that every Copy of S. & S.
is sold & that it has brought me £140 besides the
Copyright, if that sh^d ever be of any value. I have
now therefore written myself into £250[2]—which only
makes me long for more. I have something in hand[3]—
which I hope on the credit of P. & P. will sell well, tho'
not half so entertaining. And by the bye—shall you
object to my mentioning the Elephant in it, & two or
three other of your old Ships?[4] I *have* done it, but it
shall not stay, to make you angry. They are only just
mentioned.

[1] See p. 12.
[2] Including £110 for *Pride and Prejudice*, see p. 125.
[3] *Mansfield Park*.   [4] She borrowed three.

July 6.

Now my dearest Frank I will finish my Letter. I
have kept it open on the chance of what a Tuesday's
post might furnish in addition, & it furnishes the likelihood of our keeping our neighbours at the G^t House
some weeks longer than we had expected. Mr. Scudamore, to whom my Brother referred, is very decided
as to G^{m1} not being fit to be inhabited at present; he
talks even of two months more being necessary to
sweeten it, but if we have warm weather I dare-say
less will do. My Brother will probably go down & sniff
at it himself & receive his rents. The rent-day has been
postponed already. *We* shall be gainers by their stay,
but the young people in general are disappointed, and
therefore we c^d wish it otherwise. Our Cousins Colonel
Thos Austen & Margaretta are going Aid-de-camps to
Ireland & Lord Whitworth goes in their Train as Lord
Lieutenant; good appointments for each. God bless
you. I hope you continue beautiful & brush your hair,
but not all off. We join in an infinity of Love.

Y^{rs} very affec^{ly}

Jane Austen

91. *To Cassandra Austen. Saturday* 6 *Nov.* ⟨1813⟩

Saturday Novr 6—Godmersham Park

My dearest Cassandra

Having half an hour before breakfast (very snug, in
my own room, lovely morn^g, excellent fire, fancy me)
I will give you some account of the last two days. And
yet, what is there to be told? I shall get foolishly
minute unless I cut the matter short. We met only the

---

¹ Godmersham.

Brittons at Chilham Castle, besides a Mr. & Mrs. Osborne & a Miss Lee staying in the House, & were only 14 altogether. My B^r & Fanny thought it the pleasantest party they had ever known there & I was very well entertained by bits & scraps. I had long wanted to see Dr. Britton, & his wife amuses me very much with her affected refinement & elegance. Miss Lee I found very conversible; she admires Crabbe as she ought. She is at an age of reason, ten years older than myself at least. She was at the famous Ball at Chilham Castle, so of course you remember her. By the bye, as I must leave off being young, I find many Douceurs in being a sort of Chaperon for I am put on the Sofa near the Fire & can drink as much wine as I like. We had Music in the Even^g, Fanny & Miss Wildman played, & Mr. James Wildman sat close by & listened, or pretended to listen. Yesterday was a day of dissipation all through, first came Sir Brook to dissipate us before breakfast—then there was a call from Mr. Sherer, then a regular morn^g visit from Lady Honeywood in her way home from Eastwell—then Sir Brook & Edward set off—then we dined (5 in number) at ½ past 4—then we had coffee, & at 6 Miss Clewes, Fanny & I draved away. We had a beautiful night for our frisks. We were earlier than we need have been, but after a time Lady B. & her two companions appeared, we had kept places for them & there we sat, all six in a row, under a side wall, I between Lucy Foote & Miss Clewes. Lady B. was much what I expected, I could not determine whether she was rather handsome or very plain. I liked her, for being in a hurry to have the Concert over & get away, & for getting away at last with a great deal of decision & promtness, not waiting to compliment & dawdle & fuss about seeing *dear*

Fanny, who was half the even^g in another part of the room with her friends the Plumptres. I am growing too minute, so I will go to Breakfast.

When the Concert was over, Mrs. Harrison[1] & I found each other out & had a very comfortable little complimentary friendly chat. She is a sweet Woman, still quite a sweet Woman in herself, & so like her Sister! I could almost have thought I was speaking to Mrs. Lefroy. She introduced me to her Daughter, whom I think pretty, but most dutifully inferior to la Mere Beauté.[2] The Faggs & the Hammonds were there, Wm Hammond the only young Man of renown. *Miss* looked very handsome, but I prefer her little, smiling, flirting Sister Julia. I was just introduced at last to Mary Plumptre, but should hardly know her again. She was delighted with *me* however, good enthusiastic Soul! And Lady B. found me handsomer than she expected, so you see I am not so very bad as you might think for. It was 12 before we reached home. We were all dog-tired, but pretty well to-day, Miss Clewes says she has not caught cold, & Fanny's does not seem worse. I was so tired that I began to wonder how I should get through the Ball next Thursday, but there will be so much more variety then in walking about, & probably so much less heat that perhaps I may not feel it more. My China Crape is still kept for the Ball. Enough of the Concert. I had a Letter from Mary Yesterday. They travelled down to Cheltenham last Monday very safely & are certainly to be there a month. Bath is still Bath. The H. Bridges' must quit them early next week, & Louisa seems not quite to despair of their all moving together, but to

---

[1] Charlotte, *née* Brydges.
[2] Originally of Mme de Sévigné.

those who see at a distance there appears no chance
of it. Dr. Parry does not want to keep Lady B. at Bath
when she can once move. That is lucky. You will see
poor Mr. Evelyn's death. Since I wrote last, my 2^d
Edit.[1] has stared me in the face. Mary tells me that
Eliza[2] means to buy it. I wish she may. It can hardly
depend upon any more Fyfield Estates. I cannot help
hoping that *many* will feel themselves obliged to buy
it. I shall not mind imagining it a disagreable Duty to
them, so as they do it. Mary heard before she left
home, that it was very much admired at Cheltenham,
& that it was given to Miss Hamilton. It is pleasant to
have such a respectable Writer named. I cannot tire
you I am sure on this subject, or I would apologise.
What weather! & what news! We have enough to do
to admire them both. I hope you derive your full share
of enjoyment from each.

I have extended my Lights and increased my acquaintance a good deal within these two days. Lady
Honeywood, you know; I did not sit near enough to be
a perfect Judge, but I thought her extremely pretty &
her manners have all the recommendations of ease &
goodhumour & unaffectedness; & going about with 4
Horses, & nicely dressed herself—she is altogether a
perfect sort of Woman. Oh! & I saw Mr. Gipps last
night—the useful Mr. Gipps, whose attentions came
in as acceptably to us in handing us to the Carriage, for
want of a better Man, as they did to Emma Plumptre.
I thought him rather a good-looking little Man. I long
for your Letter tomorrow, particularly that I may know
my fate as to London. My first wish is that Henry sh^d
really chuse what he likes best; I shall certainly not be
sorry if he does not want me. Morning church to-

---

[1] Of *Sense and Sensibility*.   [2] Fowle.

morrow. I shall come back with impatient feelings.
The Sherers are gone, but the Pagets are not come, we
shall therefore have Mr. S. again. Mr. Paget acts like
an unsteady Man. Dr. Mant however gives him a very
good Character; what is wrong is to be imputed to the
Lady. I dare say the House likes Female Government.
I have a nice long Black & red Letter from Charles,
but not communicating much that I did not know.
There is some chance of a good Ball next week, as far
as Females go. Lady Bridges may perhaps be there
with some Knatchbulls. Mrs. Harrison perhaps with
Miss Oxenden & the Miss Papillons—& if Mrs. Harrison, then Lady Fagg will come. The shades of Evening
are descending & I resume my interesting Narrative.
Sir Brook & my Brother came back about 4, & Sir
Brook almost immediately set forward again for Goodnestone. We are to have Edwd B. tomorrow, to pay us
another Sunday's visit—the last, for more reasons than
one; they all come home on the same day that we go.
The Deedes' do not come till Tuesday. Sophia is to be
the Comer. She is a disputable Beauty that I want
much to see. Lady Eliz. Hatton & Anna-maria called
here this morn^g; Yes, they called,—but I do not think
I can say anything more about them. They came &
they sat & they went. *Sunday.*—Dearest Henry! What
a turn he has for being ill! & what a thing Bile is!
This attack has probably been brought on in part by
his previous confinement & anxiety; but however it
came, I hope it is going fast, & that you will be able
to send a very good account of him on Tuesday. As I
hear on Wednesday, of course I shall not expect to
hear again on friday. Perhaps a Letter to Wrotham
would not have an ill effect. We are to be off on Saturday before the Post comes in, as Edward takes his own

Horses all the way. He talks of 9 o'clock. We shall bait
at Lenham. Excellent sweetness of you to send me
such a nice long Letter; it made its appearance, with
one from my Mother, soon after I & my impatient feelings walked in. How glad I am that I did what I did!
I was only afraid that *you* might think the offer super-
fluous, but you have set my heart at ease. Tell Henry
that I *will* stay with him, let it be ever so disagreable
to him. Oh! dear me!—I have not time or paper for
half that I want to say. There have been two Letters
from Oxford, one from George yesterday. They got
there very safely, Edw[d1] two hours behind the Coach,
having lost his way in leaving London. George writes
cheerfully & quietly—hopes to have Utterson's rooms
soon, went to Lecture on wednesday, states some of
his expences, and concludes with saying, 'I am afraid
I shall be poor.' I am glad he thinks about it so soon.
I beleive there is no private Tutor yet chosen, but my
Brother is to hear from Edw[d] on the subject shortly.—
You, & Mrs. H.[2] & Catherine & Alethea going about
together in Henry's carriage seeing sights! I am not
used to the idea of it yet. All that you are to see of
Streatham, seen already! Your Streatham & my Bookham may go hang. The prospect of being taken down
to Chawton by Henry, perfects the plan to me. I was
in hopes of your seeing some illuminations, & you *have*
seen them. 'I thought you would came, and you *did*
came.'[3] I am sorry *he* is not to *came* from the Baltic
sooner. Poor Mary[4]! My Brother has a Letter from
Louisa[5] today, of an unwelcome nature; they are to

---

[1] Edward's boys, now at St. John's College, Oxford.
[2] Mrs. Heathcote, *née* Bigg, and her sister Alethea, staying with their
sister Mrs. Hill at Streatham.
[3] Quoted from Frank as a child; see Letter 68.
[4] Mrs. F. A.   [5] Bridges.

spend the winter at Bath. It was just decided on. Dr. Parry wished it, not from thinking the Water necessary to Lady B. but that he might be better able to judge how far his Treatment of her, which is totally different from anything she had been used to—is right; & I suppose he will not mind having a few more of her Ladyship's guineas. His system is a Lowering one. He took twelve ounces of Blood from her when the Gout appeared, & forbids wine &c. Hitherto, the plan agrees with her. *She* is very well satisfied to stay, but it is a sore disappointment to Louisa & Fanny.

The H. Bridges leave them on Tuesday, & they mean to move into a smaller House. You may guess how Edward feels. There can be no doubt of his going to Bath now; I should not wonder if he brought Fanny Cage back with him.—You shall hear from me once more, some day or other.

Yours very affec:ly   J. A.

We do not like Mr. Hampson's scheme.

92. *To Cassandra Austen. Wednesday* 2 *March* ⟨1814⟩

Henrietta St Wednesday March 2d

My dear Cassandra

You were wrong in thinking of us at Guildford last night: we were at Cobham. On reaching G. we found that John and the horses were gone on. We therefore did no more there than we had done at Farnham—sit in the carriage while fresh horses were put in, and proceeded directly to Cobham, which we reached by seven, and about eight were sitting down to a very nice roast fowl, &c. We had altogether a very good journey, and everything at Cobham was comfortable. I could not pay Mr. Herington! That was the only alas! of the business. I shall therefore return his bill, and my mother's 2*l*., that you may try your luck. We did not begin reading till Bentley Green. Henry's approbation hitherto is even equal to my wishes. He says it is very different from the other two, but does not appear to think it at all inferior. He has only married Mrs. R. I am afraid he has gone through the most entertaining part. He took to Lady B. and Mrs. N. most kindly, and gives great praise to the drawing of the characters. He understands them all, likes Fanny, and, I think, foresees how it will all be. I finished the 'Heroine'[1] last night, and was very much amused by it. I wonder James did not like it better. It diverted me exceedingly. We went to bed at ten. I was very tired, but slept to a miracle, and am lovely to-day, and at present Henry seems to have no complaint. We left Cobham at half-past eight, stopped to bait and breakfast at Kingston, and were in this house considerably before two quite in the style of Mr. Knight. Nice smiling Mr. Barlowe met us at the door and, in reply to enquiries after news, said that peace was generally expected. I have taken possession of my bedroom, unpacked my bandbox, sent Miss P.'s two letters to the twopenny post, been visited by M^d B.[2] and am now writing by myself at the new table in the front room. It is snowing. We had some snowstorms yesterday, and a smart frost at night, which gave us a hard road from Cobham to Kingston; but as it was then getting dirty and heavy, Henry had a pair of leaders put on from the latter place to the bottom of Sloane St. His own horses, therefore, cannot have had hard work. I watched for *veils* as we drove

---

[1] By E. S. Barrett.
[2] Bigeon, Henry's French servant.

through the streets, and had the pleasure of seeing several upon vulgar heads. And now, how do you all do?—you in particular, after the worry of yesterday and the day before. I hope Martha had a pleasant visit again, and that you and my mother could eat your beef-pudding. Depend upon my thinking of the chimney-sweeper as soon as I wake tomorrow. Places are secured at Drury Lane for Saturday, but so great is the rage for seeing Kean that only a third and fourth row could be got; as it is in a front box, however, I hope we shall do pretty well—Shylock, a good play for Fanny—she cannot be much affected, I think. Mrs. Perigord has just been here & I have paid her a shilling for the willow. She tells me that we owe her master for the silk-dyeing. My poor old muslin has never been dyed yet. It has been promised to be done several times. What wicked people dyers are. They begin with dipping their own souls in scarlet sin. Tell my mother that my £6. 15. was duly received, but placed to my account instead of hers, & I have just signed a something which makes it over to her. It is evening; we have drank tea, and I have torn through the third vol. of the 'Heroine.' I do not think it falls off. It is a delightful burlesque, particularly on the Radcliffe style. Henry is going on with 'Mansfield Park.' He admires H. Crawford: I mean properly, as a clever, pleasant man. I tell you all the good I can, as I know how much you will enjoy it. John Warren and his wife are invited to dine here, and to name their own day in the next fortnight. I do not expect them to come. Wyndham Knatchbull is to be asked for Sunday and if he is cruel enough to consent, somebody must be contrived to meet him. We hear that Mr. Keen is more admired than ever. The two vacant places of our two rows are likely to be filled

by Mr. Tilson and his brother General Chownes. I shall
be ready to laugh at the sight of Frederick again. It
seems settled that I have the carriage on Friday to pay
visits, I have therefore little doubt of being able to get
to Miss Hares. I am to call upon Miss Spencer: Funny
me! There are no good places to be got in Drury Lane
for the next fortnight; but Henry means to secure some
for Saturday fortnight when you are reckoned upon.
I wonder what worse thing than Sarah Mitchell you
are forced upon by this time! Give my love to little
Cassandra![1] I hope she found my Bed comfortable last
night and has not filled it with fleas. I have seen nobody
in London yet with such a long chin as Dr. Syntax, nor
anybody quite so large as Gogmagoglicus.

Yours affec^{tely}

J. Austen

Thursday. My Trunk did not come last night—I
suppose it will this morning—if not I must borrow
stockings & buy shoes & gloves for my visit. I was
foolish not to provide better against such a possibility.
I have great hope however that writing about it in this
way will bring the trunk presently.

93. *To Cassandra Austen.* *Sunday* 5 *March* ⟨1814⟩

Henrietta St Saturday March 5.

My dear Cassandra

Do not be angry with me for beginning another
Letter to you. I have read the Corsair, mended my
petticoat, & have nothing else to do.—Getting out is
impossible. It is a nasty day for everybody. Edward's

---

[1] 'Cassy', Charles's daughter, who was much at Chawton. Frank's
Cassandra was still an infant.

spirits will be wanting Sunshine, & here is nothing but Thickness & Sleet; and tho' these two rooms are delightfully warm I fancy it is very cold abroad.—Young Wyndham[1] accepts the Invitation. He is such a nice, gentlemanlike, unaffected sort of young Man, that I think he may do for Fanny; has a sensible, quiet look which one likes. Our fate with Mrs. L. and Miss E.[2] is fixed for this day senight. A civil note is come from Miss H. Moore, to apologise for not returning my visit today & ask us to join a small party this Even^g. Thank ye, but we shall be better engaged. I was speaking to M^de B. this morn^g about a boil'd Loaf, when it appeared that her Master has no raspberry Jam; *She* has some, which of course she is determined he shall have; but cannot you bring him a pot when you come?

Sunday.—I find a little time before breakfast for writing. It was considerably past 4 when they arrived yesterday; the roads were so very bad!—as it was, they had 4 Horses from Cranford Bridge. Fanny was miserably cold at first, but they both seem well. No possibility of Edwd.'s writing. His opinion however inclines *against* a second prosecution; he thinks it would be a vindictive measure. He might think differently perhaps on the spot.—But things must take their chance.

We were quite satisfied with Kean. I cannot imagine better acting; but the part was too short, & excepting him and Miss Smith, & *she* did not quite answer my expectation, the parts were ill filled & the Play heavy. We were too much tired to stay for the whole of Illusion (Nour-jahad) which has 3 acts; there is a great deal of

---

[1] Knatchbull. Fanny did better in marrying his elder brother, who became Sir Edward.

[2] Latouche and East.

finery & dancing in it, but I think little merit. Elliston
was Nour-jahad, but it is a solemn sort of part, not at
all calculated for his powers. There was nothing of the
best Elliston about him. I might not have known him,
but for his voice.—A grand thought has struck me as to
our Gowns. This 6 weeks mourning[1] makes so great a
difference that I shall not go to Miss Hare, till you can
come & help chuse yourself; unless you particularly
wish the contrary. It may be hardly worth while perhaps to have the Gowns so expensively made up; we
may buy a cap or a *veil* instead; but we can talk more
of this together. Henry is just come down, he seems
well, his cold does not increase. I expected to have
found Edward seated at a table writing to Louisa, but
I was first. Fanny I left fast asleep. She was doing
about last night, when *I* went to sleep, a little after
one. I am most happy to find there were but *five* shirts.
She thanks you for your note, & reproaches herself for
not having written to you, but I assure her there was
no occasion. The accounts are not capital of Lady B.
Upon the whole I beleive Fanny liked Bath very well.
They were only out three Even^gs, to one Play & each
of the Rooms; Walked about a good deal, & saw a
good deal of the Harrisons & Wildmans. All the
Bridgeses are likely to come away together, & Louisa
will probably turn off at Dartford to go to Harriot.
Edward is quite ⟨*about five words cut out*⟩. Now we
are come from Church, & all going to write. Almost
everybody was in mourning last night, but my brown
gown did very well. Genl: Chowne was introduced
to me; he has not much remains of Frederick. This
young Wyndham does not come after all; a very long
& very civil note of excuse is arrived. It makes one

[1] For the Queen's brother.

moralize upon the ups & downs of this Life. I have determined to trim my lilac sarsenet with black sattin ribbon just as my China Crape is, 6ᵈ width at the bottom, 3ᵈ or 4ᵈ at top. Ribbon trimmings are all the fashion at Bath, & I dare say the fashions of the two places are alike enough in that point, to content *me*. With this addition it will be a very useful gown, happy to go anywhere. Henry has this moment said that he likes my M. P. better & better; he is in the 3ᵈ volume. I beleive *now* he has changed his mind as to foreseeing the end; he said yesterday at least, that he defied anybody to say whether H. C.[1] would be reformed, or would forget Fanny in a fortnight. I shall like to see Kean again excessively, & to see him with you too; it appeared to me as if there were no fault in him anywhere; & in his scene with Tubal there was exquisite acting. Edward has had a correspondence with Mr. Wickham on the Baigent business, & has been shewing me some Letters enclosed by Mr. W. from a friend of his, a Lawyer, whom he had consulted about it, & whose opinion is *for* the prosecution for assault, supposing the Boy is acquitted on the first, which he rather expects.—Excellent Letters; & I am sure he must be an excellent Man. They are such thinking, clear, considerate Letters as Frank might have written. I long to know who he is, but the name is always torn off. He was consulted only as a friend. When Edwᵈ gave me *his* opinion against the 2ᵈ prosecution, he had not read this Letter, which was waiting for him here. Mr. W. is to be on the Grand Jury. This business must hasten an Intimacy between his family & my Brother's. Fanny cannot answer your question about button holes till she gets home. I have never told you, but soon after

[1] Henry Crawford.

159

Henry & I began our Journey, he said, talking of Yours, that he sh^d desire you to come post at his expence, & added something of the Carriage meeting you at Kingston. He has said nothing about it since. Now I have just read Mr. Wickham's Letter, by which it appears that the Letters of his friend were sent to my Brother quite confidentially—therefore do'nt tell. By his expression, this friend must be one of the Judges.

A cold day, but bright and clean. I am afraid your planting can hardly have begun. I am sorry to hear that there has been a rise in tea. I do not mean to pay Twining till later in the day, when we may order a fresh supply. I long to know something of the Mead— & how you are off for a Cook. *Monday.* Here's a day! —The Ground covered with snow! What is to become of us? We were to have walked out early to near shops, & had the Carriage for the more distant. Mr. Richard Snow is dreadfully fond of us. I dare say he has stretched himself out at Chawton too. Fanny & I went into the Park yesterday & drove about & were very much entertained; and our Dinner & Even^g went off very well. Messrs. J. Plumptre and J. Wildman called while we were out; & we had a glimpse of them both & of G. Hatton too in the Park. *I* could not produce a single acquaintance. By a little convenient Listening, I now know that Henry wishes to go to G^m for a few days before Easter, & has indeed promised to do it. This being the case, there can be no time for your remaining in London after your return from Adlestrop. You must not put off your coming therefore; and it occurs to me that instead of my coming here again from Streatham, it will be better for you to join me there. It is a great comfort to have got at the truth.

Henry finds he cannot set off for Oxfordshire before
the Wednes^y which will be ye 23^d; but we shall not
have too many days together here previously. I shall
write to Catherine[1] very soon. Well, we have been out,
as far as Coventry S^t—; Edwd escorted us there &
back to Newtons, where he left us, & I brought Fanny
safe home. It was snowing the whole time. We have
given up all idea of the Carriage. Edward & Fanny
stay another day; & both seem very well pleased to
do so. Our visit to the Spencers is of course put off.
Edwd heard from Louisa this morn^g. Her Mother does
not get better, & Dr. Parry talks of her beginning the
Waters again; this will be keeping them longer in Bath,
and of course is not palateable. You cannot think how
much my Ermine Tippet is admired both by Father &
Daughter. It was a noble Gift. Perhaps you have not
heard that Edward has a good chance of escaping his
Lawsuit. His opponent knocks under. The terms of
agreement are not quite settled.[2] We are to see 'the
Devil to pay' to night. I expect to be very much
amused. Excepting Miss Stephens, I daresay Artaxerxes
will be very tiresome. A great many pretty Caps in the
Windows of Cranbourn Alley! I hope when you come,
we shall both be tempted. I have been ruining myself
in black sattin ribbon with a proper perl edge; & now
I am trying to draw it up into kind of roses, instead of
putting it in plain double plaits. Tuesday. My dearest
Cassandra in ever so many hurries I acknowledge the
receipt of your Letter last night, just before we set off
for Covent Garden. I have no Mourning come, but it
does not signify. This very moment has Rich^d put it

[1] Hill.
[2] In the event he paid a large sum to a rival claimant for Chawton
Manor.

on the Table. I have torn it open & read your note.
Thank you, thank you, thank you.

Edwd is amazed at the 64 Trees. He desires his Love
& gives you notice of the arrival of a Study Table for
himself. It ought to be at Chawton this week. He begs
you to be so good as to have it enquired for, & fetched
by the Cart; but wishes it not to be unpacked till he
is on the spot himself. It may be put in the Hall. Well,
Mr. Hampson dined here & all that. I was very tired
of Artaxerxes, highly amused with the Farce, & in an
inferior way with the Pantomime that followed. Mr. J.
Plumptre joined in the latter part of the Even^g—
walked home with us, ate some soup, & is very earnest
for our going to Cov: Gar: again to night to see Miss
Stephens in the Farmers Wife. He is to try for a Box.
I do not particularly wish him to succeed. I have had
enough for the present. Henry dines to day with Mr.
Spencer.

Yours very affec^ly   J. Austen

98. *To Anna Austen. Wednesday* 10 *Aug.* ⟨1814⟩

Chawton Wednesday Aug: 10

My dear Anna

I am quite ashamed to find that I have never
answered some questions of yours in a former note.
I kept the note on purpose to refer to it at a proper
time, & then forgot it. I like the name 'Which is the
Heroine?' very well, & I dare say shall grow to like it
very much in time—but 'Enthusiasm' was something
so very superior that every common Title must appear
to disadvantage. I am not sensible of any Blunders
about Dawlish. The Library was particularly pitiful &

wretched 12 years ago, & not likely to have anybody's publication. There is no such Title as Desborough— either among the Dukes, Marquisses, Earls, Viscounts or Barons. These were your enquiries. I will now thank you for your Envelope, received this morning. I hope Mr W. D. will come. I can readily imagine Mrs H. D.[1] may be very like a profligate young Lord—I dare say the likeness will be 'beyond every thing.' Your Aunt Cass: is as well pleased with St. Julian as ever. I am delighted with the idea of seeing Progillian again.

Wednesday 17. We have just finished the 1st of the 3 Books I had the pleasure of receiving yesterday; I read it aloud—& we are all very much amused, & like the work quite as well as ever. I depend upon getting through another book before dinner, but there is really a great deal of respectable reading in your 48 Pages. I was an hour about it. I have no doubt that 6 will make a very good sized volume. You must be quite pleased to have accomplished so much. I like Lord P. & his Brother very much; I am only afraid that Lord P.—'s good nature will make most people like him better than he deserves. The whole Portman Family are very good—& Lady Anne, who was your great dread, you have succeeded particularly well with. Bell Griffin is just what she should be. My Corrections have not been more important than before; here & there, we have thought the sense might be expressed in fewer words—and I have scratched out Sir Tho: from walking with the other Men to the Stables &c the very day after his breaking his arm—for though I find your Papa *did* walk out immediately after *his* arm was set, I think it can be so little usual as to *appear* unnatural in a book—& it does not seem to be material that Sir

[1] William and Harry Digweed.

Tho: should go with them. Lyme will not do. Lyme is towards 40 miles distance from Dawlish & would not be talked of there. I have put Starcross instead. If you prefer *Exeter*, that must be always safe. I have also scratched out the Introduction between Lord P. & his Brother, & Mr. Griffin. A Country Surgeon (dont tell Mr. C. Lyford) would not be introduced to Men of their rank. And when Mr. Portman is first brought in, he w^d not be introduced as *the Honble. That* distinction is never mentioned at such times; at least I beleive not. Now, we have finished the 2^d book—or rather the 5th—I *do* think you had better omit Lady Helena's post-script; to those who are acquainted with P. & P. it will seem an Imitation. And your Aunt C. & I both recommend your making a little alteration in the last scene between Devereux F. and Lady Clanmurray & her Daughter. We think they press him too much—more than sensible Women or well-bred Women would do. *Lady C.* at least, should have discretion enough to be sooner satisfied with his determination of not going with them. I am very much pleased with Egerton as yet. I did not expect to like him, but I do; & Susan is a very nice little animated Creature—but St. Julian is the delight of one's Life. He is quite interesting. The whole of his Break-off with Lady H. is very well done.

Yes—Russel Square is a very proper distance from Berkeley S^t. We are reading the last book. They must be *two* days going from Dawlish to Bath; They are nearly 100 miles apart.

Thursday. We finished it last night, after our return from drinking tea at the G^t House. The last chapter does not please us quite so well, we do not thoroughly like the *Play*; perhaps from having had too much of

Plays[1] in that way lately. And we think you had better not leave England. Let the Portmans go to Ireland, but as you know nothing of the Manners there, you had better not go with them. You will be in danger of giving false representations. Stick to Bath & the Foresters. There you will be quite at home. Your Aunt C. does not like desultory novels, & is rather fearful yours will be too much so, that there will be too frequent a change from one set of people to another, & that circumstances will be sometimes introduced of apparent consequence, which will lead to nothing. It will not be so great an objection to *me*, if it does. I allow much more Latitude than she does—& think Nature and Spirit cover many sins of a wandering story —and People in general do not care so much about it—for your comfort.

I should like to have had more of Devereux. I do not feel enough acquainted with him. You were afraid of meddling with him I dare say. I like your sketch of Lord Clanmurray, and your picture of the two poor young girls enjoyments is very good. I have not yet noticed St. Julian's serious conversation with Cecilia, but I liked it exceedingly; what he says about the madness of otherwise sensible Women, on the subject of their Daughters coming out, is worth it's weight in gold. I do not see that the language sinks. Pray go on.

Yours very affec:^{ly}   J. Austen

Twice you have put Dorsetshire for Devonshire. I have altered it. Mr Griffin must have lived in Devonshire; Dawlish is half way down the County.

---

[1] In *Mansfield Park*.

99.1. *To Martha Lloyd. Friday 2 Sept.* 1814.

23 Hans Place Friday Sepr. 2^d.

My dear Martha

The prospect of a long quiet morning determines
me to write to you. I have been often thinking of it
before, but without being quite able to do it—and
You are too busy, too happy and too *rich* I hope, to
care much for Letters. It gave me very great pleasure
to hear that your money was paid, it must have been
a circumstance to increase every enjoyment you can
have had with your friends—and altogether I think
you must be spending your time most comfortably.
The weather can hardly have incommoded you by it's
heat. We have had many evenings here so cold, that
I was sure there must be fires in the Country. How
many alterations you must perceive in Bath![1] and how
many People and Things gone by must be recurring to
you! I hope you will see Clifton. Henry takes me home
tomorrow; I rather expect at least to be at Chawton
before night, tho' it may not be till early on Sunday,
as we shall lengthen the Journey by going round by
Sunning Hill; his favourite Mrs Crutchley lives there,
and he wants to introduce me to her. We offered a
visit in our way, to the Birches, but they cannot receive
us, which is a disappointment. He comes back again
on Wednesday, and perhaps brings James with him;
so it was settled, when James was here; he wants to
see Scarman again, as his Gums last week were not in
a proper state for Scarman's operations. I cannot tell
how much of all this may be known to you already.
I shall have spent my 12 days here very pleasantly, but

[1] Martha was at Bath with the Deans Dundases.

166

with not much to tell of them; two or three *very* little
Dinner-parties at home, some delightful Drives in the
Curricle, and quiet Tea-drinkings with the Tilsons, has
been the sum of my doings. I have seen no old acquaintances I think, but Mr Hampson. Henry met with
Sir Brook and Lady Bridges by chance, and they were
to have dined with us yesterday, had they remained
in Town. I am amused by the present style of female
dress; the coloured petticoats with braces over the
white Spencers and enormous Bonnets upon the full
stretch, are quite entertaining. It seems to me a more
marked *change* than one has lately seen. Long sleeves
appear universal, even as *Dress*, the Waists short, and
as far as I have been able to judge, the Bosom covered.
I was at a little party last night at Mrs Latouche's,
where dress is a good deal attended to, and these are
my observations from it. Petticoats short, and generally, tho' not always, flounced. The broad-straps belonging to the Gown or Boddice, which cross the front
of the Waist, over white, have a very pretty effect I
think. I have seen West's famous Painting, and prefer
it to anything of the kind I ever saw before. I do not
know that it *is* reckoned superior to his 'Healing in the
Temple'. but it has gratified *me* much more, and indeed
is the first representation of our Saviour which ever at
all contented me. 'His Rejection by the Elders', is the
subject. I want to have You and Cassandra see it. I am
extremely pleased with this new House of Henry's, it
is everything that could be wished for him, and I have
only to hope he will continue to like it as well as he
does now, and not be looking out for anything better.
He is in very comfortable health; he has not been so
well, he says, for a twelvemonth. *His* view, and the
view of those he mixes with, of Politics, is not chearful

—with regard to an American war I mean; they consider it as certain, and as what is to ruin us. The 〈   〉 cannot be conquered, and we shall only be teaching them the skill in War which they may now want. We are to make them good Sailors and Soldiers, and gain nothing ourselves. If we *are* to be ruined, it cannot be helped—but I place my hope of better things on a claim to the protection of Heaven, as a Religious Nation, a Nation in spite of much Evil improving in Religion, which I cannot beleive the Americans to possess. However this may be, Mr Barlowe is to dine with us today, and I am in some hope of getting Egerton's[1] account before I go away—so we will enjoy ourselves as long as we can. My Aunt does not seem pleased with Capt. and Mrs D. D. for taking a House in Bath, I was afraid she would not like it, but I 〈   〉 do. When I get home, I shall hear 〈more. I sh〉all be very happy to find myself at 〈   〉 Miss Benn 〈   〉 to hear Mrs Digweed's goodhumoured communications. The language of London is flat; it wants her phrase. Dear me! I wonder if you have seen Miss Irvine! At this time of year, she is more likely to be out of Bath than in.

One of our afternoon drives was to Streatham, where I had the pleasure of seeing Mrs Hill as well and comfortable as usual; but there is a melancholy disproportion between the Papa and the little Children.[2]—She told me that the Audrys have taken that sweet St. Bo〈niface〉 hoped he 〈   〉 Ventnor 〈*two lines missing, with the conclusion*〉.

Pray give my best 〈com〉pts. to your Friends. I have

---

[1] Not, I think, Henry's friend, but J A's first publisher, who would owe her an *account* for *S. and S.* and *M.P.*

[2] See p. 92.

not forgotten their parti⟨cular⟩ claim to my Gratitude
as an Author. We have j⟨ust learn⟩ed that Mʳˢ C.
Austen is safe in bed with a Girl.—It happened on
board, a fortnight before it was expected.

100. *To Anna Austen.* ⟨*Friday*⟩ 9 *Sept.* ⟨1814⟩

Chawton Sept: 9.
My dear Anna
    We have been very much amused by your 3 books,
but I have a good many criticisms to make—more than
you will like. We are not satisfied with Mrs. F.'s settling herself as Tenant & near Neighbour to such a Man
as Sir T. H. without having some other inducement to
go there; she ought to have some friend living thereabouts to tempt her. A woman, going with two girls
just growing up, into a Neighbourhood where she
knows nobody but one Man, of not very good character, is an awkwardness which so prudent a woman as
Mrs. F. would not be likely to fall into. Remember,
she is very prudent; you must not let her act inconsis-
tently. Give her a friend, & let that friend be invited
to meet her at the Priory, & we shall have no objection
to her dining there as she does; but otherwise, a woman
in her situation would hardly go there, before she had
been visited by other Families. I like the scene itself,
the Miss Lesleys, Lady Anne, & the Music, very much.
Lesley *is* a noble name. Sir T. H. you always do very
well; I have only taken the liberty of expunging one
phrase of his, which would not be allowable. 'Bless my
Heart'—It is too familiar & inelegant. Your G. M. is
more disturbed at Mrs. F.'s not returning the Egertons
visit sooner, than anything else. They ought to have
called at the Parsonage before Sunday. You describe

a sweet place, but your descriptions are often more minute than will be liked. You give too many particulars of right hand & left. Mrs. F. is not careful enough of Susan's health; Susan ought not to be walking out so soon after Heavy rains, taking long walks in the dirt. An anxious Mother would not suffer it. I like your Susan very much indeed, she is a sweet creature, her playfulness of fancy is very delightful. I like her as she is *now* exceedingly, but I am not so well satisfied with her behaviour to George R. At first she seemed all over attachment & feeling, & afterwards to have none at all; she is so extremely composed at the Ball, & so well-satisfied apparently with Mr. Morgan. She seems to have changed her Character. You are now collecting your People delightfully, getting them exactly into such a spot as is the delight of my life; 3 or 4 Families in a Country Village is the very thing to work on—& I hope you will write a great deal more, & make full use of them while they are so very favourably arranged. You are but *now* coming to the heart & beauty of your book; till the heroine grows up, the fun must be imperfect—but I expect a great deal of entertainment from the next 3 or 4 books, & I hope you will not resent these remarks by sending me no more. We like the Egertons very well, we see no Blue Pantaloons, or Cocks & Hens; there is nothing to *enchant* one certainly in Mr. L. L—but we make no objection to him, & his inclination to like Susan is pleasing. The Sister is a good contrast—but the name of Rachael is as much as I can bear. They are not so much like the Papillons as I expected. Your last chapter is very entertaining—the conversation on Genius &c. Mr. St. J. & Susan both talk in character & very well. In some former parts, Cecilia is perhaps a little too solemn & good, but

upon the whole, her disposition is very well opposed
to Susan's—her want of Imagination is very natural.
I wish you could make Mrs. F. talk more, but she must
be difficult to manage & make entertaining, because
there is so much good common sence & propriety about
her that nothing can be very *broad*. Her Economy and
her Ambition must not be staring. The Papers left by
Mrs. Fisher is very good. Of course, one guesses something. I hope when you have written a great deal more
you will be equal to scratching out some of the past.
The scene with Mrs. Mellish, I should condemn; it is
prosy & nothing to the purpose—& indeed, the more
you can find in your heart to curtail between Dawlish
& Newton Priors, the better I think it will be. One
does not care for girls till they are grown up. Your
Aunt C. quite enters into the exquisiteness of that
name. Newton Priors is really a Nonpareil. Milton w^d
have given his eyes to have thought of it. Is not the
Cottage taken from Tollard Royal?

Sunday 18th—I am very glad dear Anna, that I
wrote as I did before this sad Event[1] occurred. I have
now only to add that your G.Mama does not seem the
worse now for the shock. I shall be very happy to
receive more of your work, if more is ready; & you
write so fast, that I have great hopes Mr. D.[2] will come
freighted back with such a Cargo as not all his Hops
or his Sheep could equal the value of.

Your Grandmama desires me to say that she will
have finished your Shoes tomorrow & thinks they will
look very well; and that she depends upon seeing you,
as you promise, before you quit the Country, & hopes
you will give her more than a day. Yrs affec^ly

J. Austen

[1] The death of Charles Austen's wife.   [2] Digweed.

103. *To Fanny Knight. Friday* 18 *Nov* ⟨1814⟩

Chawton Nov: 18.—Friday

I feel quite as doubtful as you could be my dearest
Fanny as to *when* my Letter may be finished, for I can
command very little quiet time at present, but yet I
must begin, for I know you will be glad to hear as soon
as possible, & I really am impatient myself to be writing
something on so very interesting a subject, though I
have no hope of writing anything to the purpose. I shall
do very little more I dare say than say over again, what
you have said before. I was certainly a good deal surprised *at first*—as I had no suspicion of any change in
your feelings, and I have no scruple in saying that you
cannot be in Love. My dear Fanny, I am ready to
laugh at the idea—and yet it is no laughing matter to
have had you so mistaken as to your own feelings—
And with all my heart I wish I had cautioned you on
that point when first you spoke to me; but tho' I did
not think you then so *much* in love as you thought
yourself, I did consider you as being attached in a
degree—quite sufficiently for happiness, as I had no
doubt it would increase with opportunity. And from
the time of our being in London together, I thought
you really very much in love—But you certainly are
not at all—there is no concealing it. What strange
creatures we are! It seems as if your being secure of
him (as you say yourself) had made you Indifferent.—
There was a little disgust I suspect, at the Races—& I
do not wonder at it. His expressions there would not
do for one who had rather more Acuteness, Penetra-
tion & Taste, than Love, which was your case. And
yet, after all, I *am* surprised that the change in your
feelings should be so great. He is, just what he ever

172

was, only more evidently & uniformly devoted to *you*.
This is all the difference. How shall we account for it?
My dearest Fanny, I am writing what will not be of
the smallest use to you. I am feeling differently every
moment, & shall not be able to suggest a single thing
that can assist your Mind. I could lament in one sentence & laugh in the next, but as to Opinion or Counsel
I am sure none will be extracted worth having from
this Letter. I read yours through the very even^g I
received it—getting away by myself—I could not bear
to leave off, when I had once begun. I was full of
curiosity & concern. Luckily your Aunt C. dined at the
other house, therefore I had not to manœuvre away
from *her*; & as to anybody else, I do not care. Poor
dear Mr. J. P.![1]—Oh! dear Fanny, your mistake has
been one that thousands of women fall into. He was
the *first* young Man who attached himself to you. That
was the charm, & most powerful it is. Among the
multitudes however that make the same mistake with
yourself, there can be few indeed who have so little
reason to regret it; *his* Character and *his* attachment
leave you nothing to be ashamed of. Upon the whole,
what is to be done? You certainly *have* encouraged
him to such a point as to make him feel almost secure
of you—you have no inclination for any other person
—His situation in life, family, friends, & above all his
character—his uncommonly amiable mind, strict principles, just notions, good habits—*all* that *you* know so
well how to value, *All* that really is of the first importance—everything of this nature pleads his cause most
strongly. You have no doubt of his having superior
Abilities—he has proved it at the University—he is I
dare say such a scholar as your agreable, idle Brothers

[1] Plumtre.

173

would ill bear a comparison with. Oh! my dear Fanny, the more I write about him, the warmer my feelings become, the more strongly I feel the sterling worth of such a young Man & the desirableness of your growing in love with him again. I recommend this most thoroughly. There *are* such beings in the World perhaps, one in a Thousand, as the Creature You and I should think perfection, Where Grace & Spirit are united to Worth, where the Manners are equal to the Heart & Understanding, but such a person may not come in your way, or if he does, he may not be the eldest son of a Man of Fortune, the Brother of your particular friend, & belonging to your own County. Think of all this Fanny. Mr. J. P. has advantages which do not often meet in one person. His only fault indeed seems Modesty. If he were less modest, he would be more agreable, speak louder & look Impudenter; and is not it a fine Character of which Modesty is the only defect? I have no doubt that he will get more lively & more like yourselves as he is more with you; he will catch your ways if he belongs to you. And as to there being any objection from his *Goodness*, from the danger of his becoming even Evangelical, I cannot admit *that*. I am by no means convinced that we ought not all to be Evangelicals, & am at least persuaded that they who are so from Reason and Feeling, must be happiest & safest. Do not be frightened from the connection by your Brothers having most wit. Wisdom is better than Wit, & in the long run will certainly have the laugh on her side; & don't be frightened by the idea of his acting more strictly up to the precepts of the New Testament than others. And now, my dear Fanny, having written so much on one side of the question, I shall turn round & entreat you not to commit

yourself farther, & not to think of accepting him unless
you really do like him. Anything is to be preferred or
endured rather than marrying without Affection; and
if his deficiencies of Manner &c &c strike you more
than all his good qualities, if you continue to think
strongly of them, give him up at once. Things are now
in such a state, that you must resolve upon one or the
other, either to allow him to go on as he has done, or
whenever you are together behave with a coldness
which may convince him that he has been deceiving
himself. I have no doubt of his suffering a good deal
for a time, a great deal, when he feels that he must
give you up;—but it is no creed of mine, as you must
be well aware, that such sort of Disappointments kill
anybody. Your sending the Music was an admirable
Device, it made everything easy, & I do not know how
I could have accounted for the parcel otherwise; for
tho' your dear Papa most conscientiously hunted about
till he found me alone in the Din^g-parlour, your Aunt
C. had seen that he *had* a parcel to deliver. As it was
however, I do not think anything was suspected. We
have heard nothing fresh from Anna. I trust she is very
comfortable in her new home. Her Letters have been
very sensible & satisfactory, with no *parade* of happiness, which I liked them the better for. I have often
known young married Women write in a way I did not
like, in that respect.

You will be glad to hear that the first Edit: of M. P.
is all sold. Your Uncle Henry is rather wanting me to
come to Town, to settle about a 2^d Edit: but as I could
not very conveniently leave home now, I have written
him my Will and pleasure, & unless he still urges it,
shall not go. I am very greedy & want to make the
most of it; but as you are much above caring about

175

money, I shall not plague you with any particulars. The pleasures of Vanity are more within your comprehension, & you will enter into mine, at receiving the *praise* which every now & then comes to me, through some channel or other.

Saturday.—Mr. Palmer[1] spent yesterday with us, & is gone off with Cassy this morn[g]. We have been expecting Miss Lloyd the last two days, & feel sure of her today. Mr. Knight and Mr. Edw: Knight are to dine with us. And on Monday they are to dine with us again, accompanied by their respectable Host & Hostess.[2] *Sunday.* Your Papa had given me messages to you, but they are unnecessary, as he writes by this post to Aunt Louisa. We had a pleasant party yesterday, at least *we* found it so. It is delightful to see him so chearful & confident. Aunt Cass: & I dine at the G[t] House today. We shall be a snug half dozen. Miss Lloyd came, as we expected, yesterday, & desires her Love. She is very happy to hear of your learning the Harp.—I do not mean to send you what I owe Miss Hare, because I think you would rather not be paid beforehand.

Yours very affec[ly]
J. Austen

Your trying to excite your own feelings by a visit to his room amused me excessively. The dirty Shaving Rag was exquisite! Such a circumstance ought to be in print. Much too good to be lost. Remember me particularly to Fanny C.[3]—I thought you w[d] like to hear from me, while you were with her.

[1] Charles's father-in-law.
[2] Edward had lent his house to Frank, so was a guest in his own house.
[3] Cage.

106. *To Fanny Knight. Wednesday* 30 *Nov.* ⟨1814⟩

23 Hans Place, Wednesday Nov: 30.

I am very much obliged to you my dear Fanny for
your letter, & I hope you will write again soon that I
may know you to be all safe & happy at home. Our
visit to Hendon[1] will interest you I am sure, but I need
not enter into the particulars of it, as your Papa will
be able to answer *almost* every question. I certainly
could describe her bed-room, & her Drawers & her
Closet better than he can, but I do not feel that I can
stop to do it. I was rather sorry to hear that she *is* to
have an Instrument; it seems throwing money away.
They will wish the 24 Gs. in the shape of Sheets &
Towels six months hence; and as to her playing, it
never can be anything. Her purple Pelisse rather surprised me. I thought we had known all Paraphernalia
of that sort. I do not mean to blame her, it looked very
well & I dare say she wanted it. I suspect nothing
worse than it's being got in secret, & not owned to
anybody. She is capable of that you know. I received
a very kind note from her yesterday, to ask me to come
again & stay a night with them; I cannot do it, but I
was pleased to find that she had the *power* of doing
so right a thing.[2] My going was to give them *both*
Pleasure very properly. I just saw Mr. Hayter at the
Play, & think his face would please me on acquaintance. I was sorry he did not dine here. It seemed
rather odd to me to be in the Theatre, with nobody to
watch for. I was quite composed myself, at leisure for
all the agitation Isabella could raise.

[1] Anna, now Mrs. Ben Lefroy.
[2] See note, p. 214.

Now my dearest Fanny, I will begin a subject which comes in very naturally. You frighten me out of my wits by your reference. Your affection gives me the highest pleasure, but indeed you must not let anything depend on my opinion. Your own feelings & none but your own, should determine such an important point. So far however as answering your question, I have no scruple. I am perfectly convinced that your present feelings supposing you were to marry *now*, would be sufficient for his happiness; but when I think how very, very far it is from a *Now*, & take everything that *may be*, into consideration, I dare not say, 'Determine to accept him.' The risk is too great for *you*, unless your own Sentiments prompt it. You will think me perverse perhaps; in my last letter I was urging everything in his favour, & now I am inclining the other way; but I cannot help it; I am at present more impressed with the possible Evil that may arise to *you* from engaging yourself to him—in word or mind—than with anything else. When I consider how few young Men you have yet seen much of—how capable you are (yes, I do still think you *very* capable) of being really in love —and how full of temptation the next 6 or 7 years of your Life will probably be—(it is the very period of Life for the *strongest* attachments to be formed)—I cannot wish you with your present very cool feelings to devote yourself in honour to him. It is very true that you never may attach another Man, his equal altogether, but if that other Man has the power of attaching you *more*, he will be in your eyes the most perfect. I shall be glad if you *can* revive past feelings, & from your unbiassed self resolve to go on as you have done, but this I do not expect, and without it I cannot wish you to be fettered. I should not be afraid of your

marrying him; with all his worth, you would soon love
him enough for the happiness of both; but I should
dread the continuance of this sort of tacit engagement,
with such an uncertainty as there is, of *when* it may be
completed. Years may pass, before he is Independant.
You like him well enough to marry, but not well
enough to wait. The unpleasantness of appearing fickle
is certainly great—but if you think you want Punish-
ment for past Illusions, there it is—and nothing can be
compared to the misery of being bound *without* Love,
bound to one, & preferring another. *That* is a Punish-
ment which you do *not* deserve. I know you did not
meet—or rather will not meet today—as he called
here yesterday—& I am glad of it. It does not seem
very likely at least that he sh^d be in time for a Dinner
visit 60 miles off. We did not see him, only found his
card when we came home at 4. Your Uncle H. merely
observed that he was a day after the Fair. He asked
your Brother on Monday, (when Mr. Hayter was talked
of) why he did not invite *him* too?—saying, 'I know he
is in Town, for I met him the other day in Bond St.'
Edward answered that he did not know where he was
to be found.—'Don't you know his chambers?' 'No.'
—I shall be most glad to hear from you again my
dearest Fanny, but it must not be later than Saturday,
as we shall be off on Monday long before the Letters
are delivered—and write *something* that may do to be
read or told. I am to take the Miss Moores back on
Saturday, & when I return I shall hope to find your
pleasant, little, flowing scrawl on the Table. It will be
a relcif to me after playing at Ma'ams—for though I
like Miss H. M. as much as one can at my time of Life
after a day's acquaintance, it is uphill work to be
talking to those whom one knows so little. Only *one*

comes back with me tomorrow, probably Miss Eliza, & I rather dread it. We shall not have two Ideas in common. She is young, pretty, chattering, & thinking cheifly (I presume) of Dress, Company, & Admiration. Mr. Sanford is to join us at dinner, which will be a comfort, and in the even^g while your Uncle and Miss Eliza play chess, he shall tell me comical things & I will laugh at them, which will be a pleasure to both. I called in Keppel Street & saw them all, including dear Uncle Charles, who is to come & dine with us quietly today. Little Harriot sat in my lap—& seemed as gentle and affectionate as ever, & as pretty, except not being quite well. Fanny is a fine stout girl, talking incessantly, with an interesting degree of Lisp and Indistinctness—and very likely may be the handsomest in time. That puss Cassy, did not shew more pleasure in seeing me than her Sisters, but I expected no better; she does not shine in the tender feelings. She will never be a Miss O'Neal; more in the Mrs. Siddons line.

Thank you—but it is not settled yet whether I *do* hazard a 2^d Edition.[1] We are to see Egerton today, when it will probably be determined. People are more ready to borrow & praise, than to buy—which I cannot wonder at; but tho' I like praise as well as anybody, I like what Edward calls *Pewter* too. I hope he continues careful of his eyes & finds the good effect of it.

I cannot suppose we differ in our ideas of the Christian Religion. You have given an excellent description of it. We only affix a different meaning to the Word *Evangelical*.

Yours most affec^ly

J. Austen

Miss Gibson is very glad to go with us.

[1] No second edition of *M.P.* appeared until John Murray's in 1816.

117. *To Cassandra Austen. Sunday* 26 *Nov.* ⟨1815⟩

Hans Place. Sunday Nov: 26.

My Dearest

The Parcel arrived safely, & I am much obliged to you for your trouble. It cost 2ˢ 10—but as there is a certain saving of 2ˢ 4½ on the other side, I am sure it is well worth doing. I send 4 pʳ of silk stockᵍˢ—but I do not want them washed at present. In the 3 neck-handfs. I include the one sent down before. These things perhaps Edw. may be able to bring, but even if he is not, I am extremely pleased with his returning to you from Steventon. It is much better—far prefer-able. I *did* mention the P. R.[1]—in my note to Mr. Murray, it brought me a fine compliment in return; whether it has done any other good I do not know, but Henry thought it worth trying. The Printers continue to supply me very well, I am advanced in vol. 3. to my *arra*-root, upon which peculiar style of spelling there is a modest *qu:ʳʸ?* in the Margin.[2] I will not forget Anna's arrow-root. I hope you have told Martha of my first resolution of letting nobody know that I *might* dedicate, &c for fear of being obliged to do it—& that she is thoroughly convinced of my being influenced now by nothing but the most mercenary motives. I have paid nine shillings on her account to Miss Palmer; there was no more oweing. Well—we were very busy all yesterday, from ½ past 11 to 4 in the Streets, work-ing almost entirely for other people, driving from Place to Place after a parcel for Sandling which we could never find, & encountering the miseries of Grafton

[1] The Regent's Chaplain had assured her that H.R.H. would welcome the dedication of *Emma*, which he (Clarke) had suggested.
[2] It was corrected in proof.

House to get a purple frock for Eleanor Bridges. We got to Keppel St.[1] however, which was all I cared for & though we could stay only a q^r of an hour, Fanny's calling gave great pleasure & her Sensibility still greater, for she was very much affected at the sight of the Children. Poor little F. looked heavy. We saw the whole party. Aunt Har^r hopes Cassy will not forget to make a pincushion for Mrs. Kelly—as *she* has spoken of its being promised her several times. I hope we shall see Aunt H. & the dear little Girls here on Thursday.

So much for the morn^g; then came the dinner & Mr. Haden who brought good Manners & clever conversation; from 7 to 8 the Harp; at 8 Mrs. L. & Miss E.[2] arrived—& for the rest of the even^g the Draw^g-room was thus arranged, on the Sopha-side the two Ladies Henry & myself making the best of it, on the opposite side Fanny & Mr. Haden in two chairs (I *believe* at least they had *two* chairs) talking together uninterruptedly. Fancy the scene! And what is to be fancied next? Why that Mr. ·H. dines here again tomorrow. To-day we are to have Mr. Barlow. Mr. H. is reading Mansfield Park for the first time and prefers it to P. & P. A Hare & 4 Rabbits from Gm.[3] yesterday, so that we are stocked for nearly a week. Poor Farmer Andrews! I am very sorry for him, & sincerely wish his recovery. A better account of the Sugar than I could have expected. I should like to help you break some more. I am glad you cannot wake early, I am sure you must have been under great arrears of rest. Fanny & I have been to B.[4] Chapel, & walked back with Maria Cuthbert. We have been very little plagued with visitors

[1] Charles, his children, and his sister-in-law Harriet.
[2] Latouche East.
[3] Godmersham.   [4] Belgrave.

this last week, I remember only Miss Herries the Aunt,
but I am in terror for to-day, a fine bright Sunday,
plenty of Mortar[1] & nothing to do. Henry gets out in
his Garden every day, but at present his inclination for
doing more seems over, nor has he now any plan for
leaving London before Dec: 18, when he thinks of
going to Oxford for a few days; to-day indeed, his
feelings are for continuing where he is, through the
next two months. One knows the uncertainty of all
this, but should it be so, we must think the best &
hope the best & do the best—and my idea in that case
is, that when *he* goes to Oxford *I* should go home &
have nearly a week of you before *you* take my place.
This is only a silent project you know, to be gladly
given up, if better things occur. Henry calls himself
stronger every day & Mr. H. keeps on approving his
Pulse which seems generally better than ever—but
still they will not let him be well. The fever is not yet
quite removed. The Medicine he takes (the same as
before you went) is chiefly to improve his Stomach, &
only a little aperient. He is so well, that I cannot think
why he is not perfectly well. I should not have supposed his Stomach at all disordered but *there* the
Fever speaks probably; but he has no headake, no
sickness, no pains, no Indigestions! Perhaps when
Fanny is gone he will be allowed to recover faster.
I am not disappointed, I never thought the little girl
at Wyards[2] very pretty, but she will have a fine complexion & curling hair & pass for a beauty. We are
glad the Mama's cold has not been worse—& send her
our Love—& good wishes by every convenient oppor-

[1] Not explained.
[2] The Ben Lefroys lived at W. near Alton; but the child must be
Frank's, staying with them.

tunity. Sweet amiable Frank! why does *he* have a cold too? Like Capt Mirvan to Mᶜ Duval,[1] 'I wish it well over with him.'

Fanny has heard all that I have said to you about herself & Mr. H. Thank you very much for the sight of dearest Charles's Letter to yourself. How pleasantly & how naturally he writes! and how perfect a picture of his Disposition & feelings, his style conveys! Poor dear Fellow!—not a Present!—I have a great mind to send him all the twelve Copies which were to have been dispersed among my near Connections—beginning with the P. R. & ending with Countess Morley. Adieu. Yʳˢ affecˡʸ

Give my Love to Cassy &   J. Austen
Mary Jane. Caroline will
be gone when this reaches you.

120. *To James Stanier Clarke.* ⟨*Monday*⟩ 11 *Dec.* 1815
(JA's copy)

Dec. 11.
Dear Sir

My 'Emma' is now so near publication that I feel it right to assure you of my not having forgotten your kind recommendation of an early copy for Carlton House, and that I have Mr. Murray's promise of its being sent to His Royal Highness, under cover to you, three days previous to the work being really out. I must make use of this opportunity to thank you, dear Sir, for the very high praise you bestow on my other novels. I am too vain to wish to convince you that you have praised them beyond their merits. My greatest

[1] In *Evelina.*

anxiety at present is that this fourth work should not disgrace what was good in the others. But on this point I will do myself the justice to declare that, whatever may be my wishes for its success, I am very strongly haunted with the idea that to those readers who have preferred 'Pride and Prejudice' it will appear inferior in wit, and to those who have preferred 'Mansfield Park' very inferior in good sense. Such as it is, however, I hope you will do me the favour of accepting a copy. Mr. Murray will have directions for sending one. I am quite honoured by your thinking me capable of drawing such a clergyman as you gave the sketch of in your note of Nov. 16th. But I assure you I am *not*. The comic part of the character I might be equal to, but not the good, the enthusiastic, the literary. Such a man's conversation must at times be on subjects of science and philosophy, of which I know nothing; or at least be occasionally abundant in quotations and allusions which a woman who, like me, knows only her own mother tongue, and has read very little in that, would be totally without the power of giving. A classical education, or at any rate a very extensive acquaintance with English literature, ancient and modern, appears to me quite indispensable for the person who would do any justice to your clergyman; and I think I may boast myself to be, with all possible vanity, the most unlearned and uninformed female who ever dared to be an authoress.

Believe me, dear Sir,
Your obliged and faithful humbl Sert.
Jane Austen

120a. *From James Stanier Clarke. Thursday ⟨? 21⟩ Dec.* 1815

Carlton House Thursday, 1815

My dear Madam

The Letter you were so obliging as to do me the Honour of sending, was forwarded to me in Kent, where in a Village, Chiddingstone near Sevenoaks, I had been hiding myself from all bustle and turmoil —and getting Spirits for a Winter Campaign—and Strength to stand the sharp knives which many a Shylock is wetting to cut more than a Pound of Flesh from my heart, on the appearance of James the Second.

On Monday I go to Lord Egremonts at Petworth— where your Praises have long been sounded as they ought to be. I shall then look in on the Party at the Pavilion for a couple of nights—and return to preach at Park Street Chapel Green St. on the Thanksgiving Day.

You were very good to send me Emma—which I have in no respect deserved. It is gone to the Prince Regent. I have read only a few Pages which I very much admired—there is so much nature—and excellent description of Character in every thing you describe.

Pray continue to write, & make all your friends send Sketches to help you—and Memoires pour servir—as the French term it. Do let us have an English Clergyman after *your* fancy—much novelty may be introduced—shew dear Madam what good would be done if Tythes were taken away entirely, and describe him burying his own mother—as I did—because the High Priest of the Parish in which she died—did not pay her remains the respect he ought to do. I have never recovered the Shock. Carry your Clergyman to Sea

as the Friend of some distinguished Naval Character
about a Court—you can then bring foreward like Le
Sage many interesting Scenes of Character & Interest.

But forgive me, I cannot write to you without wishing to elicit your Genius;—& I fear I cannot do that,
without trespassing on your Patience and Good Nature.

I have desired Mr. Murray to procure, if he can, two
little Works I ventured to publish from being at Sea—
Sermons which I wrote & preached on the Ocean—&
the Edition which I published of Falconers Shipwreck.

Pray, dear Madam, remember, that besides My Cell
at Carlton House, I have another which Dr Barne procured for me at N^o: 37. Golden Square—where I often
hide myself. There is a small Library there much at
your Service—and if you can make the Cell render
you any service as a sort of Half-way House, when you
come to Town—I shall be most happy. There is a Maid
Servant of mine always there.

I hope to have the honour of sending you James the
2^d when it reaches a second Ed:—as some few Notes
may possibly be then added.

Yours dear Madam, very sincerely

J. S. Clarke.

134. *To J. Edward Austen. Monday* 16 *Dec.* ⟨1816⟩

Chawton, Monday Dec: 16.

My dear Edward

One reason for my writing to you now, is that I may
have the pleasure of directing to you *Esqre*. I give
you Joy of having left Winchester. Now you may own,
how miserable you were there; now, it will gradually
all come out—your Crimes & your Miseries—how
often you went up by the Mail to London & threw

away Fifty Guineas at a Tavern, & how often you were on the point of hanging yourself—restrained only, as some illnatured aspersion upon poor old Winton has it, by the want of a Tree within some miles of the City. Charles Knight & his companions passed through Chawton about 9 this morning; later than it used to be. Uncle Henry and I had a glimpse of his handsome face, looking all health & good-humour.

I wonder when you will come & see us. I know what I rather speculate upon, but I shall say nothing. We think Uncle Henry in excellent Looks. Look at him this moment & think so too, if you have not done it before; & we have the great comfort of seeing decided improvement in Uncle Charles, both as to Health, Spirits & Appearance. And they are each of them so agreable in their different way, & harmonize so well, that their visit is thorough enjoyment. Uncle Henry writes very superior Sermons. You and I must try to get hold of one or two, & put them into our Novels; it would be a fine help to a volume; & we could make our Heroine read it aloud of a Sunday Evening, just as well as Isabella Wardour in the Antiquary, is made to read the History of the Hartz Demon in the ruins of St. Ruth—though I beleive, upon recollection, Lovell is the Reader. By the bye, my dear Edward, I am quite concerned for the loss your Mother mentions in her Letter; two Chapters & a half to be missing is monstrous! It is well that *I* have not been at Steventon lately, & therefore cannot be suspected of purloining them; two strong twigs & a half towards a Nest of my own, would have been something. I do not think however that any theft of that sort would be really very useful to me. What should I do with your strong, manly, spirited Sketches, full of Variety and Glow?

How could I possibly join them on to the little bit
(two Inches wide) of Ivory on which I work with
so fine a Brush, as produces little effect after much
labour?

You will hear from uncle Henry how well Anna is.
She seems perfectly recovered. Ben was here on Saturday, to ask Uncle Charles & me to dine with them, as
tomorrow, but I was forced to decline it, the walk is
beyond my strength (though I am otherwise very well)
& this is not a Season for Donkey Carriages; & as we
do not like to spare Uncle Charles, he has declined
it too.

Tuesday. Ah, ha!—Mr Edward, I doubt your seeing
Uncle Henry at Steventon today. The weather will
prevent your expecting him I think. Tell your Father,
with Aunt Cass:'s Love & mine, that the Pickled
Cucumbers are extremely good, & tell him also—'tell
him what you will'; No, do'nt tell him what you will,
but tell him that Grandmama begs him to make Joseph
Hall pay his Rent if he can. You must not be tired of
reading the word *Uncle*, for I have not done with it.
Uncle Charles thanks your Mother for her Letter; it
was a great pleasure to him to know the parcel was
received & gave so much satisfaction; & he begs her
to be so good as to give *Three Shillings* for him to
Dame Staples, which shall be allowed for in the payment of her debt here.

I am happy to tell you that Mr. Papillon will soon
make his offer, probably next Monday, as he returns on
Saturday. His *intention* can be no longer doubtful in
the smallest degree, as he has secured the refusal of
the House which Mrs Baverstock at present occupies
in Chawton & is to vacate soon, which is of course
intended for Mrs Elizth Papillon.

Adeiu Amiable! I hope Caroline behaves well to you.

Yours affec^ly

J. Austen

140. *To Fanny Knight. Thursday 20 Feb.* ⟨1817⟩

Chawton Feb: 20

My dearest Fanny,

You are inimitable, irresistable. You are the delight of my Life. Such Letters, such entertaining Letters as you have lately sent! Such a description of your queer little heart! Such a lovely display of what Imagination does. You are worth your weight in Gold, or even in the new Silver Coinage. I cannot express to you what I have felt in reading your history of yourself, how full of Pity & Concern & Admiration & Amusement I have been. You are the Paragon of all that is Silly & Sensible, common-place & eccentric, Sad & Lively, Provoking & Interesting. Who can keep pace with the fluctuations of your Fancy, the Capprizios of your Taste, the Contradictions of your Feelings? You are so odd!—& all the time, so perfectly natural—so peculiar in yourself, & yet so like everybody else! It is very, very gratifying to me to know you so intimately. You can hardly think what a pleasure it is to me, to have such thorough pictures of your Heart. Oh! what a loss it will be when you are married. You are too agreable in your single state, too agreable as a Neice. I shall hate you when your delicious play of Mind is all settled down into conjugal & maternal affections.

Mr. J. W.[1] frightens me. He will have you. I see you at the Altar. I have *some* faith in Mrs. C. Cage's

[1] James Wildman.

190

observation, & still more in Lizzy's; & besides, I know
it *must* be so. He must be wishing to attach you. It
would be too stupid & too shameful in him, to be
otherwise; & all the Family are seeking your acquaintance. Do not imagine that I have any real objection,
I have rather taken a fancy to him than not, & I like
Chilham Castle for you; I only do not like you sh^d
marry anybody. And yet I do wish you to marry very
much, because I know you will never be happy till you
are; but the loss of a Fanny Knight will be never made
up to me; My 'affec: Neice F. C. Wildman' will be but
a poor Substitute. I do not like your being nervous &
so apt to cry: it is a sign you are not quite well, but I
hope Mr. Scud[1]—as you always write his name, (your
Mr. *Scuds:* amuse me very much) will do you good.
What a comfort that Cassandra should be so recovered!
—It is more than we had expected.—I can easily
beleive she was very patient & very good. I always
loved Cassandra,[2] for her fine dark eyes & sweet
temper.—I am almost entirely cured of my rheumatism; just a little pain in my knee now and then, to
make me remember what it was, & keep on flannel.
Aunt Cassandra nursed me so beautifully! I enjoy your
visit to Goodnestone, it must be a great pleasure to
you, You have not seen Fanny Cage in any comfort so
long. I hope she represents & remonstrates & reasons
with you, properly. Why should you be living in dread
of his[3] marrying somebody else? (Yet, how natural!)
You did not chuse to have him yourself; why not allow
him to take comfort where he can? In your conscience
you *know* that he could not bear a comparison with a

[1] Scudamore.
[2] Edward's fifth d.
[3] 'he' is now the John Plumtre of the 1814 letters.

more animated Character. You cannot forget how you felt under the idea of it's having been possible that he might have dined in Hans Place. My dearest Fanny, I cannot bear you should be unhappy about him. Think of his Principles, think of his Father's objection, of want of Money, of a coarse Mother, of Brothers & Sisters like Horses, of sheets sewn across &c. But I am doing no good—no, all that I urge against him will rather make you take his part more, sweet perverse Fanny. And now I will tell you that we like your Henry to the utmost, to the very top of the Glass, quite brimful. He is a very pleasing young Man. I do not see how he could be mended. He does really bid fair to be everything his Father and Sister could wish; and William I love very much indeed, & so we do all, he is quite our own William. In short we are very comfortable together—that is, we can answer for *ourselves*. Mrs. Deedes is as welcome as May, to all our Benevolence to her Son; we only lamented that we c^d not do more, that the £50 note we slipt into his hand at parting was necessarily the Limit of our Offering. Good .Irs. Deedes! I hope she will get the better of this Marianne, & then I w^d recommend to her & Mr. D. the simple regimen of separate rooms. Scandal & Gossip;— yes I dare say you are well stocked; but I am very fond of Mrs. C. Cage, for reasons good. Thank you for mentioning her praise of Emma &c. I have contributed the marking to Uncle H.'s shirts, & now they are a complete memorial of the tender regard of many.

Friday. I had no idea when I began this yesterday, of sending it before your B^r went back, but I have written away my foolish thoughts at such a rate that I will not keep them many hours longer to stare me in the face. Much obliged for the *Quadrilles*, which I am grown to think pretty enough, though of course they are very inferior to the Cotillions of my own day. Ben & Anna walked here last Sunday to hear Uncle Henry,[1] & she looked so pretty, it was quite a pleasure to see her, so young & so blooming & so innocent, as if she had never had a wicked Thought in her Life—which yet one has some reason to suppose she must have had, if we believe the Doctrine of original Sin, or if we remember the events of her girlish days.

I hope Lizzy will have her Play. Very kindly arranged for her. Henry is generally thought very good-looking, but not so handsome as Edward. I think *I* prefer his face. Wm. is in excellent Looks, has a fine appetite & seems perfectly well. You will have a great Break-up at G^m in the Spring, You *must* feel their all going. It is very right however. One sees many good causes for it. Poor Miss C.[2] I shall pity her, when she begins to understand herself. Your objection to the Quadrilles delighted me exceedingly. Pretty well, for a Lady irrecoverably attached to *one* Person! Sweet Fanny, beleive no such thing of yourself. Spread no such malicious slander upon your Understanding, within the Precincts of your Imagination. Do not speak ill of your Sense, merely for the Gratification of your Fancy. Yours is Sense, which deserves more honourable Treatment. You are *not* in love with him. You never have been really in love with him. Y^{rs} very affec^{ly}

J. Austen

Uncle H. & Miss Lloyd dine at Mr. Digweed's today, which leaves us the power of asking Uncle & Aunt F. to come & meet their Nephews here.

[1] Bankrupt 1816, he lost no time in taking orders, and is 'now curate of Bentley near Alton'.
[2] Clewes?

141. *To Fanny Knight. Thursday* 13 *March* ⟨1817⟩

Chawton, Thursday March 13.

As to making any adequate return for such a Letter as yours my dearest Fanny, it is absolutely impossible; if I were to labour at it all the rest of my Life & live to the age of Methuselah, I could never accomplish anything so long & so perfect; but I cannot let William go without a few Lines of acknowledgement & reply. I have pretty well done with Mr. Wildman. By your description he can*not* be in love with you, however he may try at it, & I could not wish the match unless there were a great deal of Love on his side. I do not know what to do about Jemima Branfill. What does her dancing away with so much spirit, mean? that she does not care for him, or only wishes to *appear* not to care for him? Who can understand a young Lady? Poor Mrs. C. Milles, that she should die on a wrong day at last, after being about it so long! It was unlucky that the Goodnestone Party could not meet you, & I hope her friendly, obliging, social Spirit, which delighted in drawing People together, was not conscious of the division and disappointment she was occasioning. I am sorry & surprised that you speak of her as having little to leave, & must feel for Miss Milles, though she *is* Molly, if a material loss of Income is to attend her other loss. Single Women have a dreadful propensity for being poor—which is one very strong argument in favour of Matrimony, but I need not dwell on such arguments with *you*, pretty Dear, you do not want inclination. Well, I shall say, as I have often said before, Do not be in a hurry; depend upon it, the right Man will come at last; you will in the course of the next two or three years, meet with somebody more generally unexceptionable than anyone you have yet known, who will love you as warmly as ever *He* did, and who will so completely attach you, that you will feel you never really loved before. And then, by not beginning the business of Mothering quite so early in life, you will be young in Constitution, spirits, figure & countenance, while Mrs Wm Hammond is growing old by confinements & nursing. Do none of the Plumtres ever come to Balls now? You have never mentioned them as being at any? And what do you hear of the Gipps or of Fanny[1] and her Husband?—Mrs F. A. is to be confined the middle of April, & is by no means remarkably Large for *her.*—Aunt Cassandra walked to Wyards yesterday with Mrs. Digweed. Anna has had a bad cold, looks pale, & we fear something else. She has just weaned Julia. How soon, the difference of temper in Children appears! Jemima has a very irritable bad Temper (her Mother says so)—and Julia a very sweet one, always pleased & happy. I hope as Anna is so early sensible of it's defects, that she will give Jemima's disposition the early & steady attention it must require. *I* have also heard lately from your Aunt Harriot, & cannot understand their plans in parting with Miss S—whom she seems very much to value, now that Harriot & Eleanor are both of an age for a Governess to be so useful to;—especially as when Caroline was sent to School some years, *Miss Bell* was still retained, though the others were then mere Nursery Children. They have some good reason I dare say, though I cannot penetrate it, & till I know what it is I shall invent a bad one, and amuse myself with accounting for the difference of measures by supposing

[1] Plumtre?

Miss S. to be a superior sort of Woman, who has never stooped to recommend herself to the Master of the family by Flattery, as Miss Bell did. I *will* answer your kind questions more than you expect. Miss Catherine[1] is put upon the Shelve for the present, and I do not know that she will ever come out; but I have a something[2] ready for Publication, which may perhaps appear about a twelvemonth hence. It is short, about the length of Catherine.—This is for yourself alone. Neither Mr. Salusbury nor Mr. Wildman are to know of it.

I am got tolerably well again, quite equal to walking about & enjoying the Air; and by sitting down & resting a good while between my Walks, I get exercise enough. I have a scheme however for accomplishing more, as the weather grows springlike. I mean to take to riding the Donkey. It will be more independant & less troublesome than the use of the carriage, & I shall be able to go about with A^t Cassandra in her walks to Alton and Wyards. I hope you will think Wm. looking well. He was bilious the other day, and Aunt Cass: supplied him with a Dose at his own request, which seemed to have good effect. I was sure *you* would have approved it. Wm. & I are the best of friends. I love him very much. Everything is so *natural* about him, his affections, his Manners & his Drollery. He entertains & interests us extremely. Max: Hammond and A. M. Shaw are people whom I cannot care for, in themselves, but I enter into their situation & am glad they are so happy. If I were the Duchess of Richmond, I should be very miserable about my son's choice. What can be expected from a Paget, born & brought up in

---

[1] The heroine of *Northanger Abbey* is Catherine.
[2] *Persuasion.*

the centre of conjugal Infidelity & Divorces? I will *not* be interested about Lady Caroline. I abhor all the race of Pagets. Our fears increase for poor little Harriet[1]; the latest account is that Sir Ev: Home[2] is confirmed in his opinion of there being water on the brain. I hope Heaven in its mercy will take her soon. Her poor Father will be quite worn out by his feelings for her. He cannot spare Cassy at present, she is an occupation & a comfort to him.

Adieu my dearest Fanny. Nothing could be more delicious than your Letter; & the assurance of your feeling releived by writing it, made the pleasure perfect. But how could it possibly be any new idea to you that you have a great deal of Imagination? You are all over Imagination. The most astonishing part of your Character is, that with so much Imagination, so much flight of Mind, such unbounded Fancies, you should have such excellent Judgement in what you do! Religious Principle I fancy must explain it. Well, good bye & God bless you.

Y^{rs} very affec^{ly}
J. Austen

142. *To Fanny Knight. Sunday* 23 *March* ⟨1817⟩

Chawton, Sunday March 23.

I am very much obliged to you my dearest Fanny for sending me Mr. Wildman's conversation, I had great amusement in reading it, & I *hope* I am not affronted & do not think the worse of him for having a Brain so very different from mine, but my strongest sensation of all is *astonishment* at your being able to

---

[1] Charles's daughter.
[2] Sir Everard, a fashionable physician.

H

press him on the subject so perseveringly—and I agree
with your Papa, that it was not fair. When he knows
the truth he will be uncomfortable. You are the oddest
Creature!—Nervous enough in some respects, but in
others perfectly without nerves!—Quite unrepulsible,
hardened & impudent. Do not oblige him to read any
more. Have mercy on him, tell him the truth & make
him an apology. He & I should not in the least agree of
course, in our ideas of Novels and Heroines; pictures
of perfection as you know make me sick & wicked—
but there is some very good sense in what he says, &
I particularly respect him for wishing to think well
of all young Ladies; it shews an amiable & a delicate
Mind. And he deserves better treatment than to be
obliged to read any more of my Works. Do not be
surprised at finding Uncle Henry acquainted with my
having another ready for publication. I could not say
No when he asked me, but he knows nothing more of
it. You will not like it, so you need not be impatient.
You may *perhaps* like the Heroine,[1] as she is almost
too good for me. Many thanks for your kind care for
my health; I certainly have not been well for many
weeks, and about a week ago I was very poorly, I have
had a good deal of fever at times & indifferent nights,
but am considerably better now, & recovering my
Looks a little, which have been bad enough, black &
white & every wrong colour. I must not depend upon
being ever very blooming again. Sickness is a danger-
ous Indulgence at my time of Life. Thank you for
everything you tell me; I do not feel worthy of it by
anything I can say in return, but I assure you my
pleasure in your Letters is quite as great as ever, & I
am interested & amused just as you could wish me.

[1] Of *Persuasion.*

If there is a *Miss* Marsden, I perceive whom she will marry.

Even^g. I was languid & dull & very bad company when I wrote the above; I am better now—to my own feelings at least—& wish I may be more agreable. We are going to have Rain, & after that, very pleasant genial weather, which will exactly do for me, as my Saddle will then be completed—and air & exercise is what I want. Indeed I shall be very glad when the event at Scarlets[1] is over, the expectation of it keeps us in a worry, your Grandmama especially; she sits brooding over Evils which cannot be remedied & Conduct impossible to be understood. Now, the reports from Keppel St. are rather better; little Harriet's headaches are abated, & Sir Ev^d: is satisfied with the effect of the Mercury, & does not despair of a Cure. The Complaint I find is not considered Incurable nowadays, provided the Patient be young enough not to have the Head hardened. The Water in that case may be drawn off by Mercury. But though this is a new idea to us, perhaps it may have been long familiar to you, through your friend Mr. Scud:—I hope his high renown is maintained by driving away William's cough. Tell William that Triggs is as beautiful & condescending as ever, & was so good as to dine with us today, & tell him that I often play at *Nines* & think of him. Anna has not a chance of escape; her husband called here the other day, & said she was *pretty* well but not *equal* to so long a walk; she *must come in* her *Donkey Carriage*. Poor Animal, she will be worn out before she is thirty. I am very sorry for her. Mrs Clement too is in that way again. I am quite tired of so many Children. Mrs Benn has a 13th. The Papillons

---

[1] The death of James Leigh-Perrot, Mrs. Austen's brother.

came back on friday night, but I have not seen them yet, as I do not venture to Church. I cannot hear however, but that they are the same Mr. P. & his sister they used to be. She has engaged a new Maidservant in Mrs. Calker's room, whom she means to make also Housekeeper under herself. Old Philmore was buried yesterday, & I, by way of saying something to Triggs, observed that it had been a very handsome Funeral, but his manner of reply made me suppose that it was not generally esteemed so. I can only be sure of *one* part being very handsome, Triggs himself, walking behind in his Green Coat. Mrs. Philmore attended as chief Mourner, in Bombasin, made very short, and flounced with Crape.

Tuesday. I have had various plans as to this Letter, but at last I have determined that Un: Henry shall forward it from London. I want to see how Canterbury[1] looks in the direction. When once Unc. H. has left us I shall wish him with you. London is become a hateful place to him, & he is always depressed by the idea of it. I hope he will be in time for your sick. I am sure he must do that part of his Duty as excellently as all the rest. He returned yesterday from Steventon, & was with us by breakfast, bringing Edward with him, only that Edwd staid to breakfast at Wyards. We had a pleasant family-day, for the Altons dined with us;— the last visit of the kind probably, which *she* will be able to pay us for many a month; Very well, to be able to do it so long, for she *expects* much about this day three weeks, & is generally very exact. I hope your own Henry is in France & that you have heard from him. The Passage once over, he will feel all Happiness. I took my 1st ride yesterday & liked it very much.

---

[1] Instead of the usual Faversham.

I went up Mounters Lane, & round by where the new
Cottages are to be, & found the exercise & everything
very pleasant, and I had the advantage of agreable
companions, as A^t Cass: and Edward walked by my
side. A^t Cass. is such an excellent Nurse, so assiduous
& unwearied! But you know all that already.

Very affec^{ly} Yours   J. Austen

145. *To Anne Sharp.* ⟨*Thursday*⟩ 22 *May* ⟨1817⟩

Chawton May 22^d

Your kind Letter my dearest Anne found me in bed,
for in spite of my hopes & promises when I wrote to
you I have since been very ill indeed. An attack of my
sad complaint seized me within a few days afterwards
—the most severe I ever had—& coming upon me
after weeks of indisposition, it reduced me very low.
I have kept my bed since the 13. of April, with only
removals to a Sopha. *Now*, I am getting well again,
& indeed have been gradually tho' slowly recovering
my strength for the last three weeks. I can sit up in
my bed & employ myself, as I am proving to you at this
present moment, & *really* am equal to being out of
bed, but that the posture is thought good for me. How
to do justice to the kindness of all my family during
this illness, is quite beyond me! Every dear Brother
so affectionate & so anxious!—and as for my Sister!—
Words must fail me in any attempt to describe what a
Nurse she has been to me. Thank God! she does not
seem the worse for it *yet*, & as there was never any
sitting-up necessary, I am willing to hope she has no
after-fatigues to suffer from. I have so many alleviations & comforts to bless the Almighty for! My head
was always clear, & I had scarcely any pain; my cheif

201

sufferings were from feverish nights, weakness and Languor. This Discharge was on me for above a week, & as our Alton Apoth^y did not pretend to be able to cope with it, better advice was called in. Our nearest *very good,* is at Winchester, where there is a Hospital & capital Surgeons, & one of them attended me, & *his* applications gradually removed the Evil. The consequence is, that instead of going to Town to put myself into the hands of some Physician as I sh^d otherwise have done, I am going to Winchester instead, for some weeks to see what Mr Lyford can do farther towards re-establishing me in tolerable health. On Sat^y next, I am actually going thither—my dearest Cassandra with me I need hardly say—and as this is only two days off you will be convinced that I am now really a very genteel, portable sort of an Invalid. The Journey is only 16 miles, we have comfortable Lodgings engaged for us by our kind friend Mrs Heathcote who resides in W. & are to have the accomodation of my elder Brother's Carriage which will be sent over from Steventon on purpose. Now, that's a sort of thing which Mrs J. Austen does in the kindest manner! But still she is in the main *not* a liberal-minded Woman, & as to this reversionary Property's[1] amending that part of her Character, expect it not my dear Anne;— too late, too late in the day;—& besides, the Property may not be theirs these ten years. My Aunt is very stout. Mrs F. A. has had a much shorter confinement than I have—with a Baby to produce into the bargain. We were put to bed nearly at the same time, & she has been quite recovered this great while.—I hope *you* have not been visited with more illness my dear Anne,

[1] James Austen died 1819. His son J. Edward inherited the Leigh-Perrot property in 1837, when he became Austen-Leigh.

either in your own person or your Eliza's. I must not attempt the pleasure of addressing her again, till my hand is stronger, but I prize the invitation to do so. Beleive me, I was interested in all you wrote, though with all the Egotism of an Invalid I write only of myself. Your Charity to the poor Woman[1] I trust fails no more in effect, than I am sure it does in exertion. What an interest it must be to you all! & how gladly sh^d I contribute more than my good wishes, were it possible! But how you are worried! Wherever Distress falls, you are expected to supply Comfort. Ly P— writing to you even from Paris for advice! It is the Influence of Strength over Weakness indeed.—Galigai de Concini[2] for ever & ever. Adieu. Continue to direct to Chawton, the communication between the two places will be frequent. I have not mentioned my dear Mother; she suffered much for me when I was at the worst, but is tolerably well. Miss Lloyd too has been all kindness. In short, if I live to be an old Woman, I must expect to wish I had died now; blessed in the tenderness of such a Family, & before I had survived either them or their affection. You would have held the memory of your friend Jane too in tender regret I am sure. But the Providence of God has restored me—& may I be more fit to appear before him when I *am* summoned, than I sh^d have been now! Sick or Well, beleive me ever y^r attached friend

J. Austen

Mrs Heathcote will be a great comfort, but we shall not have Miss Bigg,[3] she being frisked off like half England, into Switzerland.

---

[1] Miss S., formerly governess at Godmersham, was now with a widowed Lady Pilkington in Yorkshire.   [2] See note, p. 214.
[3] Alethea, normally with Mrs. H. at Winchester.

V. WINCHESTER

1817: *Forty-one*

═══

IN May 1817 she writes of the decision that she and
Cassandra shall go to Winchester for medical atten-
tion. We have only two letters from 'College Street,
Winton', where she died peacefully on 18 July.

I add two moving letters from Cassandra to Fanny,
written a few days later.

146. *To J. Edward Austen. Tuesday 27 May* 1817

Mrs. Davids, College Street—Winton

Tuesday May 27.

I know no better way my dearest Edward, of thanking you for your most affectionate concern for me
during my illness, than by telling you myself as soon
as possible that I continue to get better. I will not
boast of my handwriting; neither that, nor my face
have yet recovered their proper beauty, but in other
respects I am gaining strength very fast. I am *now* out
of bed from 9 in the morn^g to 10 at night—upon the
sopha t'is true—but I eat my meals with aunt Cass: in
a rational way, & can employ myself, and walk from
one room to another. Mr. Lyford says he will cure me,
& if he fails I shall draw up a Memorial and lay it

Tuesday 27 May 1817

before the Dean & Chapter, & have no doubt of redress
from that Pious, Learned, and Disinterested Body. Our
Lodgings are very comfortable. We have a neat little
Drawing room with a Bow-window overlooking Dr.
Gabell's garden. Thanks to the kindness of your Father
& Mother in sending me their carriage, my Journey
hither on Saturday was performed with very little
fatigue, & had it been a fine day I think I should have
felt none, but it distressed me to see uncle Henry &
Wm. K— who kindly attended us on horseback, riding
in rain almost all the way. We expect a visit from them
tomorrow, & hope they will stay the night, and on
Thursday, which is Confirmation & a Holiday, we are
to get Charles[1] out to breakfast. We have had but one
visit yet from *him* poor fellow, as he is in sick room,
but he hopes to be out to-night.

We see Mrs. Heathcote every day, & William[2] is to
call upon us soon. God bless you my dear Edward.
If ever you are ill, may you be as tenderly nursed as
I have been, may the same Blessed alleviations of
anxious, simpathising friends be yours, & may you
possess—as I dare say you will—the greatest blessing
of all, in the consciousness of not being unworthy of
their Love. *I* could not feel this.

Your very affec: Aunt

J. A.

Had I not engaged to write to you, you w[d] have
heard again from your Aunt Martha, as she charged
me to tell you with her best Love.

[1] Edward's fifth son, now at Winchester.
[2] Heathcote.

147. *To* ———— ⟨*end of May?* 1817⟩[1]

My attendant is encouraging, and talks of making
me quite well. I live chiefly on the sofa, but am allowed
to walk from one room to the other. I have been out
once in a sedan-chair, and am to repeat it, and be
promoted to a wheel-chair as the weather serves. On
this subject I will only say further that my dearest
sister, my tender, watchful, indefatigable nurse, has
not been made ill by her exertions. As to what I owe
to her, and to the anxious affection of all my beloved
family on this occasion, I can only cry over it, and
pray to God to bless them more and more.

[She next touches with just and gentle animadversion on
a subject of domestic disappointment.[2] Of this the particulars do not concern the public. Yet in justice to her character-
istic sweetness and resignation, the concluding observation
of our authoress thereon must not be suppressed.]

But I am getting too near complaint. It has been the
appointment of God, however secondary causes may
have operated. . . .

You will find Captain ———— a very respectable, well-
meaning man, without much manner, his wife and
sister all good humour and obligingness, and I hope
(since the fashion allows it) with rather longer petticoats than last year.

---

[1] This letter is known only from Henry's *Biographical Notice*
prefixed to *Northanger Abbey and Persuasion.*

[2] James Leigh-Perrot had left nothing to his sister, JA's mother.

APPENDIX

*Letters from Cassandra Austen to Fanny
Knight on Jane Austen's death*

—————

My dearest Fanny—doubly dear to me now for her
dear sake whom we have lost.

She did love you most sincerely, & never shall I
forget the proofs of love you gave her during her illness
in writing those kind, amusing letters at a time when
I know your feelings would have dictated so different
a style. Take the only reward I can give you in my
assurance that your benevolent purpose *was* answer'd;
you *did* contribute to her enjoyment. Even your last
letter afforded pleasure, I merely cut the seal & gave
it to her; she opened it & read it herself, afterwards
she gave it me to read, & then talked to me a little
& not unchearfully of its contents, but there was then
a languor about her which prevented her taking the
same interest in any thing, she had been used to do.

Since Tuesday evening, when her complaint returnd,
there was a visible change, she slept more & much
more comfortably, indeed during the last eight & forty
hours she was more asleep than awake. Her looks
altered & she fell away, but I perceived no material
diminution of strength & tho' I was then hopeless of a
recovery I had no suspicion how rapidly my loss was

approaching.—I *have* lost a treasure, such a Sister, such a friend as never can have been surpassed,—she was the sun of my life, the gilder of every pleasure, the soother of every sorrow, I had not a thought concealed from her, & it is as if I had lost a part of myself. I loved her only too well, not better than she deserved, but I am conscious that my affection for her made me sometimes unjust to & negligent of others, & I can acknowledge, more than as a general principle, the justice of the hand which has struck this blow. You know me too well to be at all afraid that I should suffer materially from my feelings, I am perfectly conscious of the extent of my irreparable loss, but I am not at all overpowerd & very little indisposed, nothing but what a short time, with rest & change of air will remove. I thank God that I was enabled to attend her to the last & amongst my many causes of self-reproach I have not to add any wilfull neglect of her comfort. She felt herself to be dying about half an hour before she became tranquil and aparently unconscious. During that half hour was her struggle, poor soul! she said she could not tell us what she sufferd, tho she complaind of little fixed pain. When I asked her if there was any thing she wanted, her answer was she wanted nothing but death & some of her words were 'God grant me patience, Pray for me oh Pray for me'. Her voice was affected but as long as she spoke she was intelligible. I hope I do not break your heart my dearest Fanny by these particulars, I mean to afford you gratification whilst I am relieving my own feelings. I could not write so to any body else, indeed you are the only person I have written to at all excepting your Grandmama, it was to her not your Uncle Charles I wrote on Friday.—Immediately after dinner on Thursday I went into the Town to do an

errand which your dear Aunt was anxious about. I returnd about a quarter before six & found her recovering from faintness & oppression, she got so well as to
be able to give me a minute account of her seisure &
when the clock struck 6 she was talking quietly to me.
I cannot say how soon afterwards she was seized again
with the same faintness, which was followed by the
sufferings she could not describe, but Mr. Lyford had
been sent for, had applied something to give her ease
& she was in a state of quiet insensibility by seven
oclock at the latest. From that time till half past four,
when she ceased to breathe, she scarcely moved a
limb, so that we have every reason to think, with gratitude to the Almighty, that her sufferings were over.
A slight motion of the head with every breath remaind
till almost the last. I sat close to her with a pillow in my
lap to assist in supporting her head, which was almost
off the bed, for six hours,—fatigue made me then
resign my place to Mrs J. A. for two hours & a half
when I took it again & in about one hour more she
breathed her last. I was able to close her eyes myself
& it was a great gratification to me to render her these
last services. There was nothing convulsed or which
gave the idea of pain in her look, on the contrary, but
for the continual motion of the head, she gave me the
idea of a beautiful statue, & even now in her coffin,
there is such a sweet serene air over her countenance as
is quite pleasant to contemplate. This day my dearest
Fanny you have had the melancholly intelligence & I
know you suffer severely, but I likewise know that you
will apply to the fountain-head for consolation & that
our merciful God is never deaf to such prayers as you
will offer.

The last sad ceremony is to take place on Thursday

morning, her dear remains are to be deposited in the cathedral—it is a satisfaction to me to think that they are to lie in a Building she admird so much—her precious soul I presume to hope reposes in a far superior Mansion. May mine one day be reunited to it.—Your dear Papa, your Uncles Henry & Frank & Edwd Austen instead of his Father will attend, I hope they will none of them suffer lastingly from their pious exertions.—The ceremony must be over before ten o'clock as the cathedral service begins at that hour, so that we shall be at home early in the day, for there will be nothing to keep us here afterwards.—Your Uncle James came to us yesterday & is gone home to day— Uncle H. goes to Chawton to-morrow morning, he has given every necessary direction here & I think his company there will do good. He returns to us again on Tuesday evening. I did not think to have written a long letter when I began, but I have found the employment draw me on & I hope I shall have been giving you more pleasure than pain.

Remember me kindly to Mrs J. Bridges (I am so glad she is with you now) & give my best love to Lizzy & all the others. I am my dearest Fanny

Most affect^ly yrs

CASS. ELIZ^TH AUSTEN

I have said nothing about those at Chawton because I am sure you hear from your Papa.

Chawton: Tuesday (July 29, 1817).

My dearest Fanny,

I have just read your letter for the third time, and thank you most sincerely for every kind expression to myself, and still more warmly for your praises of her

210

who I believe was better known to you than to any human being besides myself. Nothing of the sort could have been more gratifying to me than the manner in which you write of her, and if the dear angel is conscious of what passes here, and is not above all earthly feelings, she may perhaps receive pleasure in being so mourned. Had *she* been the survivor I can fancy her speaking of *you* in almost the same terms. There are certainly many points of strong resemblance in your characters; in your intimate acquaintance with each other, and your mutual strong affection, you were counterparts.

Thursday was not so dreadful a day to me as you imagined. There was so much necessary to be done that there was no time for additional misery. Everything was conducted with the greatest tranquillity, and but that I was determined I would see the last, and therefore was upon the listen, I should not have known when they left the house. I watched the little mournful procession the length of the street; and when it turned from my sight, and I had lost her for ever, even then I was not overpowered, nor so much agitated as I am now in writing of it. Never was human being more sincerely mourned by those who attended her remains than was this dear creature. May the sorrow with which she is parted with on earth be a prognostic of the joy with which she is hailed in heaven!

I continue very tolerably well—much better than any one could have supposed possible, because I certainly have had considerable fatigue of body as well as anguish of mind for months back; but I really am well, and I hope I am properly grateful to the Almighty for having been so supported. Your grandmamma, too, is much better than when I came home.

211

I did not think your dear papa appeared unwell, and I understand that he seemed much more comfortable after his return from Winchester than he had done before. I need not tell you that he was a great comfort to me; indeed, I can never say enough of the kindness I have received from him and from every other friend.

I get out of doors a good deal and am able to employ myself. Of course those employments suit me best which leave me most at leisure to think of her I have lost, and I do think of her in every variety of circumstance. In our happy hours of confidential intercourse, in the cheerful family party which she so ornamented, in her sick room, on her death-bed, and as (I hope) an inhabitant of heaven. Oh, if I may one day be re-united to her there! I know the time must come when my mind will be less engrossed by her idea, but I do not like to think of it. If I think of her less as on earth, God grant that I may never cease to reflect on her as inhabiting heaven, and never cease my humble endeavours (when it shall please God) to join her there.

In looking at a few of the precious papers which are now my property I have found some memorandums, amongst which she desires that one of her gold chains may be given to her god-daughter Louisa, and a lock of her hair be set for you. You can need no assurance, my dearest Fanny, that every request of your beloved aunt will be sacred with me. Be so good as to say whether you prefer a brooch or ring. God bless you, my dearest Fanny.

Believe me, most affectionately yours,

Cass. Elizth. Austen.

Miss Knight, Godmersham Park,
      Canterbury.

NOTES

19. *Martha.* It has been inferred that Jane and Cassandra were making a match between Martha and Frank. But there might be another naval officer in the offing.

20. *Calland.* The rector of Bentworth's behaviour may have given a hint for Darcy's at another ball.

40. *Sir Thomas* Williams, RN. He had lost his first wife, the Austen's cousin Jane Cooper, and did (1800) marry a Miss Wapshare.

72. *treaty.* A 'compromise' (p. 145), between the Leigh-Perrots and the Adlestrop Leighs, of a money dispute.

76. *Mary's.* Of Scotland. JA might find this in her copy of Goldsmith's *History of England*, 1771, ii, 85.

78. *Hastings.* Mrs Henry Austen (Eliza) was a protégée of Warren Hastings; Egerton was her friend. [Some contemporaries surmised that Hastings was Eliza's father. For an examination of the question see G. H. Tucker, *A Goodly Heritage* (Manchester, 1983), pp. 37–50. M. B.]

79. *visit.* The young Henry seems at one time to have been engaged, or nearly, to marry a Pearson.

81. *Johnson.* See his letter to Boswell 4 July 1774. The reference is to his *Journey to the Western Islands*.

119, 121, 122. 'My' and 'our' in this letter must be quotations. Margaret Beckford (d. of *Vathek*) was not related to anyone likely to be quoted, unless indeed the quotation is of Mrs James, whose husband's first wife was a Bertie on her mother's side; Berties and Beckfords were connected.

132. *ordination* is hardly the *subject* of *Mansfield Park*, though Edmund's taking orders is important. So is the disposal of livings, on which Cassandra's host the rector of Steventon would be an authority. [Chapman probably misreads JA's letter by assuming a stop after 'ordination'. It seems more

213

probable that she intended a break after 'subject' and before 'ordination'. 'Ordination' is then not the subject of *MP*, but merely the topic Cassandra has been asked to enquire about. This influential (mis)interpretation by Chapman was the subject of an article by H. Brogan and of subsequent correspondence, *TLS*, 19 Dec. 1968–30 Jan. 1969. M. B.]

Hedgerows is interesting; no doubt JA thought of using the piece of machinery which she used so effectively in *Persuasion*.

177. *right a thing*. One of Anna's daughters explained that the Lefroys lived at Hendon with Ben's brother Edward—so that Anna might not have been in a position to invite guests.

203. *Concini*. Eléonore Galigai, a maid of honour to Marie de Medici, was burned as a sorcerer in 1617. Her claim to strength of mind is quoted by Voltaire; but JA perhaps got it from Chesterfield's letter of 30 April 1752, or (as Miss Talmadge suggests) from Maria Edgeworth's *The Absentee*, 1812, ch. 3.

136. This letter is addressed only 'Miss Lloyd'. Martha was evidently staying with the Dundases at Barton (and her letter directed to D., an MP, would be in a franked cover). Mrs D. D. is their daughter.

124. *Miss W.* Wallop. Camilla, good-humoured and merry, and small. For a husband, it happened, was at her last stake, And having in vain danced at many a ball Is not very happy to jump at a Wake.

When the lines were published in the *Memoir*, 1870, Camilla was disguised as Maria.

125. *P. & P. is sold*. It was published in 1813. The outright sale explains why misprints detected by JA were not corrected in the second edition of the same year. She was doubtless not consulted.

INDEXES

I. JANE AUSTEN'S FAMILY

References are to the pages.

In this index the generations are thus distinguished:

> *AUSTEN, GEORGE*
> AUSTEN, JAMES
> Austen, James Edward
> *Lefroy, Anna Jemima*

For collateral Austens, Leighs, &c., see Index II.

AUSTEN, Rev. *GEORGE*, 1731–1805, s. of William A., surgeon; scholar 1747 and fellow 1751 of St. John's Coll. Oxon.; rector of Steventon, Hants, from 1761, and of Deane, Hants, from (?)1773 to 1805; m. 1764 Cassandra Leigh, q.v.; 6 s. 2 d. *passim*

AUSTEN, CASSANDRA, 1739–1827, y.d. of Rev. Thomas Leigh of Harpsden (who d. 1763; for his other children see James Leigh-Perrot and Jane Cooper); m. 1764 Rev. George A. q.v.; *passim*

I. AUSTEN, JAMES, 1765–1819, e.s. of Rev. George A.; scholar 1779 of St. John's Coll. Oxon.; curate at Overton, and at Deane, Hants; Rector of Steventon, Hants, 1805–19; m. (1) 1792 Anne, d. of General and Lady Jane Mathew, who d. 1795; 1 d.; (2) 1797 Mary y.d. of Rev. Nowes Lloyd; 1 s. 1 d.: *passim*, esp. 14 his birth, 81 'walking about and banging the doors'

AUSTEN, ANNE, 1st w. of James A., q.v.

   1. Austen, Jane Anna Elizabeth, 1793–1872, e.d. of James A. (and o.c. of his 1st wife), b. 1793, m. 8 Nov. 1814 Ben Lefroy, q.v. in Index II; 1 s. 6 d.: *passim*. Letters to her 162, 169, 'an Anna with variations' 116, 'as if she had never had a wicked Thought' 193

   i. *Lefroy, Anna Jemima*, 20 Oct. 1815, e.d. of Ben and Anna L.: 195

   ii. *Lefroy, Julia Cassandra*, 27 Sept. 1816, 2nd d. of Ben and Anna L.: 195

AUSTEN, MARY,   –1843, 2nd w. of James A., q.v.

2. Austen (-Leigh 1837), Rev. James Edward, 1798–1874, o.s. of James A.; b. 17 Nov. 1798; commoner of Winchester 1814–16; Exeter Coll. Oxon.; Vicar of Bray 1851; author of the *Memoir* 1870; in his youth usually 'Edward'; *passim*; letters to him 134, 204

3. Austen, Caroline Mary Craven, 1805–80, y.d. of James A.; b. Steventon 18 June 1805; god-d. of Cassandra A.; author of *My Aunt Jane Austen*, published 1952 by the Jane Austen Society

III. AUSTEN (KNIGHT 1812), EDWARD, 1768–1852, 3rd s. of George A.; of Godmersham Park, Kent, and Chawton, Hants; m. 1791, Elizabeth, 3rd d. of Sir Brook Bridges III; 6 s. 5 d.: *passim*; his wife's death 87 ff.; 'I must learn to make a better K' 124

AUSTEN, ELIZABETH, 1773–10 Oct. 1808, w. of Edward A., q.v.:

1. Austen (Knight), Fanny Catherine, 1793–1882, e.d. of Edward A.; m. 1820 Sir Edward Knatchbull Bt. of Mersham Hatch, Kent (their son the first Lord Brabourne edited 1884 the letters of JA in his mother's possession): *passim*; 'dearest Fanny' 87, 90; letters to her 172, 177, 190, 194, 197; with Haden 'in two chairs' 182

2. Austen (Knight), Edward, 10 May 1794–1879, e.s. of Edward A.; commoner of Winchester 1807–11; St. John's Coll. Oxon. 1811: 18 'little Edward', 82 'Edward Junr', 90 ff., 173 'agreable idle Brothers'

3. Austen (Knight), George, 22 Nov. 1795–1867, 2nd s. of Edward A.; commoner of Winchester 1808–12; St. John's Coll. Oxon. 1813: 91, 144

4. Austen (Knight), Henry, 1797–1843, 3rd s. of Edward A.; commoner of Winchester 1810–14: 192

5. Austen (Knight), William, 1798– , 4th s. of Edward A.; commoner of Winchester 1813–14: 192

6. Austen (Knight), Elizabeth (Lizzy), 1800– , 2nd d. of Edward A.; 71, 87

7. Austen (Knight), Marianne, 1801–96, 3rd d. of Edward A.: 102

8. Austen (Knight), Charles Bridges, 1803–67, 5th s. of Edward A.; commoner of Winchester 1816–20: 144, 188; 205

9. Austen (Knight), Louisa, 1804–89, 4th d. of Edward A., JA's god-d. (*Brabourne*, ii 341): 118

10. Austen (Knight), Cassandra Jane, 1806–42, 5th d. of Edward A.: 104, 191

11. Austen (Knight), Brook John, 1808–78, 6th s. of Edward A.: 90, 99

IV. AUSTEN, Rev. HENRY THOMAS, 1771–1850, 4th s. of George A.; scholar 1788 of St. John's Coll. Oxon.; Lieutenant Oxford Militia 1793, Captain and Adjutant 1797; Partner in Austen, Maunde and Tilson, bankers of 10 Henrietta-street, Covent Garden, 1807–16, and in Austen, Gray and Vincent, bankers of Alton, Hants; Receiver-General for Oxfordshire 1813; bankrupt March 1816; took orders and became curate of Bentley near Alton, Dec. 1816; m. (1) 1797 his cousin Eliza, q.v.; (2) 1820, Eleanor Jackson: *passim*, esp. 5, 16, 144 'not a Mind for affliction'

AUSTEN, ELIZA, 1761–25 Apr. 1813, o.d. of Tysoe Saul Hancock of Fort St. David (Madras) and of Philadelphia, o.s. of George Austen; m. (1) 1781 Jean Capotte Comte de Feuillide (guillotined 1794); 1 s., Hastings, 1786–1801; (2) 31 Dec. 1797, Henry Thomas Austen, q.v.

V. AUSTEN, CASSANDRA ELIZABETH, 9 Jan. 1773–1845, e.d. of George A.; engaged (?1795) to Rev. Thomas Fowle (q.v.), who d. Feb. 1797: 'does not like desultory novels' 165; 'my dearest sister, my tender . . . nurse' 201, 206; her letters to Fanny Knight after JA's death 207

VI. AUSTEN, Sir FRANCIS WILLIAM, 1774–1865, 5th s. of George A.; G.C.B. (K.C.B. 1837), Admiral of the Fleet; m. (1) at Ramsgate 24 July 1806, Mary, e.d. of John Gibson, who d. 1823; 6 s. 5 d.; (2) 1828, Martha Lloyd, q.v.: *passim*, esp. 8, 18, 23 appointments and promotion, 107 his childish saying (quoted also 141, 152); letters to him 60, 61, 68, 81

AUSTEN, MARY (Gibson), 'Mrs. F. A.', 1st w. of Francis A.:

1. Austen, Mary Jane, b. 27 Apr. 1807, o.d. of Francis A.: 82, 107

2. Austen, Francis William, b. 1809, e.s. of Francis A.: 107, 136

3. Austen, Henry Edgar, b. 1811, 2nd s. of Francis A.: 136

4. Austen, George, b. Deal 20 Oct. 1812, 3rd s. of Francis A.

5. Austen, Cassandra Eliza, b. Portsmouth 8 Jan. 1814, 2nd d. of Francis A.

6. Austen, Herbert Grey, b. Chawton 8 Nov. 1815, 4th s. of Francis A.

7. Austen, Elizabeth, b. Alton 15 Apr. 1817, 3rd d. of Francis A.

217

Jane Austen's Family

AUSTEN, MARTHA,   —1843, e.d. of Rev. Nowes Lloyd,
q.v. in Index II; 2nd w. (1828) of Francis A.

VII. AUSTEN, JANE, 16 Dec. 1775–18 July 1817, y.d. of George
A.

General: 'his prodigal Daughter' 9; 'flirtation' with Tom
Lefroy, q.v.; see also Blackall; 'to sit in idleness . . . in a
well-proportioned room' 34; 'dependent upon the communications of our friends, or my own wits' 100; 'preference
for Men and Women' 109; opinion on marriage, 'mothering',
and too many children 175, 179, 195, 199; 'consciousness
of not being unworthy of their Love. *I* could not feel this'
205; 'the sun of my life' (Cassandra in 1817, of JA) 208

On writing, her own and others': Does not write for 'dull elves'
132; cannot help being 'a wild Beast' 140; on Anna A.'s
novels, letters 98 (162), 100 (169), 'Nature and Spirit cover
many sins of a wandering story' 165; ' 3 or 4 Families in a
Country Village is the very thing to work on' 170; 'the most
unlearned and uninformed female who ever dared to be an
authoress' 185; 'pictures of perfection make me sick and
wicked' 198; 'The little bit . . . of Ivory on which I work'
189

Her novels:

Sense and Sensibility ('begun Nov. 1797', note by Cassandra,
who added that an earlier version was 'called Elinor and
Marianne'. Published by Egerton Nov. 1811, second edition
Nov. 1813). Proof-corrections ('sucking child'; 'my Elinor')
114; profits of first edition 146; second edition 150; 'given
to Miss Hamilton' 150

Pride and Prejudice ('First Impression begun in Oct. 1796.
Finished in Aug. 1797', note by Cassandra; see p. 2. Sold
to Egerton and published Jan. 1813). Sold to Egerton for
£110, 125; 'my own darling child' read aloud at Chawton
131; Elizabeth 132; 'lop't and crop't' 132; Cassandra's
praise 133; 'too light and bright and sparkling' 134;
anonymity 134; Mrs. Bingley's portrait 139, none of Mrs.
Darcy 139, 142 'the sort of Letter that Miss D. [Darcy]
would write' 141; 'the credit of P. & P.' 146

Mansfield Park (published by Egerton May 1814; second
edition, John Murray, 1816). 'Mrs. Grant's round table'
128; 'a complete change of subject—ordination' 132;
inquiry about Northamptonshire 132, 137; 'not half so
entertaining' as *P. and P.* 146; borrows names of Frank's

218

II. OTHER PERSONS, PLACES, AUTHORS, ETC. (SELECTIVE)

Other Persons, Places, Authors, etc.

1762–1837, baronet, b. of
Anne Lefroy and of Char-
lotte Harrison: their widow
mother Jemima B., of the
Precincts, Canterbury, 1727–
1809. His *Arthur Fitzalbini*
1798: 16; Mrs. B. 81

Buchanan, Claudius, 1766–
1815. JA may refer to his
popular *Christian Researches
in Asia* 1811: 127

Burney, Frances, Madame
d'Arblay,1752–1840. *Evelina*
1778: 79, 184

Burney, Sarah Harriet, 1770 ?
–1844. *Clarentine* 1798: 80

Byron, Lord, 1788–1824. *The
Corsair* 1814: 156

Cage, Lewis, of Milgate, Kent,
m. 1791 Fanny, o.d. of Sir
Brook B. III: 37 (21 is
either his wife or his mother)

Cage, Fanny, 1793 ?–1874, e.d.
of Lewis C.: 126, 153, 176,
191

Cage, Rev. Charles, y.b. of
Lewis C., m. — Graham: 190,
192

Calland, Rev. John, 1763–
1800, Rector of Bentworth,
Hants: 20 (note)

Carr, Sir John, 1772–1832.
Travels in . . . Spain 1811:
126, 127

Clarke, Rev. James Stanier,
c. 1765–1834, naval chaplain
1795–99, domestic chaplain
1799 to the Prince of Wales;
JA's correspondence with
him: 184, 186

Clarkson, Thomas, 1760–1846,

abolitionist. JA may refer
to his *Life of Penn* 1813 (too
late ?) or to his *Abolition of
the . . . Slave Trade* 1808: 127

Coffey, Charles, d. 1745. *The
Devil to Pay* 1731: 161

Combe, William, 1741–1823.
*Dr. Syntax in Search of the
Picturesque* 1812: (illustrated
by Rowlandson) 156

Cooke, Rev. Samuel, 1741–
1820, Vicar of Great Bookham, Surrey, m. Cassandra
Leigh, Mrs. A.'s first cousin;
his children George Leigh,
1780–1853, Mary: 64, 109, 115

Cooper, Rev. Dr. Edward,
1728–92, m. Jane Leigh, s.
of Mrs. A.; their s. Rev.
Edward C., 1770–1835, curate at Harpsden ('Harden')
and 1799 Rector of Ham-
stall-Ridware, Staffs., m.
1793 Caroline Lybbe Powys
(their children 6, 119); their
d. Jane, d. 1798, m. Sir
Thomas Williams, q.v.: 4, 6,
7, 88

Cowper, William, 1731–1800.
His 'Works' 17, *The Task* 17,
77

Crabbe, George, 1754–1832,
JA's admiration: 148

Crosby, Richard, of Crosby
(Crosbie) & Co., publishers:
104, 105

Deane, near Steventon, see
Harwood

Deedes, William, 1761–1834,
of Sandling, Kent, m. 1791
Sophia, 2nd d. of Sir Brook B.

Other Persons, Places, Authors, etc.

Oxford: Jane Elizabeth Scott, 1773–1824, m. 1794 the fifth Earl of Oxford, the children in their house were named the Harleian Miscellany: 137

Pasley, Sir Charles William, R.E., 1780–1861, *Military Policy and Institution of the British Empire* 1810: 127 (JA's *Police* was used in the same sense as *Policy*), 129

Plumtre, John Pemberton, 1791–1864, e.s. of John P. of Fredville, Kent; Fanny Knight's suitor; his sisters: 149, 160, 173, 174, 191, 195

Porter, Anna Maria, 1780–1832. *Lake of Killarney* 1804: 93

Prince of Wales (George IV), 1762–1830; the Princess (Queen Caroline), 1768–1821: JA on their quarrel 137, 184; dedication of *Emma*, see Index I

Radcliffe, Ann, 1764–1823; 'The Radcliffe style': 155

Reynolds, Sir Joshua, 1723–92. Exhibition of his Pictures 1813: 139, 142

Richardson, Samuel, 1689–1761. *Sir Charles Grandison* 1753: 57

Russell, Mrs.: probably a d.-in-law of Dr. R., Rector of Ashe 1720–83, whose widow d. 1785: 12

Scarlets, Berks., see Leigh-Perrot

Scott, Sir Walter, 1771–1832. *Marmion* 1808: 85; 'a critique' on him 134; *The Antiquary* 188

Seymour, —, Henry A.'s man of business: 104, 105, 115

Shakespeare, William, 1564–1616. *King John, Macbeth* 113; *Merchant of Venice* 155, 159

Sharp(e), Ann(e), governess at Godmersham and elsewhere: 66 (doubtful), 78, 83, 90, 120; JA's letter to her 201

Siddons, Sarah, 1755–1831: 117, 180

Smith, James, 1775–1839, and Horatio, 1779–1849. *Rejected Addresses* 1812: 127, 128, 129

Southampton, Castle Square: 69

Stephens, Catherine, 1794–1882: 161

Stoneleigh Abbey, Warwickshire, see Leigh

Streatham, Surrey, see Hill

Sykes, Mrs. S., *Margiana* or *Widdrington Fair* 1808: 103

Terry, Thomas, 1741–1829, of Dummer, Hants, m. Elizabeth Harding; 1751–1811, 30, 121

Terry, Stephen, 1774–1867, e.s. of Thomas T.: 29

Terry, Michael, 1776–1848, 2nd s. of Thomas T.; Rector 1811 of Dummer; perhaps the 'Brother Michael' of 130, and the 'M. T.' of 135

Oxford Paperback Reference

THE CONCISE OXFORD COMPANION TO ENGLISH LITERATURE

Edited by Margaret Drabble and Jenny Stringer

Derived from the acclaimed *Oxford Companion to English Literature*, the concise maintains the wide coverage of its parent volume. It is an indispensable, compact guide to all aspects of English literature. For this revised edition, existing entries have been fully updated and revised with 60 new entries added on contemporary writers.

* **Over 5,000 entries on the lives and works of authors, poets and playwrights**

* **The most comprehensive and authoritative paperback guide to English literature**

* **New entries include Peter Ackroyd, Martin Amis, Toni Morrison, and Jeanette Winterson**

* **New appendices list major literary prize-winners**

From the reviews of its parent volume:

'It earns its place at the head of the best sellers: every home should have one'
Sunday Times